Industrial English

Other books by T. C. Jupp (published by Heinemann)

TALK ENGLISH – T. C. Jupp, John Milne, Piers Plowright

GUIDED PARAGRAPH WRITING – T. C. Jupp & John Milne

GUIDED COURSE IN ENGLISH COMPOSITION – T. C. Jupp
& John Milne

ENGLISH SENTENCE STRUCTURE – T. C. Jupp & John Milne

ENCOUNTERS – MAIN COURSE ENGLISH: Level One –
J. Garton-Sprenger, T. C. Jupp, J. Milne, P. Prowse

THE BACKGROUND AND EMPLOYMENT OF ASIAN
IMMIGRANTS – T. C. Jupp & E. Davies
(pub. The Runnymede Trust)

Industrial English has been translated and adapted into French
under the title *Apprentissage Linguistique et Communication*
Méthodologie appliquée à l'enseignement du français aux
travailleurs immigrés – C. Heddesheimer and J. P. Lagarde

Industrial English

An example of theory and practice in functional
language teaching for elementary learners

T C Jupp and Susan Hodlin

assisted by
Jacek Opienski *and* Elizabeth Laird

HEINEMANN EDUCATIONAL BOOKS
LONDON

Heinemann Educational Books Ltd.

EDINBURGH MELBOURNE AUCKLAND TORONTO
HONG KONG SINGAPORE KUALA LUMPUR NEW DELHI
IBADAN NAIROBI LUSAKA KINGSTON

ISBN 0 435 28401 0
© T. C. Jupp and Susan Hodlin 1975
First published 1975
Reprinted (with corrections) 1978

⊗Recorded Materials for Part Two

The teaching materials in Part Two contain
eighty-nine tape items. Some of these need
to be prepared specially, but the majority
have been recorded and are available on tape.
Enquiries should be addressed to:
    ELT Department,
    Heinemann Educational Books Ltd.

Published by
Heinemann Educational Books Ltd
48 Charles Street, London W1X 8AH
Printed and bound in Great Britain by
Butler and Tanner Ltd., Frome and London
Set in Monotype Times New Roman

Contents

Part one
Principles and methods for functional language teaching

Introduction

". . . the theoretical and the practical problems converge. It
is not that there exists a body of linguistic theory that
practical research can turn to and has only to apply. It is
rather that work motivated by practical needs may help build
the theory that we need." (D. H. Hymes, *On Communicative
Competence*)

This book sets out to explore what is involved in the construction
of a functional language course in elementary English both in
principle and practice. By a functional language course, we mean
a course which has the goal of training a student to use English in
the real situations where he needs it. This is an aim which goes
beyond the usual goal of a measured level of proficiency in
pronunciation, structure, and vocabulary.

The contents of *Industrial English* arise from the very specific
situation of teaching English to adult Asian immigrants who have
settled in Britain. A unit was established at the Pathway Further
Education Centre in Southall in 1970 to experiment with English
language training for Asian employees at local places of employment. The intention was to gain the co-operation of employers by
providing language courses which would make their non-English-
speaking employees more effective workers as well as fulfilling
wider aims for the individual and the community. But we soon
found that there were no suitable published materials and that the
usual principles of course construction and methodology were
largely irrelevant to our learners' needs. So it was necessary to
think radically in terms of new principles for language course
design, and to produce the actual teaching materials. This book
represents some of the fruit of this experience after the teaching
of many such courses.

The book is in two parts. *Part One* discusses some fundamental
issues in language teaching generally and examines the principles
and methods necessary for a functional approach. In particular,
we consider the nature of language and language learning and
relate this to a student's linguistic and functional needs and to
course and classroom methodology. *Part One* also provides an
introduction to the teaching materials in the second part of the
book. *Part Two* contains some 200 graded language teaching items

with detailed guidance on teaching method and learning purpose. These items both provide the basic core for an elementary English course easily open to adaptation and variation, and demonstrate what a functional approach to language teaching can achieve at a more elementary level than has been previously attempted.

The book will serve as a useful guide to the construction of courses to meet similar needs amongst immigrants in other parts of the world, as well as being of general interest to those examining the new theories of functional language teaching. Within Britain, we hope *Industrial English* will provide a systematic approach to teaching spoken English to adult immigrants, particularly where the teaching is on the basis of in-company language training.

Note to Second Impression

Apart from corrections, we have undertaken some minor rewording and rearranging for the sake of greater clarity.

We would stress again that this book seeks to offer practical guidance and ideas derived from a case-study of functional language teaching at an elementary level. Partly for this reason we have not included a bibliography and because even a select one would have to be very long and cover a large number of topics.

Acknowledgements

This book could not have been written without the help and encouragement of Evelyn Davies or the working conditions she has created. At the crucial planning stage, we were again given valuable help by Evelyn Davies, and by Shirley Hadi and Brian Abbs. At later stages, all our colleagues have made a contribution either consciously or unconsciously, as have several other teachers.

We should also like to thank the very many people in industry who have given us time and assistance in understanding the communication needs of Asian immigrants.

The first course using these materials was supported financially by the Rubber and Plastics Processing Industry Training Board, as was some of the material development. In particular, we received practical help and advice from John Leppard and Morris Kaufman of the Board.

Rodney Goddard, as technician of the Pathway Centre, is responsible for all the taped material and slide visuals, which reflect his high standard. We are grateful to Christopher Candlin for the suggestion that we should include Appendix One.

T.C.J. and S.H.

Industrial English

Part One
Principles and methods for functional language teaching

Chapter 1
How adequate is orthodox language teaching theory and method to the communicative task?

When a language course is designed for an industrial situation or any other specialized purpose, the main aim must be for the students to use the new language effectively outside the classroom. This aim of teaching language required for real communication has also become a declared principle of much general language teaching in recent years. Most general courses in English as a foreign language now claim to teach useful spoken and written English. Yet this aim of teaching language for everyday use is seldom examined or taken to its logical conclusion by the material writer or the teacher.

The logic of such an aim must be that a teacher should not concentrate on language as an abstraction, but language in use. In other words he should give attention to language as a part of social behaviour. As Hymes says, 'There are rules of use without which rules of grammar would be useless.'

1.1 The importance of language function

If the teacher accepts that part of his job is to teach the use of language, he will require a functional language syllabus as well as a syllabus based on a description of the linguistic forms of the language. The way language can be described either from a functional or from a formal (e.g. grammatical) standpoint is illustrated by the following simplified example:

1 You're late, you know.
2 I'm sorry. I missed the bus.
3 I see. Well, get down to your section now.

Functional description

1 Criticism and demand for apology.
2 Apology and explanation.
3 Acceptance of explanation. Instruction related to job.

Grammatical description

1. Pron. + *be* (pres. simp.) + adj. pron. + V-trs (pres. simp.)

2. Pron. + *be* (pres. simp.)
   Pron. + V-trs (past. simp.) + noun

3. Pron. + V-intr (pres. simp.)
   Adv + verb (imp.) + adv. part. + adv phr. (place) + adv (time)

These descriptive labels are extremely simple and merely seek to illustrate the two approaches. The functional labels make the obvious point that in life we use language for different functions and purposes. The actual language we choose depends also upon whom we are addressing and our relationship with that person. In the example above there is the defined relationship between supervisor and factory worker. 'The rules of use' are therefore determined by such factors as function, relationship and context.

The simple but typical grammatical labels only occasionally tell us about the function of a piece of language – for example, the imperative can be used for instructions. A detailed linguistic analysis would show other important correspondences between formal features and function – for example, in intonation. However, although there are these important correlations, language functions are never confined to one set of language forms.

For the second language learner 'the rules of use' are extremely complicated. People from different countries see situations, relationships and the use of language in very different ways because these factors are the product of a whole culture of which the language is only one part. For example, the relationship between foreman and worker in an Indian factory and in a British factory will be very different, and ideas about the appropriate use of language in that relationship will also be different. Transference of the rules of use for this relationship from India to Britain will cause endless misunderstandings.

The correspondence between a particular formal language feature and a language function can also cause difficulty for the second language user. For example, there may be the same concept of a particular language function within a situation – say, a polite request – but the linguistic means for achieving this may be different in the two languages. In English, a polite request may be expressed by using a question form containing a modal auxiliary, 'Would you pass me the hammer?' The same polite request might involve an imperative in the learner's language.

6

If the learner identifies his native language imperative form with the English imperative, he may transfer his 'rules of use' for the imperative across into English and as a result fail to communicate effectively because he appears to the English listener to be speaking rudely.

We shall later describe some of the practical possibilities and difficulties in trying to teach and learn a particular area of English as an aspect of social behaviour (see Chapter 4). At this point, we merely want to argue that, if a teacher is aiming to teach 'real spoken English' this aim involves the social and cultural context of the language. This is perhaps an obvious point, but one to which syllabus and material writers have only recently started paying attention again.

In other words, what the student has to learn is not 'language' but 'communication', and the test of his success is not performance in the classroom, where attention is concentrated upon his linguistic accuracy, but successful communication in the real world which involves all the factors we have been discussing. In the real world, there is often considerable tolerance of non-standard linguistic features in pronunciation, syntax and lexis and this reduces the necessity for complete linguistic accuracy.

1.2 The importance of the learner's particular needs

A very general view of what is involved in communication through language, along the lines we have been discussing, can lead to a broad analysis of categories of meaning and of language functions; for example 'requests' and 'permission' are two contrasting types. These function labels can be applied to build up a descriptive syllabus without regard to the overall factors involved in the development of conversation and communication, such as relationships, situations, purposes and dialect. Such a description can be used for global syllabuses and courses to give a general fluency in English for unspecified learners with unspecified purposes.

But the teacher has more precise responsibilities: he should not consider some unspecified or ideal user of English; he has a group of learners in front of him who have, or will have, particular communication needs in particular situations. This, therefore, is the second major principle involved in teaching a foreign language: the centrality of the learner's needs to all the teacher's choices. This is a relevant principle for any group of learners anywhere although it is obviously more relevant in the case of adults who have themselves chosen to learn a second language. Any learner of English anywhere in the world has access to English through the media, through meeting English people, and through seeing signs and advertisements in English. Wherever there is a group learning English for a special purpose, the learners will have common needs and common opportunities.

The case of Asian immigrants at work in Britain shows the principle in a very clear and precise way. A man or woman at work has a particular set of communicative needs both social and work-specific. He is also part of a network of specified relationships and a network which would be modified if he could communicate more effectively. The teacher has to penetrate and analyse this set of needs and relationships, and then select, modify, and rewrite more broadly based materials.

1.3 The language teaching revolution

There has been a great upsurge in modern language teaching since the mid-nineteen-fifties, which has reflected a growing utilitarian demand for foreign languages as a tool of communication in work, leisure, and education. In European schools, there has been demand for language learning of a non-academic sort; many university courses throughout the world require a knowledge of a second language; and an increasing number of jobs require a working knowledge of an international language. This book arises from the fact that millions of workers have settled in industrial countries with little or no knowledge of the local language, creating another area of language teaching need.

No modern language has benefited more from all this upsurge of demand than English. The great expansion in English Language Teaching has come about as a result of people with interests and needs for learning the language; needs and interests which, particularly for adults, are central to their motivation and their response to the learning situation.

The upsurge in English language teaching was accompanied by the introduction of new methods and materials in the classroom particularly during the 1960s. These changes were often radical and can be called a language teaching revolution. But this revolution has taken little account of the situation or motivation of the learners; on the contrary it has been about *how* people learn and *what* the language is. Most of the radical innovation was based on Skinnerian learning theory and descriptions and theories of language from structural linguistics. Consideration of *why* people learn a second language or evaluation of results has been more-or-less missing except in the type of situation which would be popularly referred to as bilingual – for example the work on learners' attitudes and motivation of Lambert. Another feature of these changes has been the strong emphasis upon the difference between English as a foreign language, English as a second language, and bilingualism. They have been seen as different situations which have little to learn from each other. There has not been much consideration of these concepts in terms of individual learners and their situations. If there were, the concepts would not remain so rigidly separated into categories.

Because of the emphasis upon the *how* and the *what* of language teaching – the teacher has been encouraged and trained to *impose* his own view of the learner's needs and problems. For example, a course may present at a very early stage a description of parts of animals, or a dialogue between two young people looking at photographs of their last holiday. Such situations are chosen because they lend themselves to presenting certain structural patterns of English:

This is a dog. This is a mouth. This is a tail.

These particular structures are presented early in the course because they fit in comparatively easily with techniques based on the idea of substitution and with the various other types of drill used in the methodology. We have talked of 'imposing a view of the learner's needs and problems' because such syllabuses do not derive from an examination of the learner's situation.

Because the teacher has given little attention to the '*why*' of language learning in basic course construction, he has had to create motivation largely within the classroom itself. The emphasis has been upon making the classroom a self-motivating environment by means of 'interest', 'activity', and 'liveliness' – what has been described as 'splits and cabaret' language teaching – useful though entertainment is in a classroom. Another way of increasing motivation has always been with the concept of goals of performance. The goal cannot be real because until a comparatively late stage real situations are not touched upon, instead the goal has to be an artificial language situation. An example of such goals is any reading scheme with stages, each stage of which reflects a scheme of structural language grading which has been determined by the type of factor discussed in the previous paragraph.

1.4 An example of the structural method in practice

Adult learners are often less willing to accept a self-motivated classroom world because they usually have a conscious motivation of their own. Are teachers right to take the view that such learners should just apply themselves, that if the learners were not impatient all would be revealed? Don't people learn much more quickly if they can understand the reason for learning something, and if the item relates to the learner's long term aim? Many teachers accept that motivation is very important, but much modern methodology makes motivation a factor the teacher feels he cannot influence.

Here is an example of a situation which poses these questions. The Ministry of Foreign Trade in a small country, heavily dependent upon foreign trade, decided to give a high priority to teaching foreign languages to key personnel who had to deal with foreign business people in the capital, or who might live abroad as part of a trade mission. The Ministry was advised to release the language trainees for four hours daily every week for a year if they wanted to see really dramatic progress; which meant taking key people away from their desks, and often leaving the individual in the situation of having to catch up in his own time on vital work. The Ministry equipped two language laboratories, bought what they were advised were the most suitable materials, and trained their teachers. The materials recommended were a typical modern audio-visual course mostly based on selection and grading by structural criteria with some additional 'situational' language.

The language trainees complained that the materials and the techniques of the course were repetitious, boring and inappropriate. In fact most of the trainees made quite a lot of progress because they were reasonably disciplined and hard working. But surely the the trainees were correct and was not their attitude likely to be slowing down progress?

The following are some of the probable reasons for recommending the particular course which was used:

a Assumes some half-forgotten knowledge of the language. The trainees had learned some English at school.

b For a structural/situational course it has quite steep grading – suitable for well-motivated adults.

c Set in England – and many of the learners would expect to reside overseas in an English-speaking country.

d Contains a large amount of practice material suitable for an intensive course.

e Teaches 'spoken colloquial English'.

These criteria take no account of functional communicative needs or the learner's own immediate situation. The English setting is largely a matter of an English family and some English surroundings; there is certainly no attempt to teach the English 'rules of use' in terms of situations and relationships. The concept of 'spoken colloquial English' is one largely based upon a structural description of written English and without reference to functional uses and to roles.

The inadequacy of the criteria in relation to the learner's own immediate situation and own motivation quickly emerged. Confronted with a taped dialogue such as:

> And where's the cat?
> She's in the garden too.

teacher and learner had quite different reactions. The teacher, thinking in terms of gradual mastery of accuracy in the different aspects of the language itself, believed this was 'real spoken English'. The learner felt he was wasting his time, and thought of his needs in dealing with:

> international telephone calls
> foreign visitors
> business and social situations abroad.

Partly this is a clash over the learning process. No one can become fluent in a language immediately – to that extent the teacher is correct. But the extent of the clash here is undesirable and unnecessary. Materials and course design should seek always to measure adequacy in terms of the real world. And the learners' own functional motivation can be a most powerful ally to the language learning process; if we can harness it, many adults can more quickly reach the level of confidence and satisfaction from which learning can proceed more rapidly. Our argument is, therefore, that the contents and methods of a language course for adults should not be determined without first examining why learners should learn and in what situations they will need the new language.

The strongest argument for taking account of functional needs is that they seem a more important element in success than course structure or methodology. A comparative history of the success of language learning in various parts of the world would be most interesting in this respect. Lambert's work has suggested that a favourable attitude towards the community of the target language and a motivation to use the language in its own social context are very important to success. These factors can be increased in learners by a teacher if the learner is taught the language he needs to function within the real and relevant context of the language and the means are created for the learner actually to use this new language.

1.5 Other methods

This discussion of current methodology and practice has concentrated mainly upon 'structural methods' because these have come to underlie nearly all approaches whatever their label. However, some material mixes structuralism with attention to 'situation'. As a general theory this has a number of practical weaknesses. Language is not primarily specific to a physical context, and secondly, even if language was specific to physical situations, it would be impossible to teach the language of all the situations a person would need. But in fact 'the situational method' is not a full theory of language teaching, but more an appendix to the structural method. The idea is that 'structures should be situation-alized'. This is an artificial, but certainly useful technique, so long as confined to the status of a technique.

Much work on the teaching of English to adults for specific functional purposes is also fundamentally structural because the purpose is conceived in terms of subject areas – for example, engineering, science, medicine, banking, and so on. Work has been done on the special grammatical features of each subject, but most courses remain largely a matter of special vocabulary in the old slots of structure and methodology, or in some new structural slots.

Recent work on the teaching of English for specific purposes, particularly in the field of study skills, has recognized the necessity to use functional criteria for materials design if effective results are to be achieved in the subject areas rather than the language classroom. In these materials, there has been a shift away from only a structural analysis of language towards a much broader analysis of written discourse.

1.6 Summary

The intention of this critical analysis is not to suggest that the structural approach is useless, but that alone it is inadequate to meet the two principles outlined earlier in this chapter; the principle of teaching rules of use as well as rules of form, and the principle that the learners' needs should be central to all the choices a teacher makes. The syllabus for the teaching items contained in *Part Two* of this book has been based upon principles of communicative needs in an industrial work situation. At the same time, guidance is given, both in broad terms in *Part One* and in relation to many of the individual teaching items in *Part Two*, on how a teacher can investigate his own students' particular situation and needs with a view to selection and adaptation of the language teaching material. Undoubtely the structural approach has generated many useful techniques and methods which have been relied upon heavily in these materials, but these techniques and methods alone are not enough.

Chapter 2
Communicating at work in a second language

If we wish to concentrate our language teaching upon the learners' communicative requirements and opportunities – that is language as an aspect of social behaviour – the logical first step is to look at the type of industrial situation where foreign workers are employed, at how language is used, and at how and where communication breaks down.

2.1 The employment situations of Asian workers

Most Asian immigrants who have settled in Britain have unskilled jobs in manufacturing and processing industries. These industries are usually either ones which have expanded rapidly in areas of labour shortage, or ones which offer unattractive conditions in terms of the hours, the work, or the environment. Typical examples of such industries are plastics, rubber, food processing, building materials, foundries, metal working, laundries, and textiles. Factories in these industries usually have some labour intensive areas where many of the Asians will be working, and the environment is very noisy. Communication is largely between fellow-workers whether on social or job matters, and occasionally with supervisors, shop-stewards, and members of management. Communication skills are seldom recognized as an important part of a job at operative level, although any promotion depends very much on the ability to communicate in English. The materials in *Part Two* of this book are designed for Asian workers with elementary communications problems in English in this type of industrial situation.

Numbers of Asians are also employed in service industries which offer poor wages as well as difficult hours and conditions – for example, transport, hospitals, cleaning, and public catering. Communication with the public is often an integral part of these jobs from every point of view. Again this is often not recognized or is ignored, and Asian workers in these situations really have an even more urgent need for language training in English than those in the industrial situation.

At the outset of this discussion, it is important to note some basic distinctions in industrial work situations. Very broadly work will tend to be on the basis of either individual machines or operators, or on the basis of a flow-line usually in the form of a moving belt. The individual work often involves a slightly lengthier task than flow-line work and some responsibility for the performance of the machine as well as the completion of the task – for example, an injection moulder in plastics, many small assembly jobs, some packing jobs, or garment making. This type of worker may be on his own or part of a small team. The flow-line situation on the other hand involves larger teams, more flexibility, and the necessity never to leave the job untended – for example, car assembly, or food processing. Another very important distinction is the method of payment: flat-rate, group-bonus, individual-bonus, or piece-work. These factors of work organization and of payment have important effects upon relationships, degree of supervision, and attitudes on the shop floor, all of which are central to the language-communication situation.

2.2 A typical workplace

We shall now examine a typical work situation in some detail. We have chosen as an example the finishing and assembly department of a company making plastic electrical fittings. The department employs sixty women, of whom thirty-five do not speak English as their first language. The work situation consists of women at long benches using simple individual machines to finish or assemble the product. They have to fetch and deliver the items, they have to keep simple records for piece-work payments which are checked, they have to maintain consistent quality, and after assembling the items, they may have to pack them. There are three chargehands and one supervisor in the department, all of whom are English.

A day's work

The daily timetable is as follows:

7.50 a.m.	Arrival, clocking-in, put on overall
7.50–8.00	Preparation of work
8.00	Work begins promptly
8.00–10.00	Work

10.00	Tea from a trolley
10.15–12.50	Work
12.50	Work slows down. Wash hands. Clocking-off
1.00–1.45	Lunch
1.40	Clocking-in etc.
1.45–3.00	Work
3.00 approx.	Packing of completed work begins
4.40	Cleaning-up
4.45 p.m.	Work stops, dressing, clocking-off, leave.

Women arrive in twos and threes. They clock-in just inside the side-door and exchange greetings and walk along chatting until they reach the row of lockers in the department. Then they hang their coats in a locker which they share with someone else, and put on their overalls.

Then people drift towards their work area and if they are carrying on with a job from the previous day, check everything is ready. Otherwise they stand around waiting for a chargehand to assign them a job. They might chat about things at home or events of the previous evening. At 8.00 a.m. everyone springs to action. Some people may be put onto new jobs and an explanation may be necessary from the chargehand. Later she will check back that the work is going all right. Chargehands are constantly checking operators' work, and will reject anything they consider sub-standard which in turn affects earnings. The operator may need to ask what is wrong, or to explain she is getting a lot of faulty parts, or she may want to dispute the rejection.

Anyone arriving more than fifteen minutes late has to give the supervisor a convincing explanation or the supervisor may send an adverse report to the personnel department. During the early part of the morning, the supervisor will go around and get an explanation for absence from anyone who was away the previous day, which she will then send to Personnel with her comments.

If an operator's machine starts giving trouble, she will have to explain to a chargehand or maintenance person what is going wrong. She should also find a chargehand if there is anything generally wrong with the parts she has been given. The operator needs to make sure she always has an adequate supply of parts or she will again lose time and money. This she does by getting a general labourer to bring her what she needs from the stores.

The old hands can chat to their friend as they do a job if they

16

are close together and their small machine is not too noisy. But new workers have to stop work to talk. At 10.00 a.m. each woman gets out her mug (all rejects of a line made in the same factory), and goes up to the tea trolley which has arrived. For sale are rolls with sausages and bacon, crisps, and the usual dry packets of biscuits. After buying what they want, the women are expected to go and sit back at their work places. Most do, although groups of friends cluster together, and the Indians usually dip into packets of curried crisps which they have brought with them.

The morning's work resumes again at 10.15 a.m. and most people aim to get through more than a proportional amount of their target in the morning so that they can relax a bit in the afternoon. Occasionally someone will hurt herself on a machine. Someone may be needed to go for medical help, and the supervisor must record a report in the accident book.

Before clocking-off at lunch time, there is some chatting in the cloakroom. English people are irritated by Indians who use their own languages. Then some people go to the canteen, including some younger Indian girls. Many English women rush off to do a bit of shopping. The older Indian women have brought their own food which they eat, sitting around on the benches in the factory.

During lunchtime any social affairs of the factory are dealt with and a woman who runs a mail-order agency does her business.

Work starts up again at 1.45 p.m. and most people carry on with the same job. People with very poor English are either constantly shifted between simple jobs with poor rates, or kept in a simple and repetitive job more or less permanently.

When a particular batch is finished, the operator must pack them and make up her work rate sheet which has to be checked and signed by the supervisor. If someone can't write figures, the charge-hand will fill it in. Supervisors and chargehands are always very irate if anyone credits themselves with too much work.

The atmosphere of the afternoon is rather more relaxed. There is no tea break, but people can get a drink out of a machine. Towards the end of the afternoon the pace builds up as people try to finish a particular job. Anyone who tries to short cut by dodging a safety regulation will be in trouble if seen. Then they must clear up properly before leaving.

People stop work and are ready to leave a few minutes before time. They line-up in the corridor leading to the clock and chat. At a quarter-to-five everyone is away. Some people will walk to the bus stop with a friend.

Work in a flow-line situation is rather different. You are part of a team. You may be 'a relief' rushing around filling-in and helping out. There are crises when something goes wrong, or the line may stop and you can chat. But the broad rhythm and routine of the plastics factory we have described is fairly typical as is the broad language-communication situation.

2.3 Use of language

In most industrial work situations the use of language can be classified under the following very broad headings:

Work language

1a *Language associated with immediate job situations.*
For example: basic instructions; warnings for safety; simple messages; asking for help; apologizing for mistakes; justifying actions; identifying faults; written records.

1b *Language required for work flexibility, for unusual situations, and for increased responsibility.*
For example: following unfamiliar instructions; understanding verbally the whole process; explaining an accident; using the telephone; written notes.

Social language

2a *Language for simple social contact.*
For example: greetings; names and forms of address; talking about family and interests; gossiping about factory.

2b *Language for the individual employee to communicate about his rights and problems.*
For example: explaining an absence; discussing a major personal problem with shop steward, supervisor, or personnel manager; querying wages; completing forms.

1a and **2a** tend to have a much higher frequency than **1b** and **2b**, and usually tend to be verbally less complex. In this sense, competence in **1a** and **2a** may have to precede competence in **1b** and **2b**. On the other hand, the need for competence in communication situations **1b** and **2b** may be felt more strongly by the individual foreigner, whilst the employer may consider **1a** sufficient. In fact **1a** is unlikely to be possible without **2a** at the very least.

Obviously these very broad classifications overlap and lack clear definition. However, when a picture of a day's work in a particular place is built up and then all the occasions for language communication are put against it under these four broad classifications, a picture of the language communication needs of a worker begins to emerge in terms of function. In other words, the language teacher begins to understand the learner's needs so that he can make them central to all his choices in the way suggested in Chapter 1. A methodology for investigating and analysing a work situation is suggested in Chapter 6.

As well as considering language functions, we must also classify each situation in terms of the language skills involved, whether listening and understanding, speaking, reading, or writing.

We have examined communication needs in a factory in very broad and general terms and we have assumed that the Asian worker can potentially participate in all areas of communication in English. We appreciate that this is often not the case for reasons of concentration of Asians on particular shifts or in particular work areas, or because of cultural inhibitions. In these circumstances, needs and opportunities may be much restricted although this will vary between individuals. However, there will always be some areas of need which should be the starting point and presumably, where language training is undertaken, the aim is to achieve a much greater opportunity for using English for both efficiency and for social reasons.

Chapter 3
Communication breakdowns and inadequacies

An examination of communication breakdowns at work involving Asian workers illuminates much about the nature of the language-communication situation. Such an examination suggests priorities in selection for a language training course, and that such a course should include training in overcoming these breakdowns for native speakers as well as the foreign learners of a language.

3.1 The unpredictable pattern of problems for the foreigner

A foreign worker seldom knows no English at all unless he has just arrived. Many Asians may have learned some English before coming to England. But, as we have already discussed, the actual ability to *communicate* in English depends on much more than knowledge of the linguistic features of English. It has often been a painful and frustrating experience for more educated immigrants who thought they 'knew' English before coming to England to discover that they cannot participate in the simplest communicative situations. The point is illustrated by the story of an Indian graduate whose first job in England was at night in a bakery. Every hour or two the supervisor would walk past, shout /ɔː rai/ (All right?) and put his thumb up with the purpose of phatic greeting and encouragement. The Indian thought this must mean 'Get on with your work', and immediately looked for something more to do. The supervisor probably thought the Indian knew not a word of English and was rather stupid, and the Indian was losing confidence and feeling the supervisor was a hard task-master. If the supervisor had chosen to initiate communication in some other way, he might have succeeded.

People who have come to England with no previous knowledge of English have always picked up some language at work and often quite a lot. But it is characteristic of most immigrants that their ability to communicate is very patchy. A person can manage in one situation but is quite ineffectual in another, and what makes the difference between the situations is not only linguistic skills but many other factors. For example, an operator may understand an instruction given at the end of a break about starting up or adjusting his machine, but he may misunderstand an instruction on how to adjust his machine when it is going wrong and his work is being rejected. The second situation may not only be linguistically more complex, but is also a situation of greater stress and potential conflict. At the same time, unless the immigrant has become totally isolated and withdrawn from English-speakers, there should be a tendency over time for his ability to use English to increase gradually. However, one of the arguments for language training at work is to give this tendency a substantial boost and to create the conditions for learning to continue.

3.2 Expected patterns of communication

A characteristic of a day's factory work for an unskilled operator is how routine, repetitive, and predictable nearly everything is. Patterns of communication are part of this larger predictable pattern of behaviour. In Chapter One we analysed the different functions of language in a single verbal transaction, and if we examined some of the different sorts of transactions listed on page 18 we would find recurring functions and patterns of functions. Obviously, in a similar way, there are recurring transactions and patterns of transactions running through a whole day. A native English-speaker probably has these expectations about the pattern of communication stretching over a day (and longer). Therefore, if the immigrant fails in part of the overall pattern, he is potentially affecting all the rest of it. In this respect the failure to say anything may be a more serious communication breakdown than saying something even if it is not properly understood. A few examples will clarify this obvious point:

Never greeting English-speakers.
Not talking to a member of your work team.
Not saying anything when you take something.
Not telling people anything about yourself.
Never querying instructions.
Never raising a personal problem with the supervisor
  or shop steward.
Never attending a Union meeting or never saying
  anything at one.

The significance of these departures from the expected pattern of communication will obviously appear very different to immigrants and to English-speakers. English-speakers will tend to interpret such behaviour as rude, unfriendly, secretive, lacking in initiative, evidence of a simple and primitive person, evidence of an obsequious nature, and lack of interest in the common cause. For the immigrant on the other hand, if he knows very little English, these silences may represent inability to relate to English-speakers, loneliness, lack of any job satisfaction, a feeling that no one is interested in him as an individual, no opportunity to express his real worries and problems. For the English-speakers it is a short step to conclude that the particular immigrant is only interested in money and cares nothing for general conditions. Many English-speakers then feel on the basis of one person that the majority of Asians are rude and primitive and that all Asians are interested in is money.

3.3 Some characteristics of communication breakdowns

We shall now consider communication breakdowns on the level of particular transactions. Again the two types of breakdown occur; communication breakdowns where nothing is said, or breakdowns where the wrong thing is said or understood. Obviously the first type occurs more often when the initiation of the verbal transaction is the responsibility of an immigrant.

Examples

1 Someone says 'Yes', but carries out instruction wrongly.

2 Someone admits to doing something, but says nothing when asked for an explanation.

3 Someone tells someone, e.g. 'You must give me overtime', without having the authority to make such a statement.

4 Someone varies the sequence of a job, but denies not doing the job as instructed.

There would be no point in making a long list of such breakdowns. But in each case it would be a common reaction for an English-speaking person to consider that these are each examples of deliberate bad behaviour. This dramatically underlines the fact that language is in reality part of social behaviour. Very often, particularly in a factory situation, language and action are closely linked. The average person cannot judge the language component separately and simply draws his conclusion from the total of linguistic and non-linguistic behaviour. An example of this is a supervisor who complained that an Asian worker only understood what was in his interests and not what was in the interests of the company. He gave as an example the fact that the worker could understand when asked if he wanted to work overtime, but not when there was a fault in the running of his machine and he was told how to correct it.

One more example highlights how difficult it is to isolate the language-communication element in behaviour. A Pakistani was working in an area of a factory where there was lead dust and it was compulsory to wear a head unit with breathing apparatus. He several times was caught by the foreman breaking this regulation. As far as the foreman was concerned, it was unnecessary to seek an explanation because none was admissible. The foreman simply had to initiate the disciplinary procedure. The shop steward took no action at all as the facts were not in dispute and the Union backed total enforcement of the rules. Only when the man had achieved a record which might result in his dismissal did the shop steward look into the case. The shop steward then discovered that the man had no appreciation of the dangers in his work because of his poor English. The Pakistani knew there was a rule over wearing a breathing apparatus but, because of heat and noise, he did not keep the rule. No one liked wearing the apparatus, and no one would have bothered if they thought it was just a rule, but other people appreciated that the apparatus protected their health. In other words, other workers had a rational and emotional motivation to keep the rule, the acquisition of which depended upon communication; without communication the rules became unenforceable.

Figure 1 attempts to sum up this discussion of communication breakdowns in a diagram, which can apply to either party in a verbal transaction between a native and non-native speaker of a language.

We have examined communication breakdowns at work involving Asian workers at some length because they illuminate much about the nature of the language-communication situation, they suggest priorities in selection for a language training course, and they suggest that such a course should include training in overcoming these breakdowns for both parties.

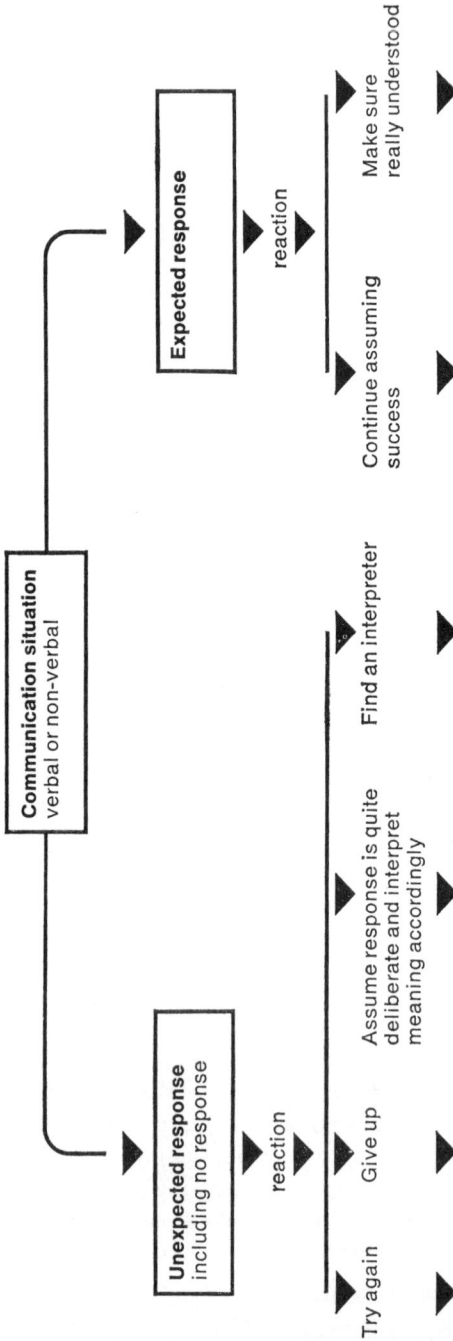

Figure 1
Communication between people with different first languages

Chapter 4
Designing language teaching items for a particular communicative need

The aim of our language teaching materials is the practical one of enabling Asian immigrants to communicate more effectively at their particular place of work. In designing them we have tried to take account of as many as possible of the different factors involved in learning to communicate in a new language. These factors are represented in Figure 2.

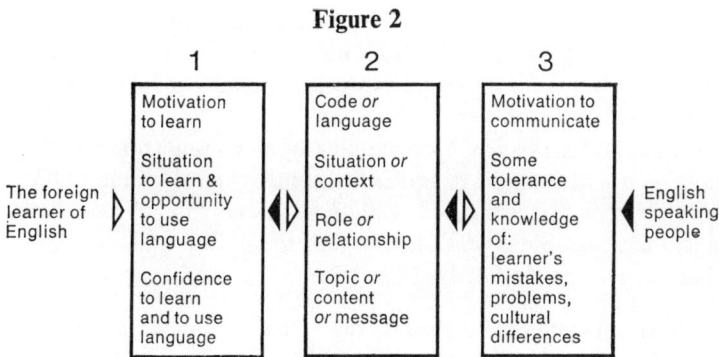

Figure 2

	1	2	3	
The foreign learner of English ▷	Motivation to learn Situation to learn & opportunity to use language Confidence to learn and to use language	Code *or* language Situation *or* context Role *or* relationship Topic *or* content *or* message	Motivation to communicate Some tolerance and knowledge of: learner's mistakes, problems, cultural differences	◀ English speaking people

The factors in boxes 1 and 3 are integral to success, but their solution is dependent upon a specific set of personal and organizational factors on both sides in the particular workplace. We shall, therefore, leave their discussion until later. Box 2 represents the factors determining the selection of language when communicating: the formal rules and the rules of use and the relationship between the two.

In order to understand the sort of things involved in the factors in box 2 and how they can be tackled systematically in language teaching materials, we shall now analyse one restricted but important area of social communication – the use of names and forms of address. We are taking this example because the code or language involved is restricted and straightforward. The rules of use in connection with situation and relationship are fairly clear and mutually exclusive. We are, therefore, taking a relatively elementary and clear-cut example which even so is difficult enough to analyse and transform into teaching items. As such, we hope the analysis and teaching scheme that follows can stand as an example of how these teaching materials seek to meet particular communicative needs, but bearing in mind that for more complex areas of language-communication it is much more difficult to analyse requirements and prepare appropriate teaching items.

4.1 Difficulties with names and forms of address

Most English as a foreign language courses give very little attention to the use of names and forms of address in English. Often names are first introduced in structural practice with the verb 'to be':

I'm John Smith. He's Fred Jones. You're Mary Davies.

No real guidance is given with use of surnames or first names. The pronoun 'you' is generally used for addressing people and occasionally an unexplained 'sir', 'darling', etc. occurs. How adequate or helpful is this for an Asian at work in Britain or for most foreign learners anywhere?

Undoubtedly this is a problem area of communication which causes misunderstandings and frustrations. Typical examples of problems are: English people calling all Asians 'Singh' plus their clock number: 'Singh 704'; the English supervisor who complained: 'They never call me Gladys.'

These difficulties arise because the systems of names and the uses of names in calling for equivalent purposes are quite different in England and in the various areas of the Asian subcontinent from which the immigrant groups have originated. Secondly, quite different linguistic means are used for a similar function or purpose when addressing people in English and in the other relevant languages. But neither English people nor Asians generally understand the existence of these differences; instead, both groups assume that the other group uses unpronounceable names in a totally unsystematic way and is often very rude in addressing people in English. It is inevitable that in this very sensitive area any departure from 'the rules of use' of each group will be considered rude unless 'sociolinguistic interference' is recognized.

4.2 Sikh Punjabi names and forms of address

A Sikh Punjabi normally has a three-part name based on the following system:

a given name	a complimentary suffix	a sub-caste name

Examples

| Harbans | Singh | Gill |
| Joginder | Kaur | Grewal |

The given name is chosen at random from the Sikh scriptures and consequently these names are not sex-specific. The given-name is used on its own in some close relationships.

The complimentary suffix is always 'Singh' for a man and 'Kaur' for a woman. These names are never used on their own, but are used after the given-name to give a degree of formality in some ways comparable to *Mr* Smith or *Mrs* Jones.

The sub-caste name belongs to the family and is inherited through the father. Families with the same sub-caste name are not necessarily related. In these respects a sub-caste name is similar to an English surname, but traditionally it is neither used nor revealed by the family because of social and religious inhibitions. If it is used, it will often only be used by the head of the joint-family. The sub-caste name would never traditionally be used on its own.

Given-name variations. Within the family variations and derivatives of the name are used and possibly nick-names. But these are rather intimate and are not used outside the family.

Calling practices and forms of address. Names (i.e. given-names) are used much less for calling purposes than amongst the English. When given-names are used a suffix of respect or affection is often added. In many relationships the name is never used – a wife never addresses or refers to her husband by name but in terms of one of his roles. Friends and kin are called 'brother' and 'sister', older friends 'uncle' and 'aunt'. Other people are more often addressed by their role – 'teacher', 'leader' etc. In addition, there is a choice of pronoun and verb form (the French *tu/vous* distinction is a comparable feature) which indicates attitude and relationship.

In most respects, the Sikh Punjabi practices of naming and address are quite different from English ones. Punjabi has fairly clearly defined practices which emphasize roles, relationships, and situations. This in turn is a reflection of a more traditional society in which relationships are often still linked to kinship and village.

4.3 The English system of names and forms of address

This is essentially a two-part system of:

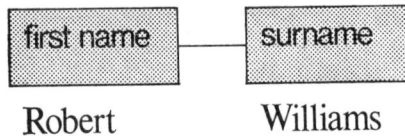

```
┌─────────────┐      ┌─────────────┐
│ first name  │──────│  surname    │
└─────────────┘      └─────────────┘
    Robert              Williams
```

The safest English name to use is always *the surname*.
The use or non-use of a title with the surname is a significant choice (Mr, Mrs, Miss). Practice in the use of first names is rapidly changing and is often at present determined by an extremely confusing mixture of factors to do with age, social standing, situation, and relationship, as well as being a purely individual matter of preference. There is often some established practice which governs the use of first names in the workplace, but the surname remains the essential form of identification which is demanded on all important occasions.

Nick-names are widely used in workplaces as well as ethnic first names – e.g. 'Paddy' and 'Jock'.

Other forms of address. Amongst women in a factory originally intimate forms are freely used: 'love', 'darling', 'dear', etc. These are also used between men and women of similar status. Men use comparable forms between themselves: 'mate', 'son', etc. Or they use abusive forms as a sign of friendship and equality: 'bastard', 'bugger' etc. Generally swearing is extremely free between men and is often a sign of friendship whereas in Punjabi it is more personally abusive.

A difficulty in English is knowing whether a relationship is being treated as one of equality or inequality. Politeness and attitude cannot be shown by pronouns and verbs, and are usually indicated by modal verbs, by tags, and by introductory phrases such as, 'Excuse me,' or, 'Can you spare a moment?'

We have given only a very general account of the two systems, but they are clearly different and with many opportunities for confusion and misunderstanding between the two. The Hindu name system is broadly similar to the Sikh Punjabi one; the name systems of Muslims from the subcontinent are somewhat different. There is plenty of evidence that these differences and confusions lead to serious misunderstandings on both sides as well as inconvenience for Asians.

4.4 A scheme of language teaching items for English names and forms of address

The use of names and forms of address in English is dealt with in the teaching materials in Part Two of this book. Obviously this is a use of language which will occur in very many teaching items, but it is particularly dealt with in the following items: 11, 13, 17, 20, 53, 55, 57, 58, 61, 68, 107 and 167. Some of these items would have to be adapted and others added depending on the custom of a particular workplace. However, we suggest that the reader looks up these items and judges how they measure up to the criteria suggested in the second box in figure 2 (page 23), and how they constitute a scheme for teaching a particular language function.

Two important factors in this scheme are that the complexity of the items develops slowly and that they are well spaced out in time. This illustrates the difference between teaching linguistic items and language functions. The learner has to grasp the actual use of the item and modify his behaviour on the shop-floor in this respect before he has 'learned' it. The presentation of all the material in a single block would be impractical in terms of changed language behaviour.

One reason for orthodox English language courses failing to cover this topic adequately is that neither a 'structural' nor 'situational' approach will suggest the importance of this topic or an adequate method of treatment, whereas a functional approach will. It may be argued that the topic is important to immigrants but peripheral to most foreign learners. But names and forms of address are extremely important in any language situation; for example, in personal contact, over the telephone and in letters. Levels of tolerance of incorrect use by different foreign groups vary but departure from the norms of practice usually affects communication.

4.5 Conclusion

We have tried to show in this chapter how certain broad principles of language learning, and the communicative needs of Asian workers can be taken account of in designing teaching items. We have examined how for one language function – naming and addressing – the factors in Figure 2 (box 2) have influenced our materials writing in twelve items. In the next chapter we shall consider the broader pattern of overall course design which has to take account of all the factors in Figure 2.

Chapter 5
A concept for a functional language learning course

In this chapter we shall consider first the construction of a learning strategy for Asian immigrant workers based on our earlier examination of needs and then the framework for preparing a functional course for such learners. We shall then suggest that a broader concept for the construction of functional language courses can be generalized from our experience with Asians, and that this concept can apply in a great variety of situations, and can apply to written needs as much as spoken ones.

5.1 A learning scheme for Asian workers

What follows is a very simplified scheme of some factors involved for Asian workers in mastering effective functional language for their work situation. This scheme is largely based on the broad classification of language-communication at work described on page 16, and the factors in Figure 2. We have represented this in Figure 3 as a 'Language Ladder'. An obvious way of constructing such a ladder would be simply in terms of the complexity and difficulty of the main areas of functional language involved. But our analysis in Chapter 3 of language breakdowns shows how complicated and involved real improvement in language behaviour must be, and how any particular language transaction, or the absence of one, may lead to further learning or may hold up further progress. The learners experience on the ladder builds up a pattern of motivation, reaction, and opportunity which may send him back to the bottom of the ladder or keep him permanently stuck at some point.

'The Language Ladder' is not meant to be a scheme for a language training course. Everyone who comes to work in a factory for the first time has a communication ladder to climb, even if in some particulars different from Figure 3. Some foreigners with considerable linguistic skills – say an Indian graduate – might nevertheless have great difficulty in progressing up the ladder. Linguistic skills are necessary for progress, but they are certainly not sufficient.

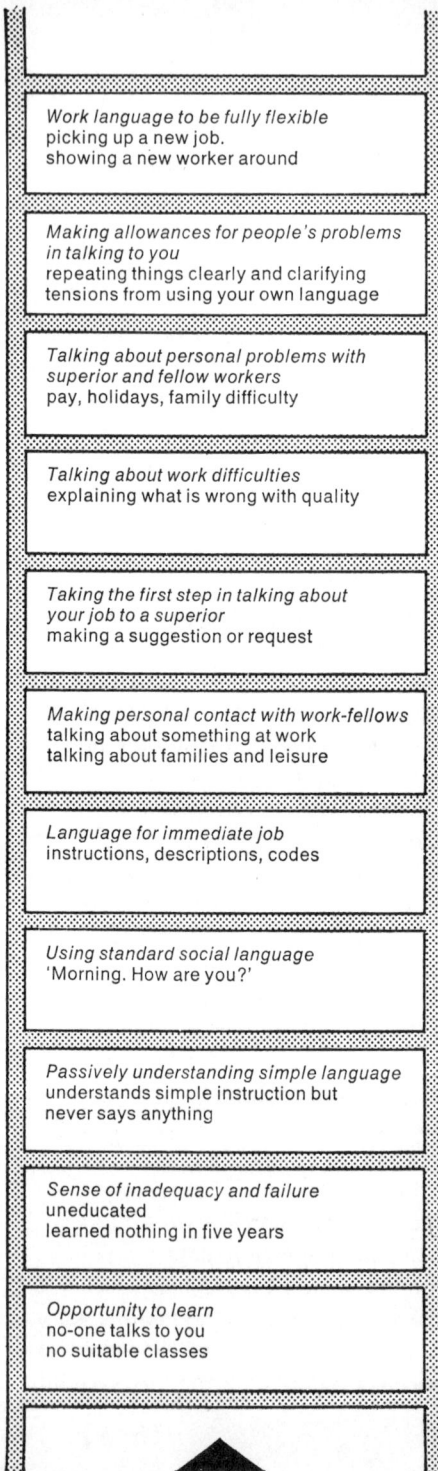

Figure 3
The language ladder
read from the bottom of the page

Note. The detailed items given
under the main heading on each
rung are only illustrations from
a very large total of possibilities

Work language to be fully flexible
picking up a new job.
showing a new worker around

*Making allowances for people's problems
in talking to you*
repeating things clearly and clarifying
tensions from using your own language

*Talking about personal problems with
superior and fellow workers*
pay, holidays, family difficulty

Talking about work difficulties
explaining what is wrong with quality

*Taking the first step in talking about
your job to a superior*
making a suggestion or request

Making personal contact with work-fellows
talking about something at work
talking about families and leisure

Language for immediate job
instructions, descriptions, codes

Using standard social language
'Morning. How are you?'

Passively understanding simple language
understands simple instruction but
never says anything

Sense of inadequacy and failure
uneducated
learned nothing in five years

Opportunity to learn
no-one talks to you
no suitable classes

A group of language trainees might be at any point of the ladder and they might be making some progress or they might be stuck. But the idea of the ladder is very relevant to the course planner because, if a reasonably accurate picture of the learners' tasks can be built up in this way, the course planner can establish his priorities and identify key obstacles to progress either in the learner himself or in his environment. The ladder may also help the course planner to understand why an individual's linguistic skills and language performance are widely disparate. In this way, it may be established that a language training programme should start with items which are elementary in linguistic terms so that the work and effort can be concentrated on language as social behaviour. If the diagnosis is correct and the teaching effective, there will be no problem of the learners thinking the course is 'too easy'. It is where time is spent on elementary linguistic items without their being relevant to communication needs that a trainee loses motivation and complains that a course is too easy.

5.2 A course scheme for Industrial English for Asian immigrants

We shall first examine aims, priorities, and constraints which must determine many points in the construction of a language training programme.

There are two principal aims in running an English course for Asians at work:

a to teach the English the learner needs for his immediate job, and to enable him to communicate more freely about the work situation in general and so to become a more effective and flexible worker able to take more responsibility.

b to teach the English needed for simple social contact within the work place between the learner and native English-speaking workers. This is essential for good industrial relations and also for attractive working conditions for employees of all origins. And besides, communication being social, aim **a** cannot be achieved without aim **b**.

These aims are functional and confined to the place of work and largely involve only spoken English. However, the wider aim of equipping an immigrant to live in Britain is achieved indirectly because for the majority of Asians the place of work is the primary place of adjustment to English society. Once the immigrant has the knowledge and confidence to communicate successfully at work, his ability to do so elsewhere will quickly follow.

Operating upon these aims **a** and **b** are two severe constraints. The amount of time available is extremely limited (usually only about 50 hours) and this is very little in terms of the time normally required to learn a foreign language. Secondly, the course is being taught inside the work place, where management and non-participants will often expect very quick and unrealistic results.

On the other hand, an in-company course offers one enormous advantage compared with orthodox part-time courses: all the learners want English for the same purposes and in the same situations. This enables the teacher to provide fairly precisely the English the learner needs, and for the learners the opportunity exists for immediate and sustained practice and reinforcement. This unique advantage goes a long way to solve the fundamental language learning problems of *motivation*, and *opportunity to use*. This is the most important justification for in-company language teaching and is probably the principal reason for our having achieved superior results with in-company courses compared with part-time evening courses of comparable length held elsewhere. To take advantage of this situation, it is essential for the teacher to understand fully the communication needs of the work situation, and for him to build up a relationship with English-speakers on the shop-floor so that he can involve them in the process of application of the new language by trainees to real communication situations.

There are many important respects in which Asian immigrants do not fit into the normal categories of learners of English. These include:

a They are living in Britain.

b They are already successfully using English to some extent, however inaccurately, and their passive knowledge of English may be fairly extensive.

c They severely lack confidence about learning English, having probably been in Britain for several years.

d They often lack educational background.

The teacher has the opportunity of access to students before the course begins and this should be used not just to assess their linguistic level, but also to find out as much as possible about their background and their experience of using and learning English.

Figure 4

Course Scheme for Industrial English
read from the bottom of the page upwards

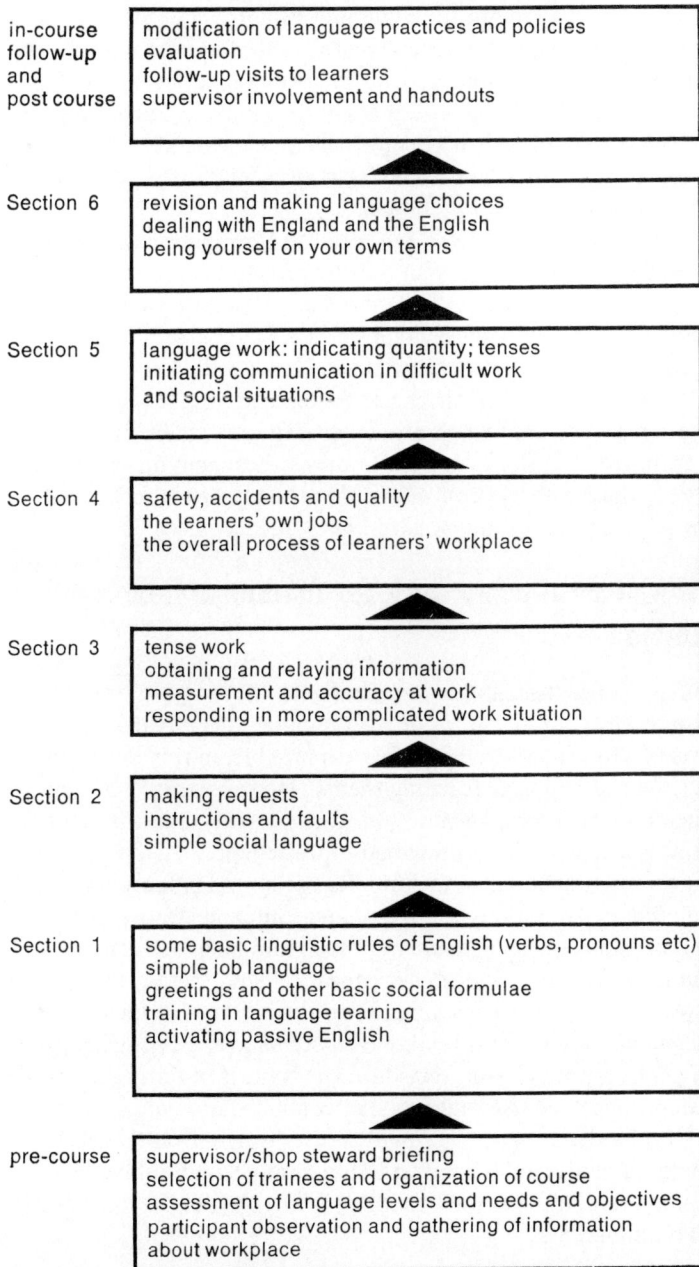

in-course follow-up and post course	modification of language practices and policies evaluation follow-up visits to learners supervisor involvement and handouts
Section 6	revision and making language choices dealing with England and the English being yourself on your own terms
Section 5	language work: indicating quantity; tenses initiating communication in difficult work and social situations
Section 4	safety, accidents and quality the learners' own jobs the overall process of learners' workplace
Section 3	tense work obtaining and relaying information measurement and accuracy at work responding in more complicated work situation
Section 2	making requests instructions and faults simple social language
Section 1	some basic linguistic rules of English (verbs, pronouns etc) simple job language greetings and other basic social formulae training in language learning activating passive English
pre-course	supervisor/shop steward briefing selection of trainees and organization of course assessment of language levels and needs and objectives participant observation and gathering of information about workplace

35

Because of the extreme limitations of time available for in-company courses, the aim in selecting language content must be to provide the learner with the minimum English he needs to function effectively in the priority situations selected. As an immigrant, and therefore in a basic language learning situation at work, the learner should be able to continue up the language ladder after the course has finished, particularly if some of the key difficulties on the way up the ladder in the form of other people's behaviour and attitudes have been modified.

We have attempted in the *Industrial English* materials to take account of all these factors and of the principles and needs discussed in earlier chapters. The materials we have provided only constitute a part of what is involved in a full course scheme. Figure 4 shows the six sections of the course within the context of all the other work the teacher has to do. This course scheme may appear neat and final when presented diagramatically, but this is far from the intention, which is to present teaching materials as part of a larger course concept so that the teacher is more easily able to adapt and change them to his students' needs.

5.3 A general framework for functional language training

We have concentrated very specifically on the language-communication needs and difficulties of Asian immigrants at work in British factories and we have only departed from this in general discussion of language teaching theory. However, many of the principles which have been discussed and the general learning and course schemes we have presented in this chapter should be relevant to any functional or communicative language teaching programme, particularly in an employment context.

There is increasing demand for functional language courses for commerce, industry, and higher education, and these are often run at work for groups with similar needs. The general principles and scheme presented in this book have been successfully applied by one of the authors in the very different context of fairly advanced written English courses within large commercial organizations in the Middle East. Figure 5 presents a very general framework for planning functional language training in any situation. But we consider parallels also exist to many of the specific factors affecting Asian immigrants.

Figure 5

A general framework for functional language training
read from the bottom of the page upwards

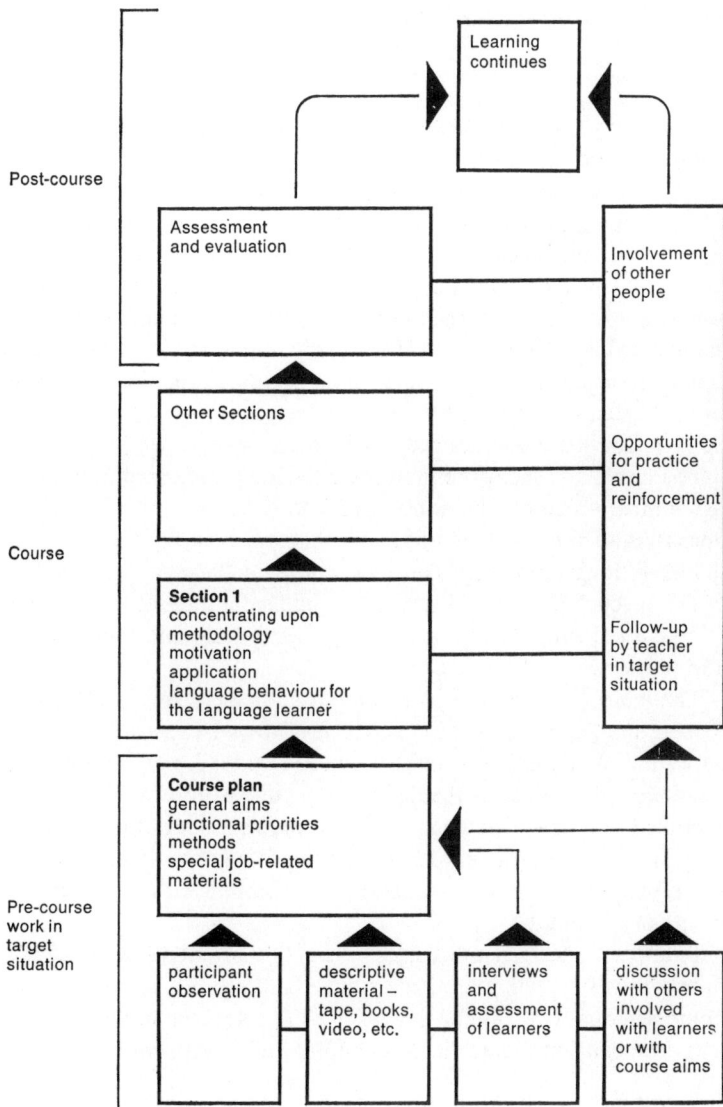

Post-course		Learning continues
	Assessment and evaluation	Involvement of other people
Course	Other Sections	Opportunities for practice and reinforcement
	Section 1 concentrating upon methodology motivation application language behaviour for the language learner	Follow-up by teacher in target situation
Pre-course work in target situation	**Course plan** general aims functional priorities methods special job-related materials	

participant observation — descriptive material – tape, books, video, etc. — interviews and assessment of learners — discussion with others involved with learners or with course aims

Chapter 6
The investigation of language requirements in an employment situation including assessment of trainees

We now turn to the first stage of the course scheme outlined in Figure 4 (page 35). It has been continually emphasized that in order to make the learners' needs central to his plans and decisions, a teacher must involve himself fully in the learners' situation. It is essential for the teacher to investigate and experience the social reality of a place of work before he can make choices about what language functions a learner in that situation needs and what linguistic skills these involve. The investigator's role is not one of a detached observer. He must develop a real 'feel' for the work place so that he can understand the experiences, tensions, and frustrations which affect communication there.

The first stage therefore involves a thorough understanding of the company or organization in order to judge what the broad objectives of the course should be in language learning terms and the likely long-term benefits for the company.

The teacher must also build up an understanding of the attitudes of English-speaking people including supervision, and the stresses and tensions of the work place.

The materials in *Part Two* contain a number of specifically job-related language teaching items which have to be specially prepared for each company where a course is taking place. There are a number of such items throughout the course, and most of Section Four of the teaching materials requires special preparation. In order to do this a teacher has to familiarize himself thoroughly with the work situation and communication requirements of the plant.

Finally, the teacher must judge the actual level and needs of the immigrants who will attend the course, and select a reasonably homogeneous class. The technical sides of selection and assessment are dealt with later in this chapter and in Appendix Two.

6.1 General plan of investigation

We suggest an investigation should take the following form:

a General and swift tour of entire site to grasp general nature of processes, products, and work, and to observe distribution of labour on site.

b Discussions with relevant management and supervision.

c English assessment interviews with all non-English speakers; *or* a representative sample; *or* those considered by management to have language/communication problems.

d Close observation and understanding of department(s) from which students will be drawn.

e Tape recording of instructions and job descriptions for a number of representative jobs at present done by potential language trainees, or which it is planned they should be able to do after the language course.

There follows a series of headings which will provide a useful scheme for such an investigation under each of the above main divisions.

6.2 General information about the firm

List of all departments.
    Work done in each.
    Main categories of jobs in each.
Size and composition of workforce.
Organization of work (shifts, bonus scheme, piece-work, etc.).

6.3 Discussion with relevant members of management and supervision

Most people cannot talk in much detail or with understanding about communication problems. For this reason, the discussion should always concentrate upon concrete examples. Even in a company which recognizes a language-communication problem, there will be people who deny it; and this will be true the closer one gets to the shop-floor where junior management will not want to suggest they have not got the situation completely under control.

Typical reactions will be: 'They all understand, but they pretend they don't when it suits them.' 'You don't need any English for this job.' These discussions are just as important for what they reveal about attitudes as for factual information. They help build up a picture of the environment in which the immigrant has to learn English.

In discussion with management and supervision, it is best to start with general questions such as:

'Do you have people who don't know much English?'
'Does it interfere with their work?'

After some unprompted talking, the following questions are important:

a Do they require closer supervision?

b Have they less job-flexibility?

c Do you have to use interpreters? (How often? How much time is wasted?)

d Is labour turnover high?

e Are there safety problems?

f Are there aspects of the job to do with waste, quality, appearance, that it may be difficult to put over?

g Are records accurate?

h Are there misunderstandings with native English-speakers?

i How well is the overall process grasped?

j What happens when there are breakdowns and emergencies?

k Are there good operators who cannot progress in the company?

l Is less initiative shown than you would like to see?

m Does the training you give assume a certain level of English?

In each case the investigator should probe as to how far language may be a cause of any of these problems.

6.4 Observation in the relevant sections or departments

This is best done by the teacher spending a day or so working at the factory – although obviously not incognito. It is important to move around a lot and understand all the main categories of work.

Social Interaction

Arrival at work.
Cloakroom, sitting, and chatting.
Assembling on the factory floor.
Assignment to job.
Tea-breaks.

Machine breakdowns.
Working close to other people.
Dinner, canteen, cloakroom, tidying-up.
Lunchtime shopping.
Afternoon (as above).
Tidying-up at the end of the day.
Leaving the factory.
Travelling home and to work.
Shift change-overs.

Language of the immediate job situation

Language used in the normal routine of the job.
Language required for regular interruptions.
Explaining a difficulty arising in the course of the job.
Requesting assistance from a supervisor.
Recognizing codes, labels, names, packets, etc. used on the job.
Understanding verbally the process in the department of which this job is a part.
Carrying out verbal instructions relating to any part of this process.
Understanding factory regulations.
Keeping written records.
Emergencies.

Language for flexibility and increased responsibility

Understanding verbally the manufacturing process of the whole plant.
Some understanding of all operations on the whole site.
Ability to carry out and give accurate instructions relating to any part of the department.
Using English with a wide variety of people.
Intelligible pronunciation.
Ability to read essential written matter in the factory.
Keeping written records.
Simple arithmetic required.

Language for simple social contact

Correct forms of greeting, parting, and address.
English for routine situations (e.g. canteen, going off to breaks, request for things, playing cards).

Discussing things that have happened in the factory.
Families, jobs, clothes, health.

Language for formal personal situations

Procedures for welfare, discipline, and grievances.
Explaining absence or lateness.
Contact with shop stewards.
Union meetings.
Contact with supervisors – wages, holidays, leave.
Contact with management.

Attitudinal factors affecting the use of English

Behaviour of supervisory staff

a Their use of English to Asians: speed, style, consistency.

b Their confidence in Asians as workers.

c Their general behaviour: attitude, demands, sociability.

d Use of interpreters.

Behaviour of fellow-workers.
Ethnic or national composition of working groups.
Length of time in U.K. and at the company.
Age.
Physical arrangement of machinery and working positions.
Transferred styles of verbal behaviour from the native language.
Cultural behaviour.

Things that are disliked by Asians and English about each other

Examples
personal habits, food, speaking Indian languages,
attitudes to cleaning up, ambition (money or position),
aggressive behaviour (particularly by English women),
relationships between the sexes.

Shift or daily timetable

6.5 Tape recording of work language

The usual supervisor, chargehand, or instructor should instruct
someone on a representative sample of jobs in the department,
and everything said should be recorded. There is usually a good

deal of overlap or similarity between jobs, so the number of key jobs can be reduced to quite a small number.

The recordings made then form the basis of the special instructional job language which is fed into the course. Here is an example of how a tape transcript can be rewritten as a simple teaching item:

Assembling a battenholder base

Look at that.

Make sure you've got no chips round the edges and cracks in it. No short mouldings and them two holes are in. Then you pick your battenholder up. Make sure that there are no cracked key holes and you've got all the screws in. Then that goes into the slot like that. You pick a ring up, put it on. Pick a short skirt up and then twist it round. You have to make sure it's not cross-threaded. Then you put it in a bin ready for packing.

Now look at teaching items 28 and 50 to see how this transcript has been utilized for teaching. For the learner to grasp the new language, a lot of other work is necessary on the present simple tense and on possessives. Although this is a simple and obvious example, in our experience, straight job descriptions can usually be utilized on the lines of this model.

It will also be useful if the department manager records an overall description of processes and purposes.

Specific job-related teaching items have to be specially prepared for each course and according to each work situation. Examples and guidance on how to do this is given under the teaching items concerned in each section.

6.6 Assessment and selection of trainees

We have found it best to base assessment on an individual face-to-face interview. The aim of this is both to select a class which is reasonably homogeneous in terms of initial knowledge of English and have similar English language needs, and to gain some initial understanding of individual linguistic and communicative weaknesses. At the same time the learners must represent the main level of communication problem which exists in the company.

There are various ways of proceeding. If the company has decided who has language difficulties and who they want to train, the teacher should ask for a list of all possible employees for language training. There should be more names put forward than places in the class. The class organizer then interviews everyone and draws up a list for the class. If the company has identified a department where there are difficulties, rather than individuals, if practical, all non-native speakers of English in that department should be interviewed. If numbers are too large, only a sample can be interviewed – the target group identified – and then others at a similar level can be identified informally and then interviewed. If the class is to be a voluntary one, everyone interested can volunteer, be interviewed, and then be told whether they can have a place.

The company may want to take into account factors other than level of language in giving employees training so that any final list must be decided after further consultation with management and supervision. But the class organizer should also reserve the right to exclude any individual from the course.

Another important reason for formal language assessment interviews before starting a course is that the results of the tests will provide a standard for measuring how much progress individuals have achieved by the end of the course. This is essential both from an academic point of view and to demonstrate what has been achieved to the company concerned and other interested companies. The whole of the pre-course and post-course assessment tests need not be the same, but there should be several identical items in both.

We have experimented quite a lot with assessment and evaluation tests and details of these are given in Appendix Two (page 317). These tests have not been standardized, so it would be misleading to provide any guidance on the interpretation of particular scores. The scoring systems provided are only for guidance, and users of the tests must build up their own experience as to the meaning of scores; and will want to introduce their own system of weighting scores.

We suggest the following criteria for any initial assessment interviews:

a Be reasonably easy and quick to administer (5–10 minutes).

b Mainly assess standard of spoken English relevant to situations at work.

c Provide recorded samples of each individual's English for later study and comparison.

d Provide crude assessment of reading and writing skills and some background information about the individual.

The assessment interviews should provide the basis for judging separately performance in the four skills of listening, speaking, reading, and writing. At an elementary level the following broad structure has proved useful:

a Simple, social chat – aimed at reassurance and some information gathering.

b Understanding and carrying out verbal instructions accurately.

c Expressing oneself about one's work.

d General level of reading and writing.

We will return later to the subject of evaluation which must include far more than a repeat assessment interview if it is to assess achievement in real communicative skills.

Chapter 7
The contents and methodology of the Industrial English teaching materials

The teaching materials which are contained in Part Two of this book are aimed at employees with fairly elementary problems of understanding and talking English and, for this reason and because of the limited time normally available, the course is almost entirely in spoken English. Although the six sections of the materials are of progressive difficulty, it is not intended that items within sections will necessarily be taught in sequence or used as they stand. Exactly how and what items are used will vary between groups of learners. A group who required a lot of time on Section One would probably not be able to reach more than one or two items of Section Six. Groups with an extensive passive knowledge of English can move quickly through Sections One and Two and greater emphasis can be given to the later sections. We have tried to produce a basic core of materials easily open to adaptation and variation in the light of the teacher's knowledge of his students' situation and needs, which we assume he will have built up in the way suggested in Chapter 6. In designing the materials we have also had in mind that at the elementary level lessons should be frequent but short – four or five times a week for up to an hour and that total time will probably be very limited (up to about 60 hours).

This chapter provides a broad introduction to the course materials themselves, and as such is less general in discussion and application than the earlier chapters. However, the emphasis is upon the broad principles of selection of contents and of the methodology because *Part Two* contains the close detail. Each of the six sections of the teaching materials begins with a detailed description of contents, and content and aims are further analysed for each group of teaching items (called 'Part 1, 2', etc.). The methodology is taken up in each teaching item because we consider methodology can be only considered in detail in relation to the particular purpose and content of an item. We have resisted drawing the methodology together because it can only be judged in relation to the group of learners, the teacher's relationship with them, and the situation for which the students are being taught English.

The methodology of the materials seeks throughout to take up the objective of functional language teaching as we have discussed it in terms of the variety of factors summarized in Figure 2 (page 25) and Figure 3 (page 32).

7.1 The scheme of subject matter and language contents

It is important to emphasize that the aims of a course at work are:

a to teach the English a learner needs for his immediate job and for simple social contact

b to teach English which will enable him to communicate more freely about the work situation in general and to express his personal problems and needs at work.

a is basic, but the extent that **b** can be realized will depend upon the particular group and the time available. These aims involve language learning in the classroom and modification of behaviour outside the classroom in the learners' common work situation. It will be obvious from the earlier discussion that we have considered the teaching of functional language for this common situation a higher priority than covering a grammatical syllabus of elementary English.

In designing the language teaching items, we found it useful at the outset to classify the language requirements of Asian people in the work situation in terms of the role in which the language was needed, and the function or purpose of the language within that role. This approach is summarized in Figure 6 on page 48. The broad scope of the items on axis A was outlined on page 18.

This scheme proved a very useful broad method of classifying many of the language situations we observed in order to judge the balance between the different roles and functions and to judge the situations of common language use within and between them. In designing a particular teaching item, it was obviously necessary to define role and function more closely so as to take the most useful decision on linguistic content and learning methodology. However, a few examples of teaching items show how the broad classifications of Figure 6 apply:

Figure 6

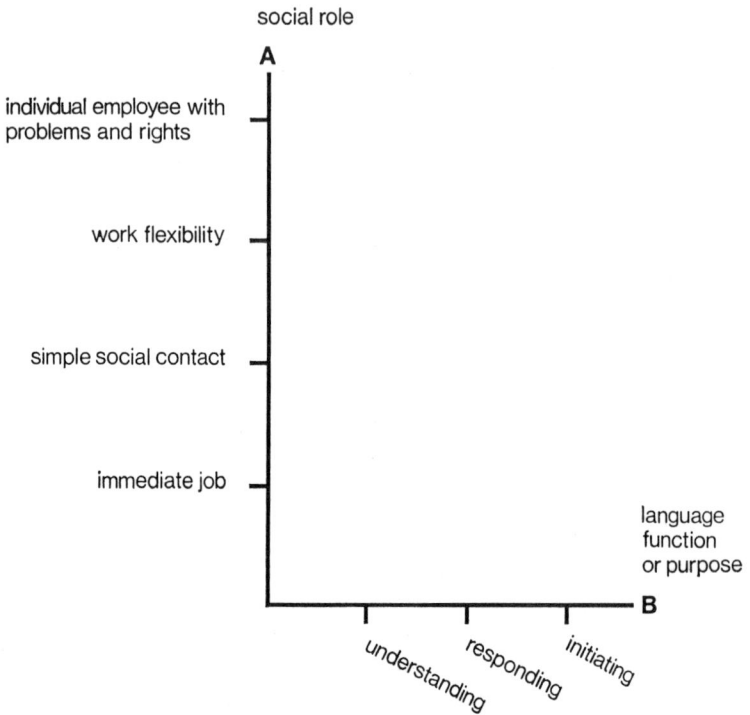

Number and title	Social role	Verbal purpose
Item 12 Factory codes	immediate job	understanding
Item 43 Arriving at work	social contact	responding
Item 71 Following unfamiliar instructions	work flexibility	understanding
Item 84 Asking for help in the factory	work flexibility	initiating

It was only after making some basic decisions on the selection of content in terms of language functions, social roles, and situations that we attempted to select and systematize linguistic content in terms of vocabulary and structure. Vocabulary selection tended to be fairly obvious, but the selection of structural material was far more difficult, particularly as we wanted to give limited time to systematic structural work.

The definition of language or code content has been approached in three ways:

a Simple language functions which recur across many situations. These are taught on their own and usually without attention to the structural components which are often very complex. In other words they are dealt with as idioms although at a later stage some of the structures may be taken up.

Examples
Item 18   expressions of meeting and parting
Items 60, 61   'Can I have . . ., please?'

After initial teaching, these language functions recur in longer stretches of multi-functional language.

b More sustained verbal situations in which a number of language functions occur, and in which considerable variations of language are possible. These cannot be usefully approached simply in terms of particular idioms or structures.

Examples
Items 94–100   Taking a message
Items 145–147 Explaning mistakes

For initial teaching purposes we have reduced this type of situation to a series of transactions each made up of several functions, some of which will have been covered in earlier items. For Items 94–100 these are:

1 Listen to the message and repeat it.
2 Say you have a message and deliver it.
3 Repeat the reply if any.
4 Say you've delivered the message and deliver the reply if any.

For language teaching purposes, there emerges from these transactions a mixture of language functions as in **a,** particular structural features (e.g. pronouns), and particular skills (e.g. accurate listening).

c Some sustained descriptive or instructional language proved structurally fairly simple and analysis pointed to obvious structural features which could be tackled in an elementary course.

Example
Item 28   Instructions – present simple tense

We applied these three approaches to our data and we found certain structural features of English stood out as very important for our purposes, and naturally quite often these are ones basic to all language teaching.

Examples

Section One	Personal pronouns and possessives
	Present simple tense (statement, question and negative forms)
Section Three	Past simple tense
Section Five	Present perfect tense
	Determiners

However, familiar though these look, it is important to emphasize that they have been selected and graded in terms of communicative needs. For the most part, structural material is taught and limited in terms of the criteria **a**, **b**, and **c** (page 49). But the very basic material of the examples above has sometimes been presented by a more orthodox language teaching method as a preliminary or follow up to its use in functional language situations.

The overall scheme of subject matter and language content aims to bring together a number of factors such as language code, role, situation, and message. A teacher planning a language course on the basis of the *Industrial English* teaching materials needs a comprehensive index of how the practice of language forms and language functions is combined in the items so that he can select and expand or reduce the material according to his students' particular needs. Such an index is provided as *Appendix One* at the back of the book.

7.2 The contents and progress of the course

A broad outline of the contents and progress of the course was given in Figure 4 (page 35). Each of the six sections are designed to last approximately two to three weeks (10–15 hours), of an intensive in-company course. Each section has its own contents and introduction and the reader who wants to familiarize himself with the material should now look at these and at Appendix One.

Section One is intended to increase the learner's confidence (probably lacking because of extended failure to communicate successfully in English), to familiarize the learner with the language teaching methods of the course, and to establish certain basic structural features of English. There are added difficulties for any learner when purely oral methods are used. Thus the items in this section are simple and many have been chosen because they will already be familiar. The learner begins to actively *use* English which he has probably been familiar with passively for some time. This will result in outwardly dramatic progress, which in turn greatly increases the learner's confidence and ability to come to grips with new and more difficult material.

Section Two exploits and extends the language of the previous section in more realistic factory situations. Tape dialogues are introduced for the first time containing characters who work in a factory. It is intended that the learner should develop some 'feel' for the way the language of these characters expresses their personality and attitude differences.

Section Three introduces the learner to much more complicated and realistic verbal situations in which he has to think out his response. This section also deals with measurement and accuracy in the work situation which involves a combination of behaviour, concept, and language, any of which may be unfamiliar.

The content of *Section Four* is entirely about the work place of the learner and his job. Most of the actual content has to be prepared by the course teacher and gathered in the factory. There is not a lot of new structural material in this section although inevitably there is a lot of vocabulary, but much of this should be familiar. This section is intended to bring home to the learner how applicable the English he is learning is to his work situation, how he can apply the same English in a variety of situations, and also how a variety of English can be used in the same situation.

Section Five moves the learner on to the role of initiating conversation in both work and social situations. Many of the situations are also ones in which serious communication breakdowns arise between English speakers and non-English speakers: mistakes on the job, and cultural and social misunderstanding.

Section Six contains a lot of difficult language needed for taking the initiative and for real flexibility at work. The emphasis is particularly upon a person being able to communicate in terms of himself as an individual: to be able to get help with his own problems, to be able to stand up for his rights, and to be able to explain things about himself and his own cultural background. Attention is also given to the need to choose the language appropriate for the situation and to revision of material in earlier sections.

Each section is fairly flexible and is specifically designed to allow for a flow of information, suggestion, and participation between teacher and factory. This should avoid an unrealistic presentation of middle-class and useless English. Of course, the fact remains that the teacher can only teach with his own pronunciation and his own variety of English, and this may be far removed from the factory floor. This is an added reason for using dialogue material recorded by local people. But this question of variety of English needs to be kept in proportion and not cause undue anxiety because the learner can adapt the style and pronunciation of his English.

We have found it reassuring and useful for the students to supply them with summary notes of the main points in each section after they have completed the section. Some students can already read English, and others can get a relation or friend to go over the notes with them. The printed word is an important symbol of education and, although it is impossible to teach reading in the time available, such notes provide help and encouragement.

7.3 Classroom methodology

The following is a broad guide to the methodology of the course; detailed guidance is included in the teaching items themselves. The teaching and learning methods used in the course have been determined by the following factors:

a Learners will already be successfully communicating in English to however limited and inaccurate an extent, and their passive knowledge will be more extensive. Materials and methods must build on this and must be credible in the sense of giving students an immediate sense of greater communicative effectiveness.

b In spite of **a**, the majority of learners will lack confidence and will already be convinced of their inability to learn English extensively and systematically because of their repeated failure to communicate in so many situations.

c This is entirely a course in spoken English – no written materials are used as an essential part of it.

d Asian learners will be unfamiliar with modern teaching methods.

e Learners must be able to transfer the language they learn to the real-situation outside and to apply it successfully.
Section One is largely concerned with introducing the methods of the course and overcoming factors **b** and **c**. The main methods which learners must initially become familiar with, and disciplined in following, are:

Language practice on their own in groups of three or four.
Carrying out activities with factory products or other objects in response to verbal instructions.
Accurate listening and repeating of material on a tape.

There are also a number of games and other 'fun' activities to develop an atmosphere of relaxation and informality.

As in any language course, much preparatory class work and initial presentation of material relies on the teacher. Often detailed suggestions are given for this work, but a teacher will need to supplement these or he may prefer to think of his own way.

Practice and exploitation of the material relies very heavily on the methods mentioned above. We do not consider the course can be used with maximum success unless these methods are followed. An individual teacher may come to the course with a dislike of any of these methods of language teaching, but as they are integral to this course we would urge the teacher to give them an honest try. The rationale behind using these methods is explained below.

Group Work

By group work is meant a period of time during a lesson when the class is divided into groups of three or four learners who practise amongst themselves language items which have been initially presented to the class as a whole and sufficiently practised for the majority of the class to have grasped the material accurately (Examples: Items 14, 76–77).

A very large number of items in the course, particularly instructional language, short dialogues, and question and answer sequences have been designed for this sort of practice. If the teacher does not practise the material in this way, he will find that there is not sufficient variety of material or examples in these items to hold the interest of the entire class. For example, the questions in Item 31 about learners' families illustrate this. If the teacher practises these questions by getting students to ask him (the teacher) all the time, the class will become very bored by hearing the same answer each time:

Where does your husband work?
What time does he arrive at work?

Some teachers may feel that the natural way to avoid this is to change elements in the question keeping 'Where?' and 'What time?' constant. Certainly, wider practice may be needed with some structural features. But, by giving it at this stage, the teacher increases the learning load and he is extending the length of the course, or excluding other items which may be more important. Teachers are used to teaching on the assumption that however long is needed to master something the learner has the time, but any in-company course has a very strict time limit. And there is a more fundamental objection to a teacher indiscriminately extending structural drilling of a piece of language because in so doing he may alter the language function. In items where the main aim is the purpose or function of the piece of language, any extension of the material must take this into account. The way around this particular lack of variety is for students to ask *each other* the questions and it is more natural and much more economic of time to do this in small groups than across the public classroom.

More importantly group work means that all the class are directly involved in the work; it is far more difficult to be a passenger in a group of four than in a class of sixteen. And the quantity of practice is greatly multiplied, because instead of the teacher and one student speaking, in four groups there are a total of eight students practising at any one moment.

Both of the above arguments for group work relate to saving time on a type of course in which there is a shortage of time. But there are also strong pedagogic arguments for using group work and for spending time on establishing it from the very outset. Some teachers have suggested that students would not have the confidence to use group work until far on in the course. But we have always successfully used it from the start and as a means of building the type of confidence that a student must acquire from the outset if he is to start using on his own the English he is learning. A group situation comes far closer to real communication than teacher/student exchanges across a classroom ever can.

Because they have been accustomed to very formal methods in the Indian sub-continent schools, learners must be weaned away from teacher-centred learning and towards accepting for themselves the more active role which is essential for learning and using spoken English. Group work forces this upon the learner. Group work also helps to overcome the shyness that Asians often feel at saying anything to one another in English when they have a more fluent language in common. This shyness about using English to one another may also arise from an inability in many immigrants to identify with the social and educational status of Indians and Pakistanis who would speak English amongst themselves in their countries of origin. Many Asian immigrants have come to England from villages. In the long run the Asian immigrant needs to be bilingual in some situations, and to do this he must overcome the feeling that he can never use English to a fellow countryman.

The group situation also provides a much more relaxed and realistic social situation than the full class does for practising English. Speaking out across a formal class in a foreign language is essentially a stress situation which does not encourage easy practice.

Since group work will be unfamiliar to the students, when it is introduced, one group should be organized first by the teacher with the rest of the class observing, so that they see what they have to do. It is also often a good idea to divide the best students between groups so they can take a lead in organizing the work, although other factors such as departments and friendships must also determine group membership. The other essential for organizing group work is to make sure the language material given for group practice at the beginning is easy and short. It is sufficient to start group work with periods of only three or four minutes. Even at a later stage, it is seldom useful to spend more than about ten minutes at a time on group work when using this course.

It will be obvious to the reader that we feel strongly that group work should be used from the outset with these materials. This fact needs to be remembered when choosing a classroom and physically arranging it. Rows or all sitting around one table should be avoided. Students are best grouped in fours or fives around individual group tables.

Practical activities

An initial difficulty which faced us in planning these course materials was how to produce sufficient variety and opportunities for relaxation in an entirely spoken English course. The normal way to achieve this in a language course is to break up oral work with some reading and writing.

One solution has been to introduce regular items in which, at least initially, students only have to listen and then carry out practical activities with factory objects or with multi-purpose objects such as paper, bricks, crayons, scales, and jars. The handling of these familiar objects gives a break from purely verbal tasks even though the student is still having to listen accurately to English (Examples: Items 15, 71, 73, 74, 75, 90).

A second reason for this type of item is that the student needs to develop accurate understanding of language (particularly instructions) which requires a non-verbal response, in other words, practical action. This is typical of one role of the operative in the work situation.

But this type of practical activity not only simulates the real world of the working imigrant, it also plays a useful teaching purpose. The most obvious role of visual aids is to help comprehension, but they are also widely used as cues for practising language. If every individual has his own set of objects, they can also serve as a secure base when he is learning and practising a language sequence. In some way, effort and tension associated with speaking the foreign language is removed for a student possibly by channelling it into the motor activity of handling things. At the simplest level, we are all familiar with the fact that it is easier to learn to count by using your fingers than looking at numerals or illustrations at the front of the class. A more advanced example is Item 71, for which every student would have his own pieces of paper. As far as possible every student should have his own set of objects for this type of item.

These objects also serve as a cue when students are working on their own in groups.

The tape recorder

Tape recorded items serve three main purposes in this material.

a To provide *ear training* with a variety of native-speaker voices. It is actually more difficult to listen to a tape recorder than a person because of the removal of all gesture and visual cue, and because there is an inevitable degree of distortion. The use of tape recorded items from the outset, even if the recorded material could be provided by the teacher, trains the learner in the effort and concentration that accurate listening demands. This is particularly important with immigrants who have grown accustomed to switching-off mentally during the floods of English which flow over them at work, or when watching television. The breaking of this 'switching-off' habit, which may have developed over several years, is an important first objective.

b To provide *a variety of context and realism* which the teacher alone cannot create in the classroom. This is done mainly in the form of dialogues set in a factory work situation. At the end of some sections there are also a series of dramatic listening dialogues which provide revision of the main language items in the whole section in a rather entertaining style not otherwise used in the course.

c To introduce students to factors of *personality, implication, and mood* which form a very important aspect of comprehension and of an individual's use of language. This is why the factory dialogues contain a set of permanent characters who have differences of role and personality. These characters are first introduced in Section Two (Items 42 and 52) and appropriate pictures should be used to bring them to life for students.

Fairly detailed instructions are given in the text on how to use the recorded items (see page 129). Use is made of choral repetition simply because this is such a time-saving means of preliminary practice. If this choral work is to be of value, careful training is needed at the outset.

The dialogues usually contain only one speaker's part as a target for the learner. The other side of the dialogue is only intended for listening comprehension (Example: Item 53). The language of the listening side of the dialogue is not tightly controlled in the way the language of the learning side is because one characteristic of the immigrant's position is that he is always subject to native speakers addressing him in a real situation. The use of one-sided learning dialogues also gives the opportunity to cast the learner in more realistic roles and situations. The dialogues are recorded three times for a three-phase use:

1 Listening.
2 Repeating individually and chorally one part.
3 Filling in one part (blanked) against the other parts on the tape.

This third use is often difficult for students and teacher to grasp. In fact very clear guidance is needed from the teacher or it will break down. This means the teacher must show conviction in the method from the outset or it may become unworkable. This would be a pity because it is only in this third phase that the student has to make a thoughtful and realistic response.

A further use of the tape recorder is for recording students speaking English (Example: Item 125). This technique should be used for building up the concept of self-cricitism and can be developed from at least the end of Section Two.

There are about eighty tape items included in the whole course,

57

and these present, or practise in some form, a large amount of the total teaching material. Since the students have no textbook, these tape items can serve in some ways as a book. They can be quickly and conveniently referred to for revision, and students will recall the context without the elaborate reassembly of aids which would be necessary for revising some ot the classroom items.

We have reservations about too extensive a use of recorded material with in-company immigrant courses, but we have found tape items can serve a purpose for which there is no other simple alternative. The reservations we feel are that the tape recorder is a machine which encourages mindless repetition in this type of learner, and that carrying on a dialogue with a tape recorder is unreal at the very least. Whereas Asian immigrants desperately need real contact with English speakers involving their personalities and feelings. This is one reason why we have seen no case for ever trying to use language laboratory facilities.

7.4 How to teach the course

The needs and levels of learners will vary substantially even within a general classification such as elementary, and the speed with which a teacher can use these materials will be determined accordingly. However, although teachers like to think that pace and level are largely determined by learners, there is plenty of research and experience to prove that teacher expectations can be crucial in determining the learners' performance and progress. We, therefore, argue that the teacher must set his expectations high.

Both management and the employees who come on the course will be expecting a really substantial and dramatic improvement. And the responsible teacher can hope for no less; he has perhaps three months in which to help the learner out of the sticky swamp of failure to communicate in English, on to some firm ground. The learner can then proceed after the course to come to terms with more and more English as a result of this momentum. This three months is probably a once-and-for-all opportunity for the learner to 'take-off' into learning English. The teacher must expect and insist upon no less.

It has already been pointed out how the immigrant learner differs significantly from the usual foreign learner of English. Most significantly the immigrant has been exposed to an enormous amount of English over a period of time and, if we can tap this 'passive' knowledge, learning will be faster. The immigrant also has experience of communicating in English in real and complex situations, and he will have established a number of incorrect uses of English – however little he knows.

All these points argue for pace and variety in organizing an in-company course. Certainly the amount of basic language contained in these materials can only be covered if the teachers maintain a fairly relentless pace and steadfastly refuse to be delayed by in-essentials. We would further argue that the materials contained here (allowing for some items not being relevant in particuar work situations, and some of Section Six not being essential) represent a basic minimum for a learner to start communicating successfully at work.

We shall now look at some examples of lessons plans. It should be remembered that within the parts of cach section, items are grouped by topic, so a satisfactory variety of material cannot be achieved by following the items consecutively – some mixing is needed. The following are specimen lesson plans, each set covers one week (five 45-minute lessons) at different stages in a course. The time allowed for each item in the lesson plan is given in brackets. Five minutes of each lesson is deliberately left unaccounted for.

Week One

Monday
Introductory talk in Punjabi about the course (10 mins)
Item 1 (10 mins), Item 14 (15 mins), Item 3 (5 mins)

Tuesday
Item 2 (5 mins), Item 17 (15 mins), Item 4 (10 mins), Item 14 (10 mins)

Wednesday
Item 9 – upper case (15 mins), Item 17 (10 mins), Item 16 (5 mins), Item 9 (10 mins)

Thursday
Item 9 (10 mins), Item 18 (15 mins), Item 7 (10 mins), Item 10 (5 mins)

Friday
Item 18 (5 mins), Item 12 (10 mins), Item 11 (10 mins), Item 20 (15 mins)

Week Four

Monday
Item 44 revision (5 mins), Item 48 (10 mins), Item 49 (15 mins), Item 53 (10 mins)

Tuesday
Item 53 (10 mins), Item 54 (5 mins), Item 55 (a) and (b) (15 mins), Item 39 (5 mins), Item 49 (5 mins)

Wednesday
Item 50 (15 mins), Item 61 (10 mins), Item 46 (5 mins), Item 55 (5 mins), Item 60 (5 mins)

Thursday
Item 56 (a) and (b) (15 mins), Item 61 (10 mins), Item 46 (5 mins), Item 55 (5 mins), Item 60 (5 mins)

Friday
Item 60 (5 mins), Item 61 (15 mins), Item 52 revision (10 mins), Items 56 and 57 (10 mins)

This sort of lesson planning may look as if it will lead to scrappy lessons. But the use of many varied items for a short time each is quite deliberate, and there is nothing scrappy about the curriculum when viewed over a period of several weeks. This type of scheme presents the learner with constant variety of content and activity which maintains a high level of interest and concentration. This type of scheme also makes great demands on the teacher in terms of pace. He really has to keep himself moving to stick to these times and needs every aid and piece of equipment ready to hand.

These teaching plans are based on three main assumptions:

a Any important item should occur in at least *three* lessons to assure thorough presentation, practice, and reinforcement. Students are not therefore expected to master it in the first lesson.

b There is extensive built-in revision in later items. This means a particular point does not require total mastery when it first occurs in the course.

c A teacher will spend a couple of days revising earlier items from time to time.

These three points merely stress the fact that this is a course and that learning must be cumulative. But we make these points strongly because many teachers insist on a degree of perfection in learning a particular language item which seems to assume they will never have an opportunity to deal with that bit of English again. Asian immigrants do not, in our experience, respond well to this type of teaching, nor is it the way languages are really learned or used. On the other hand we recognize as absolutely essential that the immigrant learner should grasp the notion of accuracy in learning a language from the outset.

Speed and variety have been emphasized in discussing how to teach these materials because time is very short and an entirely oral lesson demands great variety if the learner is to be kept at an efficient level of concentration and effort. Whenever he finds he has to spend excessive time on a particular point or teaching item, the teacher must ask himself: 'How important is this item to their needs and situations? How much will this point affect intelligibility and real communication?' For example, the -s form in the present simple tense would probably fail to meet both these criteria; but the difference between '*dark* red' and '*light* red' could be very important in one situation and of no importance in another.

What happens in the classroom is only one part of the learning situation, the other part is the work situation itself. There are two main approaches to influencing the learner in his use of English when he is actually working. First the teacher should visit every student at least once a week at his job. A variety of things can be revised then in the real situation, and often, where equipment and machinery is involved, actual teaching can most effectively take place on the work bench or in the office. Secondly the teacher can get the native English-speakers to talk to the learner and give an opportunity to practise what has actually been taught. First priority should be given to influencing chargehands and supervisors because they will influence others and they are often essential people for all operatives to communicate with.

Chapter 8
The participation of other people in communicative improvement

'In many ways a personality will only make sense in relation to the community that produced it; if judged by the standards of another community, a person's behaviour may be falsely assessed.' (Paul Christophersen *Second Language Learning: Myth and Reality*)

Finally we shall consider the role and response of the native English-speakers in the work situation as the immigrant learner tries to improve and extend his communicative competence in English; that is the third set of factors represented in Figure 2 (page 25).

8.1 The contribution and needs of English-speakers

The presence of native English-speakers and the need for an immigrant to communicate with them is one of the unique advantages of running in-company language training which must be utilized to the fullest extent for practice, reinforcement, and extension. An Asian worker will have to communicate with his chargehand, foreman, shop steward, and fellow-workers in English if they are native-speakers, and these people need to be included in the language-training process. Supervisory staff are particularly important because they can alter practice, such as the use of interpreters, and they can motivate the learners as representatives of the factory management. The language course presents a unique opportunity to give supervisory staff some permanent understanding of communication difficulties and cultural factors – an understanding which is essential to effective and fair management of a mixed workforce. This is something which will have a much wider effect among employees than just upon the course participants. It will affect all the Asians, present and future, who are employed in the department or by the company.

There are two main reasons why we have come to regard supervisory staff as so vital in creating this fair and effective management. First, the chargehand or supervisor sets the tone of a section or department. If he believes all Asians really understand

English, but pretend not to when it suits them, so will other non-Asian workers. Unhelpful attitudes to communication difficulties of Asians by English-speakers have often resulted in regression in terms of effective use of English by Asians. Secondly, the Asian worker requires accurate and confident communication with his immediate boss more than with anyone else. We must also emphasize the role of shop stewards who are uniquely placed to influence ordinary fellow workers and thus to affect the whole social atmosphere of a department for immigrant workers.

The willingness of native-English speakers to practise English with learners is not sufficient. In order for their communication with the learners and with other Asian immigrants to be permanently improved, English people must first understand something of what is involved in communicating in a second language: the type of breakdowns which will occur, the way to overcome such breakdowns, and the types of irregularity in the use of English which they must learn to accept. This is very necessary because no language training course is going to turn anyone into a totally fluent user of English, and many Asian immigrants settled in Britain will continue to have some level of language-communication difficulty all their working lives. In addition to this feel for the second language users problems when speaking English, English people, particularly supervisors and shop stewards, must know sufficient about the background and experience of such people to be able to begin to relate to them as individuals.

A useful working relationship between the teacher and supervisory staff should have been built up during the preparatory stage before teaching starts. There follow three practical suggestions about what can be done further to involve these people and to mount some formal training sessions.

8.2 Briefing on language training course

This is best provided as one seminar of about two and a half hours, a day or two before the language course begins. The briefing should not be any earlier or impact will be lost. All chargehands, supervisors, instructors, department managers, and other staff who have any direct responsibility for course participants should be involved. We have found the following scheme an effective approach to the briefing session:

a Introductory remarks

b The present level and performance of trainees for the language course. Play some tape interviews; discuss likely effect of this level of English on a person – bluffing, guessing, uncertainty, etc.; ask them to imagine working in a foreign country with this level of the language. There are three major factors involved in achieving improvement.

a psychological problem
a behaviour problem
a learning problem

c Overall analysis of communication needs and difficulties in the company arising from the investigation.

d Some examples of communication breakdowns, their nature and how they can be overcome.

e The content of the language course and why.
Very brief summary of contents; play or demonstrate some teaching items.

f The methods of the course and why.

g The contribution of supervisory staff.
Practice and reinforcement in department; attitudes and encouragement; other practical suggestions.
Explain summary sheet for first week and how it can be utilized.

h Realistic expectations and results.
Likely profile of learning; continued use of first languages.

This type of session has to be kept on a very simple level; regard must be given to the experience people have in trying to cope with the communication barrier; and there must be discussion and questioning.

8.3 Reinforcement of language course

Chargehands and supervisors, shop stewards and others interested should be spoken to at least once a week and asked to report on the progress of the workers who are on the course. The best way of getting effective co-operation is to give a weekly summary of the work done to the chargehand or supervisor along with suggestions on how it can be practised. Practical suggestions for follow-up activities are made in connection with many teaching items in Section One and thereafter a teacher should devise his own in terms of his own situation.

There may be initial reluctance to become involved, but most people will respond if the teacher perseveres. For some people, the language training will provide a source of real interest once they become involved. People should also be persuaded to drop in on classes.

The following is a specimen summary for the first week. It must, however, be stressed that summary sheets on their own have not provided sufficient involvement, and practical communication exercises with check-off points should be introduced as early as possible.

Specimen —
English Language Training   Week One

During the first week we have been teaching the trainees in the language class to *listen* carefully and to make simple answers without embarrassment.

These are some of the things taught:

1 Counting – particularly in twos.
(Sometime when you are going around ask each of your trainees to count a box of parts in English.)

2 Following simple instructions and using:
pick the . . . up, please.
put down
hold
pass
hand over
touch
(try some of these words in instructions)

3 First thing in the morning.
'Good morning . . . ' (say the name)
'How are you?'
And ways of saying goodnight.
(Are they using them to you? Make sure!)

4 What to say when someone pronounces your name incorrectly.
No. Excuse me. It's . . . . .

5 Learning to recognize and read quickly the codes used in the factory on items:
for example: 171 BW, CA 16/A1, CF 313 W
(Try a few! Asking for them and getting trainees to read them)

Obviously not all teaching points are given in the handout, but only points which will seem immediately relevant and can be easily used. Later, summary sheets become more difficult to devise and rather than write a lot of incomplete sentences and part dialogues, it is better to give a suggestion. For example:

Taking a message

Ask your trainees to take a message to an English-speaker in another department and bring back an answer or some object. Please make a note on this sheet of whether it was done correctly.

8.4 Background seminars about Asian employees

Groups of about fifteen staff attend two seminars lasting about three hours each. Careful attention is given to case study material and discussion of the participants own departments. The emphasis throughout the seminars is upon presenting information and discussing its relevance to good communication. A package is provided for all participants summarizing this background information and the contents of the seminars.

The following is the scheme of contents:

Seminar One

Part One

The need for basic information about immigrant workers, and the sort of information required.

Discussion of case study illustrating the need for information about individuals.

Open discussion in relation to participants departments.

Part Two

Countries of origin of immigrants working at the company and reasons for emigration.

Useful information:
systems of names	religions and dress
political backgrounds	languages

Illustrated material relating to the way of life of Asian immigrants in their country of origin, particularly in relation to work and social life.

Discussion on the dangers inherent in misusing information about background to form stereotypes.

Seminar Two

Part One

Immigrant workers' attitudes to authority, job insecurity, and to the supervisor in particular.

The language/communication problem at work.

Discussion of short case studies illustrating difficulties which arise in connection with attitudes and communication.

Part Two

Discussion and positive suggestions about the language training course and its effectiveness to date.

Suggestions about: initial contact, factory behaviour, attitudes of British workers.

We have found about two-thirds of the way through a language course the best time to mount these background seminars.

The suggestions contained here are very sketchy because this type of background course, while an essential complement to language training, is a very different field from the subject of this book. However, a thorough guide to running background seminars will be found in *The Background and Employment of Asian Workers*, T. C. Jupp and Evelyn Davies, published by the Runnymede Trust.

Chapter 9
Evaluation of communicative improvement

A company sponsoring an in-company language course will expect a report which presents fairly clear-cut and quantified results as is normal with industrial training. Normally in language teaching it is impossible to go beyond a formal test of certain areas of linguistic performance. However, an in-company course offers a unique opportunity to investigate more fully the real language behaviour of the learner and thus to find out how far the individuals and the company have benefited.

The following is an outline of the main ways in which we have found it feasible to evaluate the results of in-company language training.

9.1 Improvement in English language of learners

One of the clearest ways of evaluating linguistic progress is to administer some of the items in the pre-course assessment as part of the final evaluation. But the final evaluation test will also need to include a number of new items specifically related to the content of the language course. A sample final evaluation test is included in Appendix Two (page 317).

The problem arises of how to present results of such an evaluation test in a meaningful way for any outsider. We suggest each student is rated on a four-point scale on the basis of his test results as follows:

no change
a little improvement
fair improvement
substantial improvement

This rating is given under three headings:

following instructions (direct comparison)
talking about job (direct comparison)
general level of English (refers to specific course content)

This is a fairly meaningful way of presenting change. But comparative performance (before and after the course) does not answer the crucial question of whether someone now has an adequate level of English (assuming some continuing progress). So students are also rated on the following three-point scale in relation to language needs at work:

English now adequate
English greatly improved but would respond to further training
English still inadequate

This rating is determined by performance in the test and equally by the opinion of the class organizer.

9.2 Post-course language assessment administered by supervisors

This sets out to measure a student's ability to use his new English when required in the course of his work. Improvement in this respect is more important as a measure of real progress than the results of a formal language assessment interview.

The chargehands and supervisors in closest daily contact with students are asked to administer a six-item assessment the week after the course finishes. Questions are asked when the appropriate opportunity arises in the normal course of the job so that the student is unaware he is being assessed. In all cases it must be agreed with the chargehands and the supervisors that none of the students used the particular language function effectively before the course started. See Appendix Two (page 317) for an example.

9.3 Supervisor and chargehand reactions to the progress of students

A thorough evaluation of improvement in a student's ability to communicate in his work place and the effect of this on his level of efficiency could be immensely complicated and time-consuming. The only practical way to try to judge it is to ask for the opinion of each student's immediate boss.

This type of reaction evaluation is obviously unreliable, but is a very useful indicator. For example, if, in the opinion of a chargehand, two of his operators are now more useful and flexible, this indicates a lot in terms of his relationship with them and the demands he is making on them, and is likely to be reflected in real performance whether or not the opinion is objectively true.

The following questionnaire should be administered *informally* within a general and discursive chat:

a Since the course began have you noticed a change in X's English?

1 none   3 better
2 a little better   4 a lot better

b Has X made a special attempt to speak to you and his English-speaking fellow workers?

1 none   3 medium effort
2 a little   4 a lot of effort

c As a result of the course do you consider X a more useful and flexible worker?

1 about the same
2 more useful and flexible
3 a lot more useful and flexible

Of course, these questions do not touch upon many areas in which there might be significant improvement, and an informal discussion should range more widely.

9.4 The effect of the course on output and production

If students are being withdrawn from their jobs during the working day, one might expect a proportionate drop in their output. This will reveal itself either in short-work or in excess overtime in the department. Both these points should be checked, and if neither has occurred, or in less than proportion, an increase in productivity has resulted. Where a department is on piece-work, the output of each individual can be easily checked.

On different language courses we have found improvements can occur in any of the following areas:

a Use of interpreters – which in turn saves someone's time and he is therefore available to do more work on his own job.
b Waste and quality control.
c Accurate record keeping.
d Safety.

9.5 Other possible effects of language training

In some cases language training can also affect the following factors:

a Tension and frustration between English speakers and non-English speakers.
b Drift away from the company of non-Asian workers.

c Suitability for industrial training.

d Impediments to up-grading and promotion.

e Labour turnover.

These factors can be very serious in terms of personal relationships, misunderstandings, and grievances.

9.6 Further follow-up

If all these factors are evaluated at the finish of the course, a measure of the immediate impact of the course on the company is made. But for a measure to be taken of long-term effects, the evaluation needs to be repeated, after about six months.

Perhaps more importantly, this type of post-course evaluation shows an employer what has been achieved, and steps must be taken by the employer himself to make sure the benefits are reaped in terms of greater efficiency and better personal opportunities.

As a form of constructive follow-up and further work, we have experimented with fortnightly visits to students after the end of the course. At each visit students are given a task which is checked on at the next visit. The following are some examples:

a Find out the names of five *new* things in the factory.

b Speak to two English people in the factory and find out:

1 Where do you live?   3 What time do you start work?

2 How do you come to work?   4 In which section do you work?

Industrial English

Part two

Elementary course materials for immigrants

A detailed list of contents is given at the beginning of each of the six sections, and an overall analysis of the linguistic content in Appendix One.

Introduction to Part Two

The teaching materials contained in *Part Two* have been developed as a basis for in-company English language training for employees with fairly elementary problems of understanding and talking English at work. The course is almost entirely in spoken English because of the limited time normally available. At this level, lessons should be frequent but short – four or five times a week for about 45 minutes each.

These materials constitute a teachers manual of some 200 language learning items and provide a total of about 80 hours' teaching material when used intensively on an in-company basis. If used in part-time adult education classes, these materials will provide the basis of a year's course when some time is also given to reading and writing.

In practice, most in-company language training lasts only from 40 to 60 hours so careful selection across the six sections of these materials is recommended. We have tried to produce a basic core of materials easily open to adaptation and variation. Appendix One provides an overall view of contents to assist a teacher in the matter of selection.

The job vocabulary a learner needs will naturally vary between every work place, so for items concerned with the actual job we have only given examples, and a teacher has to write his own material based on these. A full understanding by the teacher of the learner's language needs at work is essential in order to adapt these materials and to plan a successful course.

The real introduction to these materials is provided by *Part One* of this book, and anyone using them in the classroom should look particularly carefully at Chapter 7, which includes some lesson plans. In addition Appendix One provides an index by item to the relationship between language forms and language functions which enables a teacher to select and supplement according to the linguistic and situational needs of his students. Appendix Two provides language assessment tests for selection of students and evaluation of their progress.

Organizing language training

There are three main factors which may result in an in-company language course being a failure:

Inappropriate teaching materials and curriculum.
Inadequate selection of trainees.
Unrealistic arrangements for the duration, frequency, and
conditions of the classes.

These materials are intended to provide the basis of a solution for
the first. An example will demonstrate the type of trouble that
can occur as a result of poor selection and organization. A
language course was organized at a bakery. Any employee was
free to volunteer for the classes and the standard of trainees
varied from 'O' level G.C.E. to complete beginners. The class was
held once a week for two hours at the end of a physically
exhausting 12-hour shift. At the end of the course, the company
were of the opinion that language training was a waste of
time.

Any language teacher organizing a course at a college or centre
would exercise careful control over entry to the class, and make
sure the duration of the course was practical in terms of the goals.
There is a natural tendency when organizing a course at the
request of a company, on their premises, and at their expense, to
assume they have the right to decide who attends and when.
Certainly the company has a right of veto, but the language
teacher is the professional who should know what he is doing and
he must exercise control over matters which can crucially affect
the learning process. If the language teacher accepts conditions
which he knows to be pedagogically unsound, he is placing his
neck in a noose because the course will fail. When a course does
fail, it is naturally the professional – the language teacher – who
will be held responsible. The resulting disillusionment of the
company will not only dissuade it from organizing any further
language training for immigrant employees, but may have
repercussions throughout a group of companies, a geographical
area, or even an industry.

An in-company language course is by its nature a very public
type of teaching which will be crudely judged by practical results.
It is not just a matter of the learner and the teacher establishing a
beneficial relationship, there is also the sponsor of the class, the
management of the company. One of the many added difficulties –
but also interests – for the in-company course organizer is the
task of educating company personnel in what is involved in
language learning, what can be achieved in a given period, and
what company personnel can contribute to good results. A vital

part of this is persuading the company that the course must be properly organized in terms of selection and duration.

Duration and timetabling of course

The work place imposes severe restraints on the total time available and the times of the day at which classes can be run. To this extent the arrangements for a course are inevitably a compromise between these practical constraints and the essential conditions needed for language learning. But we have already stressed that if the course organizer compromises too far, the course is better not run at all because there will be no worthwhile learning achieved and, in a wider sense, positive damage may result.

Experiments with different lengths of course suggest that 40 hours is the minimum duration to achieve worthwhile results. This time is preferably organized in doses of 45-minute classes daily. Following this pattern, a 40-hour course would extend over about 10 weeks. A typical course offers 50 hours spread over 12 weeks. We suggest 60 hours or 14 weeks is about the maximum length of course which should be planned at elementary level. A further course can always be arranged.

The frequency of lessons should be determined by the level of the learner and the time of the day. At an elementary level in largely spoken English, effective learning and concentration is difficult to maintain for more than about 45 minutes; at least in the early weeks of a course. With trainees who have some knowledge of the language we have found $1\frac{1}{4}$-hour sessions three times a week effective. The beginning of the day, or around the mid-morning break, or after lunch all provide suitable times for classes, particularly as they are times at which work is stopped or started anyway and therefore production losses are reduced.

With shift workers classes may have to come at the end of a long shift, but, if so, effort should be made to avoid the same individuals always having their class after work. It is quite unrealistic to expect people to concentrate for more than an hour immediately after a long working day. The often favoured 2-hour session is merely an administrative convenience which in the in-company situation totally disregards learning factors.

Teaching aids and equipment

Certain items of equipment are essential for using these materials. The teacher organizing an in-company course has to teach in non-classroom accommodation. All items have to be packed up, and often transported daily. This means weight and convenience for carrying are very important criteria in choosing any equipment.

Tape recorder
Important to have a really light and portable machine which can be operated by batteries and from the mains. A pause button is essential. A good microphone is needed for recording in the factory.

Camera
Transparencies and black and white pictures are needed of factory scenes and equipment. The best available 35-mm camera should be used and electronic flash equipment will be needed for the indoor shots.

Slide-projector
A small number of slides are shown at a time, so automatic changing is not needed. A 150-watt QI lamp is best as blackout arrangements may be poor or non-existent.

Multi-purpose objects and aids
The particular aids and pieces of equipment needed for each part of each section of the materials are listed at the beginning of the part. Many of these items can be made, improvised, or borrowed from the factory. The following will be needed on most in-company courses, and can be bought inexpensively:

a At least two sets of scales for weighing.
b Three or four clock-faces.
c A set of screw-top jars (one for each student).
d One or more glove puppets.
e Sets of coloured crayons and coloured bricks.
f Sheets of card and of tissue paper.

Considerable planning is needed to make sure the necessary equipment is available at the right time, and that visuals and aids are made or collected. On a largely spoken course these things introduce essential variety and interest.

Preparation of job-related items

Specific job-related teaching items have to be specially prepared for each course and according to each work situation. Examples and guidance on how to do this is given under the teaching items concerned in each section. The initial investigation at the company will provide the material needed for many of these without any further investigation.

Teachers are strongly advised to prepare all the special items for Sections One, Two, and Three before the course begins or very early on because these items are closely interrelated and later items modify earlier ones. In addition, the special knowledge and aids required for many of these items cannot be quickly acquired and assembled.

Section Four, however, requires a great deal of special preparation and will also require visits to the factory to take slides and make sketch-plans. This will be best prepared after the course has been running for some time and the teacher has developed a real familiarity with the position and needs of students.

The use of written materials and student notes

Asian immigrants quite often have some elementary knowledge of written English, and sometimes it is better than their spoken skills. Anyone who has attended a secondary school in the sub-continent will have started learning to read and write English. On the other hand, we have always had a number of course students quite illiterate in English so it is impractical to assume the use of any written materials as an integral part of the course without teaching literacy.

The total exclusion of written materials from the course is a disadvantage for two important reasons. Most adult learners of a language are anxious to have things in writing at least for reference and memorization. An Asian learner, in particular, often attaches importance to the written word as the very symbol of education itself, and will feel most disappointed when he is told no written work will be done on the course. From a teacher's point of view, written materials can be a useful form of reinforcement and provide a break from the strain of oral work for himself and the learners. The total exclusion of written work from the course (except for letters and numbers) has necessitated a good deal of special thought to ways in which pace and variety can be maintained.

It should be noted that sometimes particular written words on check sheets – for example, a laundry list – form an essential language requirement for the job. Under these circumstances, the teaching of recognition and understanding of this very limited number of words is an important part of an in-company language course. But 'look and say' methods can be used. Writing is probably not required. But this word recognition in no real way represents the teaching of literacy.

However, it is important to make some concession towards the Asian learner's anxiety for written materials. A useful way of doing this is to issue duplicated notes (together with a folder) at the end of work on each section. Those students who can read can use the notes for revision and reference purposes, perhaps with the help of a relation or friend. Those who cannot read can seek help from a relation or friend, and their interest may be stimulated so that they start learning to read and write in their own time.

The following is a scheme of notes for Section One. We would stress that distribution of written notes for classroom use at the time of teaching would seriously slow down and inhibit spoken performance, given inadequate literacy skills.

Section One

1 Counting
  numbers in numerals and words
  large numbers
  plus and minus

2 The alphabet

3 Instructions
  list of lexical items (mainly verbs)
  'please' and 'thank you'

4 Greetings and saying goodbye

5 How to tell someone your name
  Dialogue from Item 17

6 Referring to people
  sentences and questions demonstrating the pronouns and
  possessives: Items 20 – 27

7 Talking about your family
  Question and answer sequence
  Lexical items

8 Starting the day

The use of these materials in part-time adult classes

These materials have been successfully used in ordinary voluntary part-time classes. Although with such classes, it is difficult to concentrate upon functional needs and practical communications opportunities to the extent that these materials do, because students will have come from a variety of work situations, and it is difficult for the teacher to understand or have contact with these situations. However, the functional language teaching approach of these materials can be developed considerably in ordinary classes. For example, the job instruction items can be replaced by more general instructional material suitable in the classroom (e.g. How to operate a tape recorder), and general parallels can be found for many of the work-related items. In addition a teacher should find out about the students' work places or work aspirations and give students practical assignments related to them.

When these materials are used with part-time voluntary classes, we recognize that literacy and written work will be an important component of the course. Most teachers will choose an existing literacy scheme. Unfortunately none of these are designed for non-native English-speaking adults. If the teacher is prepared to build up his own materials, we suggest the materials should be partly built in terms of the functional needs and possibilities of the learners' environment as well as narrative interest and systematic phonic work. But in whatever way the literacy work is planned, and particularly if it draws on the language of these materials, we suggest that there should be at least ten hours exclusively spoken teaching first.

Section one

Building confidence
Establishing teaching methods
Basic grammar

Introduction

The section begins with a number of elementary language items which are likely to be known by almost any immigrant. The later parts deal with pronouns and the basic forms of the present simple tense; these are likely to be known only partially by many students and therefore to require remedial teaching of the type given here. The material in this section can be covered in ten to twelve hours.

The main aim of this section is to build up the confidence of students by making them feel that they already know a lot of useful English, and also to train the class in the methods of teaching and learning which are used throughout these materials. These methods may be rather unexpected to Indian or Pakistani learners who have been accustomed to a very passive and formal learning situation. In addition, there are particular difficulties with any language course which is exclusively oral. For all these reasons a teacher should pay particular attention to training students in the methods and classroom organization that the course requires.

It is not intended that items should be taught in exactly the order they appear here. Much more varied and interesting lessons will result from choosing items from different parts for a single lesson (see *Part One*, page 59). Equally any teacher will feel free to reject or adapt any of the material here. Language learning needs vary enormously and a course can only offer a guide to exact content and a source of ideas.

By the end of this first section, a class should be working confidently and happily with each other and their teacher, and be accustomed to the learning methods required for the rest of the course.

Written work

This material is designed to teach exclusively spoken English because this is the first priority and the only one that time usually allows on an elementary in-company course. However, when the class is literate, it is obviously sensible for them to have written summaries, after mastering the material orally, and to do written exercises for homework.

There are also some work situations for which a limited literacy is required, for example, reading a laundry list, or filling in a work sheet. In these situations the necessary words can be taught by look-and-say methods from Section Two onwards.

Contents *for section one*

Part one
Counting
items 1 – 8

Teaching points:
Spoken and written numerals.
Written numbers are in general use throughout the Asian sub-continent so their recognition is seldom a major problem.

Aims
a To revise and when necessary teach numerals.
b To develop initial confidence in the language learning process.

Teaching procedure
There are eight small items for teaching counting. Obviously these should not be taught in sequence from the beginning of the course, but should be put into a number of different lessons with items from other parts of Section One.

For most groups, these items will be very easy and the teacher should, therefore, concentrate on using them for class relaxation (between more difficult items) and for building up participants' confidence and familiarity with course methods.

Equipment
a Beans, matches, or a set of small objects for counting.
b A spinning top.
c Cards on which are written: 10's, 100's, 1000's
single very large numbers.

Practical communication exercises
In this first section of the course suggestions are made for practical follow-up exercises related to each part for use out of class. These are not primarily intended for use by the teacher, but for the teacher to set up with the co-operation of people who normally come into contact with the learner on a routine basis (chargehands, supervisors, shop stewards and co-operative fellow-workers). It is hoped that the suggested exercises will help

the teacher to generate his own ideas which will be more appropriate for the particular situation; and for this reason fewer suggestions are made in later sections of the materials.

These follow-up items are seen as an integral part of the learning process because success with communication in ordinary life is the real test and measure of achievement for the learners of a language.

1 Numbers up to 10 (and up to 20)

AIM **These numbers will usually be known. This work is simply to give confidence, get students to speak on their own in front of others, and to relax the class.**

Make sure orally that the numbers 1 to 10 are familiar. Then teach plus (+) and minus (−) by doing simple sums orally. Use fingers, beans, matchsticks, etc.

Later go on with numbers 10–20.

2 Counting in 2's

AIM **a quicker way of counting.**

2–4–6–8–10 . . .

Once learned, students can do this with one another in groups. Later go on with this up to 20.

3 Game *number lists*

AIM **Recognition of written numbers when spoken. And early introduction of games will help the class to relax and not to feel self-conscious.**

Write two prepared lists of numbers on the blackboard. Each list contains the same numbers but in a different order. Divide the class into two teams. Call out one of the numbers. The first student to strike out that number (the one called) in his team's list scores a point for his team.

4 Game *number calling*

AIM Another game for confidence and amusement.

Students all sit in one line. Each student has a number. One student calls a number, that student responds by calling another number and so on. Failure to respond means the student moves to the end of the line.

5 Game *spinning and calling out numbers*

AIM Another game for confidence and amusement.

Students sit in a circle. Each student has a number. One student spins a top and calls out a number or two numbers with plus or minus (6 + 2). The student who is that number must catch the top before it stops spinning, and then does the same. This game can be used with any numerals and can later be played with new vocabulary items.

Note Items 3, 4 and 5 can be constantly re-used with higher and more complex numbers and with letters and codes (*see* Items 9 and 12).

6 Numbers 20–100

AIM To establish total accuracy up to 100, if this is in any doubt.

The numbers can be established by counting out piles of beans, matchsticks etc. and combining them. This can be reinforced by adding together sets of cards (1–10, 20, 30, 40, 50, 60, 70, 80, 90) and on the blackboard.

Students can then practise in groups.

7 Larger round numbers

AIM To teach hundreds and thousands which students are often uncertain about.

Teach 100; 1,000; 10,000; 100,000; 200; etc. Students can count out piles of beans, matchsticks, etc., which can be used to make up piles of 100, 200, etc. Larger numbers can be made up from piles of small cards with 100; 1,000; written on them.

This work can be practised with sets of cards in groups.

When students are uncertain of numbers up to 100, this item and item 8 should obviously be left for sometime later, or a great deal of muddle may result.

8 Long numbers

AIM **Accurate reading off of long numbers which are frequently used for reference on products and other items in a factory.**

Teach numbers such as: 11,524; 2,501; 36,542; 106,342.
These are probably best taught as a string of single numerals:
   One-one-five-two-four (etc.).
Thousands and hundreds need only be used when speaking of round numbers:
   11,600 – Eleven thousand six hundred.

The main teaching point here is being able to read or report a string of numbers. Time need not be spent on hundreds and thousands if they cause difficulty, although some people seem strongly to want to be able to say 2,501 (two thousand, five hundred and one). If time is spent on establishing this, the teacher should bear in mind that this style only applies to quantities and not to the widespread use of numbers for reference and codes (see Item 12).

Practical communication exercise

Reading clock-card numbers.
Get someone to be at the clock at the beginning of a shift. This person asks students to read their own number from their card. On later occasions students can read the number on each other's cards.

Part two
Letters and numbers
Items 9 – 13

Teaching points

Recognition of letters of the alphabet on their own and in combination with numbers.

Students being able to spell their own names.

Aims

a Accurate recognition of both letters and numbers in speech and writing particularly as used in the factory for codes.
b Introduction of the tape recorder for listening and recording.

Teaching procedure

Again it would be tedious and unsatisfactory to work straight through this material. So these items should be put into lessons with other items from this section.

And as in items 1–8, the items here will be very elementary for many students and can be quickly worked through with some parts omitted.

This course does not teach literacy, but recognition of letters is usually possible without too much effort. Students who are illiterate in English usually know at least the alphabet. However, when students are totally illiterate in their own language, there may be a serious difficulty in this work (see Introduction to *Part Two*, page 77).

Equipment

a Sets of 52 small blank cards for each student for writing upper and lower case alphabet.
b Slips of paper.
c Sets of pens or pencils.

9 The alphabet

AIM **Recognition of the small and capital letters of the alphabet.**

a Write up and get the students to recognize the lower case alphabet. Refer to lower case as 'small letters'.

b Write up and get the students to recognize the upper case alphabet. Refer to upper case as 'capital letters'.

c Give each student a set of fifty-two small blank cards so that they can make their own sets of small and large alphabet.

With some classes the alphabet may be quite familiar and very little time will be taken up with this, or it may be omitted altogether. With other classes, it may only be possible to teach recognition of the letters without writing them down. Reading and writing as such are not included in the course so it is unwise to spend a long time in getting the letters written correctly. What is required is the ability to recognize and say the names of the letters of the alphabet. With a largely illiterate class it may be better to give already prepared sets of letters.

It is essential that lower case as well as upper case letters can be recognized.

10 Game letter lists

AIM **Recognition of single letters when spoken. Also another game for relaxation.**

This game is exactly the same as Item 3 except that it is played with letters instead of numbers.

Write two prepared lists of letters on the blackboard each combining the same letters but in different orders.

11 Spelling of names

AIM **For each student to be able to spell his own name.**

Present and practise the following short dialogue:

A   What's your name, please?

B   Daljit Kaur (depending on your choice and factory custom).

A   How do you spell it?

B   D-A-L-J-I-T.

A   Thank you.

This can be practised with several students, then students can practise this dialogue in groups of three or four. If this is the first time students have worked alone in groups, get one group to work first in front of the class. See page 53 for detailed suggestions on organizing group work.

After students have had some practice, they can be recorded working on this item. This will help to familiarize the class with a tape recorder and will also help to overcome shyness and gaucheness over speaking English.

Get students to establish the name with you by which they will be addressed in the class. Our own preference is for first names of both students and teachers particularly if English people use first names amongst themselves in the factory. Although students may prefer more formal use of names, particularly to a teacher, this is a small area in which classroom practice should emphasize the correct level of formality.

As a result of this item, you may become aware that some people are not apparently using the correct part of their name. This is something to be resolved later (see Item 57). See *Part One*, Chapter 4, for more information on Asian name systems.

12 Factory codes

AIM **Ability to recognize accurately in speech and writing codes using letters and numerals which are in common use in the factory.**

In many factories and other work places coding by letters and numbers is used. You should try to use real examples from the place where your students work. Typically, codes are used for warehouse pallets of wrapped products, in laundries, in the stores, stamped on each item made, and so on.

Codes given below are only meant as examples.

a Start by reading simple combinations from the blackboard, based on the same principle as those in use in the factory but probably shorter.

Examples   A 15   B 26   C 24

Then move on to real examples from the factory.

Examples BR3S G42R L510S

Insist that students work fast and accurately with these codes, but do not go on for long on any one occasion or the work is very boring. Introduce the phrase passively: 'What's the number (or) code number (or) code?'

b Collect objects from the factory (such as labels) on which are codes. Then ask a student for an item by the particular code; possibly for several objects with the same code.

Example Two BR3S, please.

Students can then have further quick practice in groups if necessary.

c Recorded codes

⊗ Tape item 1

Record a couple of minutes of factory codes on tape. Students write these down as they are played on the recorder.

If there are non-writers, it is best to work in groups. The one who can write copies down what the others remember.

Really attentive listening must be insisted upon for this work. Don't repeat the code yourself. Insist that students listen to the tape recorder because this is essential training for using the tape throughout the course.

Slips of paper and pencils or pens required.

13 Identifying yourself at work

AIM **Fluency in self-identification for factory record purposes.**

This item affords an opportunity to revise and utilize the work of this part in a more personal way.

Present and practise the following short dialogue.

A   What's your name, please?

B   Dhirajlal Pandav.

A   How do you spell it?

B   Pandav: P-A-N-D-A-V.

A   Clock number, please?

B   6-0-4-9-3.

Organize further practice with students working alone in groups. Then record some examples of the dialogue. Make sure that the name with which students practise is the surname they use in the factory and have on their records.

Practical communication exercise

Arrange for someone to get each student formally to give his name and clock number as a follow-up. For example, when giving out wage slips at the end of the week.

Part three
Following instructions
Items 14 – 16

Teaching points

a Imperative form with useful verbs:

verb + noun
verb + noun + adverbial particle

Structurally this represents a presentation of the basic verb form.

Some Asian learners incorrectly use the '-ing' form as the basic form.

b 'Please' and 'thank you'
Other points included are not primary teaching points.

Aims

a Accurate listening to, repeating, and carrying out of sequences of simple instructions.
b To associate language learning with practical activities, and thus with one of the essential functions of language at work.
c To introduce several of the basic methods of the course (see *Part One*, Chapter 7).

Teaching procedure

This material represents the first solid block of language in the course and should be used from the very beginning mixed with the material in Parts One and Two of this Section.

The sequences of simple instructions offer an opportunity to train a class carefully in both group work and choral work. Both group work and choral work are crucial to using this course successfully and time will be well spent at this point establishing these methods.

Equipment

a Set of screw-top jars for the whole class and a packet of beans.
b A glove puppet.

14 Important verbs used for instructions

AIM **To learn and accurately respond to a number of verbs in frequent use for instructions in the factory.**

Present the following verbs to the class in imperative form:

pick up, put down, hold, pass, get back, touch.

Present these verbs with the following nouns:

pencil, pen, paper, table, floor, window.

And with five very common nouns from the factory.
Or anything else you choose.

Lead up to the class understanding and being able to follow this sequence of instructions.

⊗ Tape item 2

Pick your pen up.
Hold your pen.
Put your pen down.
Pick your paper up.
Pass your paper.
Get your paper back.
Put your paper down.
Touch the table.
Touch the floor.
Touch the window.

Note Verbs with adverbial particles are used in the following pattern with nouns.

Pick your pen up.
Verb + noun + adverbial particle.

The alternative pattern:

Pick up your pen.

is never used in this section in order to avoid confusion.

When this and similar sequences can be carried out by the class, play tape item 2. In the class use 'please' and 'thank you' to a natural extent. It is important to constantly vary the details of the instructions and the sequence or there is no accurate check on comprehension.

At a later point students can repeat the instruction as they carry it out.

Finally class can divide into groups and students can take turns in instructing the rest of the group in similar sequences. See notes on group work in introduction to the course, page 53.

Note The determiners 'your' and 'the' are used, but they are not intended as special teaching points.

15 A sequence of instructions

AIM **To learn to follow accurately a sustained sequence of related instructions. To learn further verbs frequently used for instructions.**

⊗ Tape item 3

Lead up to the class understanding and being able to follow this sequence of instructions:

Fetch a jar.
Pick twenty beans up.
Put them in your jar.
Screw the cap up.
Pass your jar to your neighbour.
Unscrew the cap.
Take seven beans out.
Put the beans on the table.
Take six beans out.
Put them back in the jar.
Screw the cap up.
Shake the jar.
Put it down.
Count the beans on the table.
How many have you got?
Unscrew the cap.
Put the seven beans back in your jar.
Screw the cap up.
Pass the jar to your neighbour.
Shake the jar.
Stop!
Put it down.

There are a lot of new vocabulary items here; although many may already be familiar. Note also the pronouns 'them' and 'it', and the prepositions 'in' and 'on'. Don't give special attention to these items unless the prepositions cause confusion.

Follow the same teaching procedures as suggested for item 14. However, this being a long sequence, with some classes it will need to be broken up and perhaps presented in parts before the full taped version can be used.

There is no reason why this sequence should be followed. This would be suitable with any assembly or packaging work. But many other variations on this idea can easily be made up. For example, folding towels for laundry workers, moving cutlery and plates on a tray for catering workers. A variety of such sequences can later be exploited for work on prepositions of place.

16 Glove puppet

AIM **To introduce the use of a glove puppet to the class.**

Introduce a glove puppet to the class:

What's your name?
(Brock)
Pick the pencil up, please.
Thank you.

Carry on with similar familiar instructions.

A glove puppet is very useful because it will enable the teacher to present a two-sided dialogue to a class. But the use of glove puppets is an individual matter for teachers to decide because we recognize some teachers will not be happy with the idea. For this reason glove puppets are not an essential aid, and teachers may prefer to use some other method for demonstrating a two-sided dialogue to their class.

Part four
Meeting and greeting
Items 17 – 19

Teaching points

Sets of formulae for telling someone your name, for greetings, and for parting.

Aims

To get students to *use* with English-speakers the everyday set formulae of English greetings.

Teaching procedure

This material will be familiar to most students, so the main thing is to get students into the habit of always using the right formulae when entering and leaving the class. And to make sure they do the same in the factory.

Equipment

Only standard items.

17 How to tell someone your name

AIM **To teach a polite, but clear formula for making sure English-speakers pronounce a student's name properly.**

Present the following dialogue using a glove puppet:

A What's your name?

B Brock (use your own name or the puppet's name).

A Brit?

B No. Excuse me. It's Brock.

A Pardon?

B Brock. B-R-O-C-K.

A Oh, Brock.

B Yes. That's right.

It is important to get over the idea of mispronunciation and mis-interpretation to the class. If they are familiar with the teacher's name, this should not be difficult. As soon as they have picked up the main points of the dialogue, you can practise with members of the class making very obvious mistakes with their names. Later the class may practise in groups.

This item involves two important principles in a very simple way which are essential to student progress in the long run:

a It is the first case of the learner having to initiate a turn in the conversation rather than just responding.

b It involves a recognition that effective communication depends upon the addressee understanding, as well as upon the speaker using, the correct words.

With some classes this dialogue may be too long to grasp at once so early in the course, in which case it can be presented in two halves in consecutive lessons.

At a later stage in the course, this item should be repractised using a two-part name (see Item 57).

18 Meeting and parting

AIM To drill the class in the two-sided nature of all set forms of greeting and parting.

Present and drill the following pairs of items. A glove puppet can be used initially.

⊗ Tape item 4

Good morning Mrs X – Good morning Mrs Y

Morning – Morning

Good afternoon Mrs X – Good afternoon Mrs Y

Good evening – Good evening

Hello – Hello

I'm A – I'm B

Pleased to meet you – Pleased to meet you

'Bye – 'Bye

Goodbye – Goodbye

Cheerio – Cheerio

Ta, ta – Ta, ta

See you tomorrow – Yes, see you

See you – 'bye

(include any other set formulae in widespread local use)

Then practise: teacher says one, student other. Get the class to compete with one another to see how many they can remember in total. Practise in groups if necessary.

Generally these formulae will be familiar which is why we have not suggested presentation in a context. The important point is to make sure students use them in the real situation; whenever they enter and leave the class and in the place of work.

Note that title plus surname is used in the early phrases and only first names in the sixth phrase. Make sure students make the correct distinction when practising these phrases to each other.

19 Dialogues

AIM **To present some of the formulae in Item 18 and some others in simple dialogue form.**

⊗ Tape item 5

a A Good Morning, how are you?

  B Very well thanks. How are *you*?

  c Fine thanks.

There should be no difficulty in presenting this straight from the tape recorder. Then practise orally teacher/student, and student/student.

b A How do you do. I'm A.

  B How do you do. I'm B.

This dialogue can be extended by mispronouncing the name (see Item 17).

c A Cheerio then. See you tomorrow.

  B Yes. Night, Night. See you.

  A 'Bye.

  B 'Bye.

Part five
Personal pronouns and possessives
Items 20 – 27

Teaching points

a Subject pronouns: I, you, he, she, it, we, they.
b Possessive determiners: my, your, his, her, X's, our, their.
c Object pronouns: me, you, him, her, it, them.

If these items of pronoun reference are major problems to students to teach them in immediate sequence could be confusing, in which case work on the different groups **a**, **b**, and **c** should be spaced in time by bringing in later items from this Section and items from Section Two.

There are a number of other secondary teaching points contained in the material.

> verb 'be'; questions with: what, where, whose, who; this and there; prepositions: by, on, in, next to.

Other than the prepositions, a lot of attention should not be paid to these secondary points.

Aims

To make sure personal pronouns and possessives are accurately known and used. Very often these forms cause confusion for immigrants who have picked up a certain amount of English. Again there may be interference from the mother tongue, for example, Gujerati speakers do not have a him/her or he/she contrast. If these grammatical forms are already accurately known, there is no important behavioural or situational material in this part, so in these circumstances the teacher can leave most of the items out. The one thing not to be omitted is the new vocabulary.

Teaching procedure

Concentrate on the pronouns and possessives. Don't attempt to deal fully with the secondary points because this is highly structural and rather dull material which will become extremely boring if over-used.

Parts Five and Seven of this Section contain a lot of grammatical material. It is not intended, at this stage in the course, that any of these items will be *perfectly* mastered. Reasonably effective use is all that is required, remembering that this material is constantly practised and presented in later items. The teacher must have confidence to move on reasonably quickly, and to mix in other items, or he will turn the course into one of structure drills rather than communication.

Equipment

Factory objects for Item 21.
Personal photograph if additional material taught in Item 24.

20 Subject pronouns *I, you, he, she*

AIM **Accurate use of pronouns, I, you, he, she.**

Present and practise:

I'm Tom Jupp (Known from Item 18).

You're Parminder Kaur Atwal.

She's Ranjit Kaur Gill.

He's . . . . . . (In a single sex class use a glove puppet or a picture)

To establish this pattern accurately it may be easier to use unshortened forms at first:

I am
You are . . . . . .
She/He is

And afterwards to shorten them.

Every individual in the class should say this sequence accurately. Make sure each student refers to different people or students may only be repeating without understanding the significance of the different pronouns.

For this item use full names. Also establish that in English everyone is addressed as 'you', regardless of position or relationship.

21 Subject pronoun *it (with position of objects)*

AIM Accurate use of subject pronoun 'it'.

Present and practise chorally, individually, and in groups at least six new vocabulary items from the factory. If possible, use multiple sets of these objects.

What's this? (What is this?)

Examples

	ceiling rose.
	battenholder.
It's a	battenholder base.
	lampholder.
	piece of brass.
	ring.

Note The indefinite article used throughout.

Then teacher presents:

The *ceiling rose* is (*use vocab. from above*).	on the table. (etc.) in the box. (etc.) by the door. (etc.) next to the *battenholder*. (etc.)

Present and practise chorally, individually, and in groups:

Where's the *ceiling rose*? (etc.)
It's on the table. (etc.)

Note The definite article is used throughout. 'In' and 'on' have already been practised in Item 15.

22 Subject pronouns *I, you, he, she, we, they*

AIM As for item 18 plus 'we' and 'they'.

Present and practise chorally, individually, and in groups:

Where am I?
You are next to Mrs Bains.
You are in the Canteen. (etc.)

Where are you?
I am . . . . . .

Where is Mrs Bains?
She is . . . . . .
He is . . . . . .

Where are Mrs Bains and Mrs Gill?
They are . . . . . .
We are . . . . . .

23 Subject pronoun *they (with position of objects)*

AIM **Accurate use of subject pronoun 'they' referring to objects.**

Present and practise chorally, individually, and in groups:

What are these?

Examples

They are *battenholders*. (etc.) (Use objects from item 21.)
Where are the *battenholders*? (etc.)
They are on the table. (etc.)
Where are the *battenholders* (etc.) and the *lampholder*? (etc.)
They are in the box. (etc.)

Note omission of the article with the indefinite plural.

24 Possessive determiners *my, your, her, his, X's*

AIM **Accurate use of these possessive forms.**

Particularly at the beginning of teaching these forms it is essential
to use objects which really do belong to a particular person.

Start off:

This is   my watch.
       my pen. (etc.)

       your overall.
This is   X's coat.
       her/his . . . . . . (etc.)

Choral drilling can be only meaningfully done with 'his', 'her', and
'X's'; for 'my' and 'your' individual responses are always needed.

This is a good opportunity to teach and practise the vocabulary
for clothes and other items students always have with them.

Then go on to present and practise these forms in a question and
answer sequence:

Where is my pen? (etc.)

It's   on the table.
    in my pocket. (etc.)

This is suitable for group practice.

Go on to present and practise a new question form:

Whose pen is this?

	my pen.
	your (etc.)
It's	his
	her
	X's

Additional material

If these possessive forms are already familiar, the above material should be sufficient. But, if they cause difficulty, further practice can be given in the following way.

Bring some photographs of your family, and get the students to do the same for the next lesson.

This is my wife, husband, mother, father, son, (etc.)
Who is this? Your wife, husband, (etc.)

When the class bring their pictures, 'his', 'her', and 'x's' can be further practised in the same way.

25 Possessive determiners *your, our, their*

AIM **Accurate use of these possessive forms.**

If the forms in Item 24 are known and give no difficulty go on to present 'our', 'your', and 'their' using the same procedure. First of all give out some objects making it clear they belong to a group of two or three people. But if there is difficulty with the earlier possessive forms, leave the plural forms altogether and come back to them a week or two later, or the students will become very muddled.

26 Object pronouns *me, you, him, her, it, them*

AIM **Accurate use of object pronouns particularly with instructions.**

Present and practise these object pronouns using the instructional material in Part Three of this section (Items 14 and 15). In fact some of the pronouns already occur there. However instead of beans and jars use some of the factory objects introduced in Item 19. Also introduce at least six more vocabulary items from the factory.

Examples

Spring, backplate, short skirt, H.O. skirt, plunger. starter.

Present and practise individually and in groups sequences like these:

Pick a spring up.

	him.
Pass it to	her.
	me.

Pick the H.O. skirts up.

	him.
Give them to	her.
	me.

Put them down.

The word 'give' should be taught.

Teach the object pronoun 'you' by getting students to say:

This is for you.

when they give something to someone.

27 Possessive pronouns *mine, yours, ours, his, hers, theirs*

AIM Accurate use of possessive pronouns particularly for identifying objects.

So as not to cause confusion, this item should be taught some time later than the possessive determiners, but it is included here for the sake of completeness.

Present and practise these forms and at the same time revise the possessive determiners.

A   That's my clock card.

B   It's yours?

A   Yes, it's mine.

Similar sequences for the other pronouns.
If possible present some new vocabulary with this item, but choose objects of which everyone has a closely similar one:
e.g. wage packet, overall, locker-key, tools, etc. Collect them in and then hold them up for identification. Later the sequence can be practised in groups.

Part six
A factory process or job
Items 28 and 29

Language teaching points

Present simple tense affirmative with impersonal pronoun 'you'.

Understanding of question form and responding with short answer 'Yes, I do.'

Vocabulary of a job or process.

Aims

To get over the idea of a job description and of the way language can be used accurately in relation to a particular job.

Teaching procedure

This material is particularly well suited for group work.

Equipment

Sets of job material or visuals for each member of the class if possible.

28 Instructions for a factory process or job

AIM To teach an accurate use of English to describe the main steps of a factory job which is already familiar to the class.

The teacher has to choose a job or process for the particular factory and write this item.

The job chosen should be very familiar and one which can easily be demonstrated with the actual parts. If there are no jobs which can be easily demonstrated in the classroom, blackboard drawings or photographs can be used as cues, or the language can be taught in the actual factory where the job is always done. In any case, if the language is presented with visuals, it will probably be necessary at some point actually to go into the factory with the whole class or in groups to make sure all the language has really been understood.

The best way to put together a job description is to record a supervisor or trainer describing the job. Then by simplification this recording can be used as a basis for the teaching material. See note on collecting teaching material in the introduction.

⊗ Tape item 6

Example

Here is an example of a job description from the assembly department of a plastic moulding firm.

Assemblying a battenholder base:

You pick your battenholder up.
You pick your base up.
You slot the battenholder into the base.
You pick a ring up.
You put it on.
You screw it down.
You pick a short skirt up.
You twist it round.
Then you put it in the bin ready for packing.

At this stage of the course, this represents a much simplified version of what a supervisor actually said; but, it does represent an accurate account of the essentials.

Suggested teaching procedure

a Teacher demonstrates with the language.
b Teacher speaks description while class do it. Sets of material required for each student.
c Teacher does process again; class chorally repeat each appropriate sentence.
d Best students instruct the other members of their groups to do the job; in this way gradually every individual will master the language of the whole process.

29 Understanding questions and giving short answers

AIM **Passive understanding of questions and 'yes'/'no' responses.**

When the factory job description has been fully mastered ask incorrect questions or questions out of sequence. This is only to familiarize students with the question form and should not be difficult for them to understand.

Students reply 'Yes, you do' or 'No, you don't'.

Examples

Do you pick your battenholder up?

Response: Yes, you do.

Then do you pick a ring up?

Response: No, you don't. (Explain: do not.)

You may have to accept simply: 'Yes' and 'No' as answers.

Part seven
Daily routine
Present Simple Tense
Items 30 – 33

Language teaching points
Present simple tense in positive, negative, and question forms.
Question words: where, when, what.

Aims
To master the verb forms of this tense accurately. Immigrants who
have picked up quite a bit of English often remain unable to use
the interrogative and negative verb form. There is very little
strictly structurally based material in the course as a whole, but
this part was included because of the difficulty in the verb forms.
There is no important situational or behavioural material in this
part.

Teaching procedure
The use of the auxiliary with negative and interrogative verb
forms is the essential point to get over. This may involve rather
repetitive work, which the class will resent. However it is important in the first section of this course to be insistent on and achieve
accuracy in listening and production.

Equipment
Slides, projector, screen.
Personal photographs of the student's families.

30 A typical day

AIM **To present the English for a typical daily routine with third
person and present simple tense.**

Slides
The main emphasis is on the start of the day. A series of slides
are shown showing a man or woman travelling to and starting
work at his/her factory.

The slides can be taken anywhere, but it helps if some local points and a local bus are included. The commentary should, of course, contain appropriate place names.

Present the slides with the following sort of language commentary. Later choral and individual practice can be given with the suggested questions.

Slide 1
This is Jane (or any name you choose).
She lives in Hounslow (substitute appropriate place names).
Every day she leaves home at half-past seven.

Where does she live?
When does she leave home?

Slide 2
She works in Brentford.
She goes to work by bus.
She catches the 207 bus to Brentford.

Where does she work?
Does she go to work by car/van/bicycle/bus?

Slide 3
Here she is on the bus.
The bus takes twenty minutes.

Slide 4
Jane works at Lamptons.
Every morning she arrives at work at eight o'clock.

Where does she work?
When does she arrive?

Slide 5
She goes into the factory.
She clocks on.

Slide 6
Then she goes to her locker.
She takes off her coat.
She puts on her overall.
Then she starts work.

Where does she go?
What does she take off?
What does she put on?

Slide 7

Jane has dinner at half-past twelve.
She goes to the canteen.

When does she have dinner?
Where does she go?

Slide 8

She arrives home at half-past five.

When does she arrive home?

If further practise is needed, this can be given by putting the slides up one at a time and allowing students to practise the language in groups together.

31 Your family

AIM Talking personally about what members of a student's family do. Active use of question forms and introduction of negative form.

A similar sequence of language can be used to talk about student's families. Students can bring photographs of their families which can form the basis of initial questions.

Where does your husband / wife / son / daughter / father / mother work?

He works at . . .
He doesn't work, he . . .

Where does your son / daughter go to school?

Does he go to school / to work by bus/van/bicycle?

What time does he arrive at work?

When does he leave work?

When does he arrive home?

Where does your mother / father live?

32 Starting the day

AIM **Asking and answering truthfully about how you start your day.**

This item introduces and practises present simple forms with 'I'
for the first time. These are not different from the verb forms in
Items 25 and 26, but the question form with 'do' is practised for
the first time.

Present the following type of sequence of questions and answers
and then use them for individual and group practice.

Do you live in Y?
Where do you live?
Do you get up at six o'clock?
When do you get up in the morning?
When do you leave home?
Do you travel by bus/train/van/etc.?
What bus do you catch? (New type of question)
When do you arrive at work?
Do you clock on?
Where do you clock on?
Then where do you go?
(and any other appropriate questions).

Notice you should practise both type of questions (with question
words or with 'do'). By asking questions with 'do' you can get
negative responses. You can take any positive or negative response
of an individual student; make it third person and practise it
chorally:

TEACHER   Do you live in Greenford?
STUDENT   No/No, I don't./No, I don't live in Greenford.
TEACHER   She doesn't live in Greenford.
CLASS   (Chorally) She doesn't live in Greenford.

33 Recorded drills

AIM **Practice with present simple forms.**

⊗ Tape item 7

This is the first set of recorded drills in the course. By this time
students should be reasonably familiar with responding to a tape
recorder. However, they will need some introduction to the conventions of a drill. The teacher can make up some examples of his

112

own first. These can be about class members or someone they know.

Students listen to the information on the tape and then answer the the questions.

Note These items would be better recorded with local names of places and people.

Mr Gill
Lives in Southall.
Works in Hounslow.

Where does he live?
Does he live in Brentford?
Where does he work?
Does he work in Ealing?

Mrs Uppal
Lives in West Ealing.
Works in Greenford.

Where does she live?
Does she live in Hounslow?
Where does she work?
Does she work in Perivale?

Mr Gill
Leaves home at six o'clock.
Starts work at seven o'clock.

When does he leave home?
Does he leave home at five o'clock?
When does he start work?
Does he start work at eight o'clock?

Mrs Uppal
Leaves work at five o'clock.
Arrives home at five-thirty.

When does she leave work?
Does she leave work at three o'clock?
When does she arrive home?
Does she arrive home at seven o'clock?

As many examples of this type of drill can be provided as are needed by the class, but bearing in mind the reservation about drills explained earlier. Students can practise the 'I' and 'you' present simple form in the classroom with a similar type of drill.

Part eight
Dramatic listening dialogues
A new job
Items 34 – 37

Language teaching points

Revision of a number of the language points in this section:
greetings, numbers and counting, instructions and telling someone
your name. A few examples of pronouns and present simple tense.

Aims

Entertaining listening practice to train students in careful listening
and comprehension. If students are capable of repeating the
dialogues, the items can be used in this way, but this is not the
main aim.

Teaching procedure

Students will need to hear each dialogue several times and it may
not be possible to present all four on the same occasion. If the
dialogues go over well, they can often be played for light relief at
the end of later lessons. This way students may learn a lot of
language from them.

Equipment

Pictures of a bank, a cashier, and a policeman.
A picture of a piece of furniture with a drawer in it, if there is not
one in the place of teaching.

34 Dialogue one: *arriving at work*

Make sure students know what a bank and a cashier are. Use
illustrations.

⊗ Tape item 8

(Inside a bank manager's office.)
(Door opens.)

A   Morning.

B Morning.

A I'm Miss Tyler.

B Yes. Good morning, Miss Tyler. How are you?

A Fine thanks.

B You are the new cashier.

A Yes.

B I'll give you your money for today.

A Thank you.

B Just a minute.

A Yes.

    (Rattle of keys. Opening of safe).

B Yes. Here's the money. 1-2-3-4-5-6-7-8-9-10-11-12-13 . . .
    64-65-66-67-68-69-70-71-72-73 . . . 295-296-297-298-299-300
    Three hundred pounds.

A Yes, three hundred pounds.

B Count it please.

A Yes. 1-2-3-4-5-6-7-8-9-10-11-12-13-14-15-16 . . .

35 Dialogue two: *starting work*

⊗ Tape item 9

(At the bank counter.)

B You sit here.

A Yes, I see.

B You keep your money in this drawer. This is the key.

A Thank you.

B Unlock the drawer, please.

A Yes.

B Open it.

A Open it.

B Put the money in the drawer.

A Put the money in the drawer.

B And lock the drawer at dinner time.

A Yes, of course.

B This is Mr Jones. He sits next to you.

C Good morning.

A Good morning. I'm Elsie Tyler.

36 Dialogue three: *no money*

⊗ Tape item 10

c Hullo.

a Hullo.

c Good dinner?

a Yes, thanks.
(Takes out key and opens drawer.)
(Aside) Take the key out. Unlock the drawer. Open it. HELP. . . .

c What's the matter.

a No money.

c No money?

a NO MONEY.

c Where do you keep your money?

a In this drawer.

c It's empty.

a Yes, It's empty.

c Phone the police.

a Yes – phone the police. What's the telephone number?

c 9-9-9 of course.

a Oh yes – 9 . . . 9 . . . 9 (sound of dialling).

37 Dialogue four: *the police*

⊗ Tape item 11

d Good afternoon. I'm from the police.

a Good afternoon.

d Now what's your name?

a Elsie Tyler.

d Elsie Flyer?

a No. Excuse me. It's Tyler.

d I beg your pardon?

a Tyler. T-Y-L-E-R.

d Oh, Tyler.

a Yes, that's right.

D   Where do you live?

A   I live in Greenford.

D   And you work here?

A   Yes. I started today.

D   Today?

A   Yes.

D   I'm sorry, Miss Tyler. You must come to the police station.

A   But it's not me. Ask him.

C   No. It's not her.

A   It's not me.

D   I'm sorry.

Section two

Simple social language
Instructions and faults
Making requests

Introduction

This section mainly deals with set language forms such as those
used when arriving at work, leaving, making a request, addressing
people, identifying oneself, and meeting people. In addition, there
is a certain amount of basic language for the work situation (time,
dates, colours, and prepositions), as well as identification of faults
in a work process and starting simple social conversations. There
is not a great deal of new language material compared with
Section One, and the contents of this section can be covered in
about ten hours on an intensive in-company course.

   This section is the point at which to introduce any essential
literacy items. This should only be done in situations where some
reading or form-filling is an essential part of the job. For example,
laundry lists or some forms of stock control may require recognition of perhaps 20–30 words. On the written side, the most common requirement is to fill out a work sheet for bonus or piece-
rate purposes. This requires that an employee should write his
name, and write numerals and letters. This can be developed from
the work of Section One, with the added skill of being able to
recognize essential printed matter on such forms. In companies
where there are no such requirements, students should still
master the writing of their names and addresses.

Conversations
After a course has run for about four weeks, it has proved very

useful for the teacher to keep back two or three students at the end of each lesson for a short chat. The conversation is best taken along fairly personal lines and the objective is to improve confidence rather than to correct language.

Contents *for section two*

Part one
Dates and times
Items 38 – 41

Language teaching points
a Vocabulary of days and dates.
b Expressions of time.

Aims
Confidence and fair accuracy with times and dates. Also stress upon the significance given to time in Britain in all organized arrangements. The significance of the clock is something new to people from rural backgrounds. They will probably appreciate the need to be punctual, but may not understand the significance of time and sequence in other areas of their work. This is a point to find out about in the investigation.

Teaching procedure
These items are best taught in short sections and then frequently revised and practised.

Equipment
a Calendar.
b Set of clock faces.

38 Days of the week

AIM Accurate recognition of days and dates; also the use of terms 'weekdays' and 'weekends'.

Teach days of the week on the page of a large calendar or draw in advance on a sheet of cartridge paper.

Monday, Tuesday, Wednesday, Thursday, Friday, Saturday, Sunday.

Also teach along with the days and dates:

The weekend. Did you have a nice weekend?

Today is . . . . . .
Yesterday was . . . . . .
Tomorrow will be . . . . . .
Everyday I come to work.

At a later stage introduce names of the months

39 Telling the time

AIM **The ability to tell the time quickly and with reasonable accuracy. This is more important than precise identification of the exact number of minutes.**

Use a clock face to present and practise:

What's the time?
Five, six, seven, etc. o'clock.
quarter to . . . . . .
quarter past . . . . . .
half past . . . . . .
It's nearly . . . . . .
It's just after . . . . . .

Call out times and get students to set the clock face to the correct time.

Then get students to set clock face to the following times and afterwards to answer these questions:

What time do you catch the bus every day?
What time do you arrive at work?
What time do you begin your job?
What time do you come to the English class?
What time do you leave work?

(and other suitable questions).

Go on to present and practice on a later occasion with sets of clock faces:

Five, ten, fifteen, twenty (etc.) past/to . . . . . .

If the class want to, and have found this item easy, go on to (at a later date):

two minutes past . . . . . . (etc.)

But there is no need at all to teach this with a class who have difficulty in grasping the basic forms.

40 Daily timetables

AIM **Practising phrases of time, and talking about daily work in terms of a timetable.**

Prepare visuals (enough for group work) of students' daily routine.

Similar question and answer sequences to item 39.

What time do you have your tea-break? (etc.)

In some jobs there are vital times: for example, to do with the staggering of tea-breaks. Or the sequence of a job may be very important: for example, in catering and domestic work. Where the sequence is vital words such as 'first' and 'then' should be introduced.

41 Written timetables

AIM **Reading of printed times.**

At a much later point in the course introduce materials illustrating bus, train, or air timetables. Also use any examples of lists of times used in the workplace.

The concepts can be put over with written times and visuals, but the practical value of this item can only apply with groups who have some simple literacy or at least the ability to recognize place names. Such limited literacy would be essential for any students working in transport even as manual workers because they would be asked times by the public – for example, a London station or Heathrow airport.

Practical communication exercises

Reading clock-card times.
This can be organized at the clocking-in point at the entrance to the factory. But examples of clocking-in cards should first be looked at in the classroom as the way of printing out the time may present special problems.

Time-clocks on machinery.
Practice should be given to reading these if they exist on machines in the factory.

Part two
Arriving at work
Items 42 – 45

Language teaching points
Set formulae for use when arriving at work in the morning.

Aims
a To get students always to talk to their fellow English workers when arriving in the morning.
b To present the idea of fictional characters in recorded dialogues.
c To establish classroom methods of using recorded dialogues.

Teaching procedure
The dialogues and language presented are simple and short so they should not give real difficulty. Make sure the desired classroom methods are established from the start in using this type of material. Some past simple verb forms are introduced for the first time. These should simply be learned as set expressions. No attempt is made to present this tense as a whole until Section three.

Equipment
Visuals of fictional characters; mounted pictures and/or slides.

42 Characters in the factory dialogues

AIM **To present as convincingly as possible the first three characters who appear in the factory dialogues.**

Throughout Sections Two, Three, Five, and Six a series of fictional characters appear in many of the recorded dialogues. This traditional device has been used for two reasons: to allow personality to be established and shown to be an element in language behaviour; to make the characters in the dialogues identifiably similar to the people the students work with.

Women or men
Many of the dialogues in the course were originally developed for teaching Asian women. The sex of the characters in the dialogues

126

should obviously be chosen to suit the situation. We suggest the following sets of main characters according to the situation.

Women

Mary Williams: between 35 and 40, kind, alert.
Gurmit Kaur Gill: young Indian girl.
Sheila Richardson: young English girl, new to the job. Friendly and willing, but makes mistakes.
Beryl James (Mrs James): the supervisor. Middle-aged, formal but quite kind.
Betty: a minor character in her thirties, for when someone else is needed in a dialogue.

In our dialogues, these people work in a food processing factory.

Men

A similar set of characters.
Fred Barker: In his thirties and stuck in the job.
Davinder Singh Bhullar: young Indian – unmarried.
Tony Goddard: young Englishman – new to the job.
John Carr (Mr Carr): the supervisor. Been there a very long time and quite tough.

In our dialogues, these people work in an injection moulding factory.

Mixed

In the event of a mixed workforce, arrange characters according to the situation. Or if you just want to introduce some men, make the supervisor male and have a male general-hand or maintenance man.

Mount pictures or take slides (which make more impact) of suitable people to use as characters in the dialogues. These pictures should be shown as illustrations for each dialogue in which the characters occur. The following are examples. Rewrite and change to suit the background of your own students. This introductory material is not intended for active language learning. Try to make the characters look as different as possible, and have contrasting voices in the recorded dialogues. The type of factory should be varied as appropriate.

Slides

Use one name only for each character.

Slide 1

This is a factory.
It's called Lamptons Ltd.

Slide 2
This is Mary.
She works at Lamptons.
She lives in Hounslow.
She's married.
She has two children, David, he's seven, and Sally, she's nine.
She's thirty-five.

Slide 3
And this is Gurmit.
She works at Lamptons.
She's married.
She's young, about twenty.

43 Arriving at work

AIM **To practise standard greetings for the morning and after the weekend, To establish procedure for using recorded dialogues.**

Early, late, on time
Using times and clock face establish the meaning and use of these items:

TEACHER   What time did you come to work on Tuesday, etc.

yesterday?
this morning?

STUDENT   At . . . . . .

TEACHER   You were early/late/on time.

Present the following dialogue with pictures of the characters. Prepare and revise any vocabulary items you think necessary. Note the use of the past simple tense. Get these usages correct without going into details of the tense.

⊗ Tape item 12

Version A

NARRATOR   Mary arrived at work early on Monday. First Gurmit came in.

MARY   Morning. How are you?

GURMIT   Very well thanks. And you?

MARY   I'm fine.

GURMIT   Did you have a nice weekend?

MARY   Yes, thanks. We went for a drive.

GURMIT   That's nice.

1 *Listen.*
2 *Listen and repeat* Gurmit.
3 *Listen and fill-in* Gurmit.

2 *Listen and repeat* Mary.
3 *Listen and fill-in* Mary.

Version B

NARRATOR	Fred arrived at work early on Monday. First Davinder came in.
FRED	Hullo, Davinder.
DAVINDER	Morning, Fred. How are you?
FRED	I'm fine.
DAVINDER	Did you have a nice weekend?
FRED	Yes, thanks. I went fishing.
DAVINDER	Oh, yes.

1, 2, 3 *as for Version A.*

Groups of men and groups of women use slightly different language to each other. Therefore, when the sex of the characters is changed in a dialogue, it is necessary to make some changes to the language of the dialogue.

Procedure for classroom exploitation of recorded dialogues

Each dialogue is recorded three times to be used as follows:

1 Listen

Keep playing an item initially until it is fully understood.

2 Listen and repeat

In most dialogues (although not this one) it is intended that students should only learn the language of one character's part. The other parts they are not required to repeat. Important not to let them repeat everything, because the other parts are only intended for passive understanding.

3 Listen and fill in

The particular part which has been repeated is blanked out on the third version. Students fill in the lines for this character against the other parts which come over the tape recorder. This is a procedure that a class need a good deal of practice with.

Whenever using recorded dialogues avoid mere parroting without understanding, and insist upon accuracy with structure and pronunciation.

The use of recorded dialogues is explained more fully in Part One, Chapter 7.

44 A bad morning

AIM **Dealing with someone in a bad humour.**

Another short and easy dialogue. Present with pictures of the characters.

⊗ Tape item 13

NARRATOR Mary was late this morning.

GURMIT Hullo, Mary. How are you?

MARY I'm terrible.

GURMIT What's the matter?

MARY I'm late.

GURMIT Never mind.

1 *Listen.*
2 *Listen and repeat* Gurmit.
3 *Listen and fill-in* Gurmit.

A man would be unlikely to say 'never mind'. 'Oh, yes' would again be a more appropriate comment as in Item 43.

45 Classroom practice

AIM **To make up and practise in groups dialogues similar to Items 43 and 44.**

How are you?
Give practice with the following responses.

I'm fine.
Very well.
I feel terrible.
Not so good.

What's the matter?
Teacher acts so he looks tired, ill, unhappy, etc.

Student asks the questions. Teacher responds.

I'm tired/ill/etc.

Build up simple dialogues such as the following. Students can make up their own variations and practise them in groups.

a Morning. How are you?
Fine thanks. And you?
Very well.

b Morning. How are you?
I'm terrible.
What's the matter?
I'm tired.
Never mind.

Reinforce these the next morning when students are arriving. Better students may act in front of the class.

Practical communication exercise

Arrival greetings.
Active use should happen without difficulty or the need of a lot of active encouragement. However, it is a good idea to get one or two people to check use with each student one morning.

Part three
Colours
Items 46 and 47

46 Colours

AIM **To check that principal colours are clearly known. This item can also be used for vocabulary building.**

Note If this course is used for a factory where items or equipment are colour coded use these, if possible, for identifying colours.
Examples: Control panel buttons, packets, wire leads.

Use slides already shown, or sets of crayons for initial identification.

Prepare duplicated pictures of any objects from the factory, canteen, etc., and use these for giving colouring instructions to the class.

Examples
(Picture of the factory).
Make the walls red.
Make the doors blue.
Make the roof black (etc.)

Use 'make' rather than 'colour' to discourage use of 'red colour'.

Most classes will find this very easy so go on to present and practise shades of colour with:

pale/light/dark.

Equipment
Sets of crayons. Prepared duplicated pictures.

47 Instructions linked to colour

AIM **Establishing and practising vital colour distinctions in the work situation.**

In some work situations there are vital colour or shade distinctions in the products, and often these colours are identified by a special two-part name – for example, 'sky-blue', 'fire-red' etc.

In a situation where colours are important in this way, a sequence of instructions using the language of Item 15 can be made up in which items have to be differentiated by the appropriate colour names.

The sequence can be used and practised in groups in the same way as Item 15.

Practical communication exercise

Colours.
Chargehand or foreman can ask student to fetch him some items identified by colour.

Example

Fetch me six green bacon boxes, three red bacon boxes, and one yellow bacon box. Put them on my desk, please.

Part four
A factory process or job
including looking out for faults
Items 48 – 50

Language teaching points

a Revision of language of a job or process. Or presentation of a new set of instructions.
b Vocabulary and set phrases for key faults.
c Instructions for fetching and carrying.

Aims

Accurate verbal identification of key faults.

Teaching procedure

The material is again particularly well suited to group work. The final set of instructions will probably be quite long and will have to be led up to gradually – a chunk at a time.

Equipment

Sets of job materials or visuals for each member of the class (or at least each group).

Collections of faulty materials or visuals illustrating the faults. Again ideally a set for each member of the class.

48 Revision of factory job

Go back to Item 28 in Section One of the course and revise it completely with the class.

49 Identification of faults

AIM **Accurate verbal recognition of key faults which affect quality in a particular job or process.**

Teach the vocabulary for all possible important faults associated with the job or process used for Item 28. However, if very few faults occur with that particular job, choose another one where quality control and possible faults are more important.

Again the names of faults and means of identifying them can be taken from the job description recorded by a Supervisor or trainer.

Example

Teach the names of the defects likely to be found on a batten-holder:

> chips, cracks, short mouldings, cross-threaded.

Practise with the questions, 'What's wrong?', and accept single word replies. Also teach:

> edges, key holes, screws.

Obviously teach these with examples of defective parts from the factory, or with visuals, or if necessary in the factory itself.

Then give out sets some of which are faulty and some of which are perfect.

Teach: one crack, two cracks, no cracks (etc.). How many cracks?

Make sure 'no' is taught with multiple examples.

Then go on to teach phrases:

> Make sure there are no cracks (etc.).
> Make sure you've got six screws (etc.).

Use sets of material again.

All this vocabulary and expression can be practised in groups.

50 Instructions including looking out for faults in a factory process or job

AIM **Accurate use of English to describe a job or process including looking out for key points in identifying faults.**

Now combine the original instructions for the job in Item 28 (or another job if more suitable) with the faults identification language taught in the previous item (Item 49).

⊗ Tape item 14

Example

Assembling a battenholder.
> You pick your battenholder up.
> Make sure there are no cracked key holes.
> Make sure you've got all the screws.

Then you pick your base up.
Make sure you've got no chips round the edges.
Make sure there are no cracks in it.
Make sure there are no short mouldings.
Then you slot the battenholder into the base.
You pick a ring up.
Make sure there are no cracks in it.
Make sure there are no short mouldings, no chips.
You put it on.
You screw it down.
You pick a short skirt up.
Make sure you've got no cracks, no chips, no short mouldings.
You twist it round.
Make sure it's not cross-threaded.
Then you put it in the bin ready for packing.

Suggested teaching procedure

a Teacher demonstrates with the language.
b Teacher speaks description while class do it.
c Teacher does process again; class chorally repeat appropriate sentence.
d Best students instruct the other members of their groups; in this way every individual will gradually master the language of the whole process.

51 Fetching and carrying

AIM **Accurate understanding of instructions to collect, move, and deliver objects.**

For some jobs in some work places, matters of quality and process are of little importance to the workers – for example, general labourers, or people working in a warehouse or stores. One important aspect of these people's work is to understand and act upon instructions to fetch and carry things.

This item consists of a number of instructions (they would not in reality be a sequence) relating to instructions of this sort. Much of the language needed has already been presented in Item 15 (general instructions), Item 21 (prepositions of place), and Items 46 and 47 (colours). An important new point is: bags *of* . . . . . ., sacks *of* . . . . . ., boxes *of* . . . . . .

The following is an example of such instructions which should be written for the particular situation. When the objects are small they can be brought to the classroom. When they are large, drawings or models can be used.

⊗ Tape item 15

Fetch four bags of bacon boxes, please.
Two bags of blue boxes and two bags of pink boxes.
Bring me one bag of blue boxes.
Give Joginder one bag of blue boxes.
Take two bags of pink boxes to Jaswant.
Put them down next to the table.

Collect six packets of A42 brown labels.
Put three packets next to the two bags of pink boxes.
Give one packet to me.
Put two packets on the table next to Parminder.

Put these four blue boxes back on the shelf.

Suggested teaching procedure as for Item 50.

Practical communication exercise

Identification of faults.

Constant practice on the shop-floor is essential if the language needed for accurate identification of faults is to be established. Chargehands and foremen whenever possible should ask the question: 'What's wrong?' and accept a one-word identification of the fault as sufficient at this stage.

Part five
Introductions, personal names and leaving work
Items 52 – 58

Language teaching points
a Set formulae for use when meeting people for the first time.
b Set formulae for saying goodbye.
c Prepositional phrases of place.
d Further colours.

Aims

a For students to understand and use the English formula for meeting people at work.
b To always say goodbye when leaving work.
c To understand and use English names and other forms of address correctly.
d To introduce some more of the fictional characters in the recorded dialogues.

Teaching procedure
Again simple and short dialogues (as in Part Two) which should not present real difficulties, and should not be overtaught. Make sure students are now all familiar with listening, repeating, and filling in methods when recorded dialogues are being used.

The work on English names will be best extended over some time and revised carefully at a later stage in the course.

Equipment
a Visuals of fictional characters, mounted pictures, and/or slides.
b Pictures of useful vocabulary items.
c Sets of uniform objects of different colours (e.g. bricks).

52 More characters in the factory dialogues

AIM **To present as convincingly as possible three more characters.**

Prepare suitable mounted pictures and/or slides. Go over the old characters again before you go onto the new ones. Again the language suggested is not for active teaching.

Slides
Again use only one name for each character.

Slide 2
Who's this? It's Mary.
She's worked at Lamptons for six years.

Slide 3
And this is Gurmit.
She came to Lamptons a year ago.

Slide 4
This is Sheila.
She's a new girl.
She came to Lamptons today.

Note The introduction of a new employee gives the opportunity to present a number of unfamiliar and difficult situations at work which are similar to those often encountered by Asians with language difficulties.

Slide 5
This is Mrs James.
She's the Supervisor.

Slide 6
And this is Betty.
She also works at Lamptons.

Note Betty is a very minor character, but it is sometimes useful to have another person available.

53 Meeting new people

AIM **Behaviour and language for meeting people for the first time.**

Present the following dialogue with pictures of the characters.

⊗ Tape item 16

NARRATOR Today a new girl came to the department.

SHEILA Excuse me. I'm new.

MARY Come in, dear. We won't bite.

SHEILA Where do I put my coat?

MARY Put it over there.

SHEILA Thanks.

MARY I'm Mary, and that's Gurmit.

SHEILA Hullo. I'm Sheila.

1 *Listen.*
2 *Listen and repeat* Sheila.
3 *Listen and fill in* Sheila.

With male characters, the second line could be simply: 'Come in mate/lad.'

Introducing yourself
Now go round the class, everyone saying
I'm . . . . . .
Then divide into groups with one new girl:
A I'm . . . . . . That's . . . . . . and that's . . . . . .
B Hullo. I'm . . . . . .
The dialogue can be practised with substitutions for the word 'coat'.

54 Vocabulary game

AIM **To increase vocabulary. Useful for pronunciation too.**

Make a series of picture cards of anything you consider useful. The best way is to ask the class to cut out pictures of objects that interest them and bring them to class. The vocabulary item is then taught.

Divide the class into teams. Teacher holds up a card. The first person to identify it wins a point for her team.

55 Position

AIM **To teach some useful prepositional phrases, and more practice with language for meeting people for the first time.**

a Put the cards of the characters introduced so far face down:

> Who's in the middle?
> Who's on the right?
> Who's on the left?
> Who's over there?

b Repeat this with a variety of objects including uniform objects of different colours (e.g. bricks). These can then be identified as:

> The red/blue/yellow/green/black one, etc.

Introduce here any useful colours not covered so far.

Teach 'next to'.

> The red one is *next to* the blue one.
> 'Who is *next to* Mary?'

c Dialogue
Present the following dialogue with pictures of the characters.

⊗ Tape item 17

NARRATOR Betty came in. She saw the new girl.

BETTY Hullo. I'm Betty. Who are you?

SHEILA Hullo. I'm Sheila.

BETTY Do you know Mary and Gurmit?
That's Mary in the middle.
That's Gurmit on the left.

1 *Listen.*
2 *Listen and repeat* Betty.
3 *Listen and fill in* Betty.

56 Leaving work

AIM **To practise standard ways of saying 'goodbye' in the evening.**

a Set formulae
Go back and quickly revise the ways of saying goodbye practised in Section One, item 18.

b Dialogue practice
Present the following dialogue with pictures of the characters.

⊗ Tape item 18

Version A

NARRATOR At quarter-to-five everyone rushes to go home.

GURMIT Quick, quick. I'll miss the bus.

141

SHEILA	Excuse me, where's my coat?
GURMIT	I don't know.
SHEILA	Oh, it's all right. Here it is.
GURMIT	Cheerio, everyone.
SHEILA	'Bye, Gurmit. See you tomorrow.
GURMIT	Yes, 'bye. Goodbye, Mrs James.

1 *Listen.*
2 *Listen and repeat* Sheila.
3 *Listen and fill in* Sheila.

Version B

NARRATOR	At the end of overtime – at six o'clock – everyone rushes to go home.
DAVINDER	Mind out. I'm in a hurry.
TONY	Excuse me. Where's my clock-card?
DAVINDER	I don't know.
TONY	Oh, it's all right. Here it is.
DAVINDER	Cheers, everyone.
TONY	'Bye, Davinder. See you tomorrow.
DAVINDER	Yes, 'bye. See you, George.

1, 2, 3. Tony.

At the end of the lesson get everyone to leave in turn and to say to the class:

A 'Bye (or any alternative). See you tomorrow.
B 'Bye (or any alternative). See you tomorrow.

c Game: *Where is it?*

If extra practice is needed, this game can be used to reinforce the material in the dialogue.

Someone in the class hides something belonging to someone else. The person who it belongs to can go out of the room.

STUDENT A	Excuse me. Where's my handbag.
RESPONSES	I don't know.
	Here it is.
	It's over there/next to . . . . . ./etc.

142

57 Correct names to use with English employees

AIM **Discussion of what students call other workers and supervisors.**

Practice varies in factories as to whether people like to be called by their first names or their surnames. Immigrants are often uncertain as to correct forms of address, of the significance of different parts of names and to the names themselves (see *Part One*, Chapter 4). English workers and even supervisory staff sometimes resent the fact that Asians do not call them by any name at all.

Find out what is the practice in the factory where you are teaching and then use this dialogue or prepare a more suitable one of an incident which might occur there.

Present the following dialogue with pictures of the characters.

Establish the full name of each of the dialogue characters (see Item 42 for complete list).

Make sure everyone understands that the first name is 'the Christian name', and the second name is 'the surname'. Also establish that 'Mr', 'Mrs' and 'Miss' are only used with the surname, and that the first name alone is friendly and familiar. Revise Item 17 using full names. Explain that the surname is always the name for formal identification in Britain.

⊗ Tape item 19

NARRATOR   Mrs James, her first name is Beryl, is our supervisor.

MRS JAMES   Off you go, ladies.

MARY   'Bye, Beryl. Give me a nice job tomorrow.

MRS JAMES   Go on. 'Bye.

SHEILA   Goodbye . . . er, Beryl.

MRS JAMES   Mrs James, dear.

SHEILA   Oh, goodbye, Mrs James. See you tomorrow.

MRS JAMES   I hope so. Goodbye dear.

1 *Listening only.*

This is for listening only. Follow the dialogue with a simple discussion of the names of English employees in the factory and of supervisors. Make sure students are clear as to the correct name to

143

use. If they do not know the names of people they work with, tell them to find out for the next lesson.

58 Practising English names

AIM **To understand and recognize the difference between first and second names and to improve pronunciation of some common names.**

This item continues the discussion from Item 57 and should be used as a later follow-up. With a weaker class, the level of discussion needed will make it best to leave this until the second half of the course.

Practise pronouncing a number of common two-part English names preferably represented in the students' own departments.

Examples

Bob Williamson.
John Pearce.
Geoff Seager.

Give some names and get people to guess whether it is a first or second name.

Discuss the use of 'Mr', 'Miss' and 'Mrs'; the meaning of these titles and the fact that they are only used with surnames. It is a common mistake of Asian immigrants to call people 'Mr John', or 'Mrs Beryl'.

Emphasize that the English like to use names and be addressed by name most of the time.

Find out the complete name of each student in the class. Discuss and advise students on the use of their names by English people. Inform each student's department and personnel of the full names and style of use.

Practical communication exercise

Correct use of English names.
Make sure that all employees now ask students to call them by the name they prefer if the students have been using unusual forms of address, such as, 'Mr Bill'.

Part six
Asking politely
Items 59 – 63

Language teaching points
a Set formulae for polite requests.
b Intensive practice with 'please' and 'thank you'.
c Vocabulary for food.
d Vocabulary for money.

Aims
To get students to use polite forms when asking for things; and perhaps to encourage them to feel able to use the works canteen.

Teaching procedure
The language material in this part is very simple but needs hammering home until it becomes completely automatic. It may be found best to return to this part again after doing some later work in the section.

Equipment
a Sets of factory objects.
b Sets of pictures of food mounted on card.
c If required, cards with amount of money written on them.

59 Polite requests

AIM **Train students in a polite formula for asking for things.**

Use familiar objects preferably from the factory to present and practise. Initial presentation with a glove puppet.

Can I have *a battenholder* please? Thanks.

Practise with students individually and in groups. Nothing to be handed over unless 'please' is said. And objects to be taken back if 'thanks' not used.

At some point when teaching the material in Part Six point out that the following expressions are considered very rude by many English people:

I want . . . . . .
I must have . . . . . .

Use of these expressions by Asians sometimes leads to mis-understandings and hard feelings. Equally just pointing and naming the object can also be considered rude.

60 Game *'please'*

AIM **To establish the use of the word 'please' as quite mechanical.**

Give simple instructions to the class, such as:

Touch the desk, please.
Pass your pen to your neighbour.

Class should do things when 'please' is used and not do them when it is not. Anyone doing something when 'please' is not used is out.

Students can take it in turn to instruct the class or the game can be played in groups.

The game can be played very briefly on a number of occasions so that the point is really got home to students.

61 Asking for things in the canteen

AIM **Clear and precise use of English in the factory canteen.**

a Vocabulary items
Prepare pictures of food mounted on cards – particularly dishes regularly served in the canteen. Present and practise these items, then give out the cards for group practice in this way:

A Can I have some *eggs and bacon*, please.

B Here you are, X (hand over the card).

A Thanks.

b Dialogue
Present dialogue with visuals of characters and of the different dishes.

⊗ Tape item 20

NARRATOR	At lunchtime Sheila went to the canteen.
SHEILA	Can I have fish and chips please?
CANTEEN WOMAN	Here you are, love.
SHEILA	Thanks. And pudding please.
CANTEEN WOMAN	Yes.
SHEILA	Thanks. How much?
CANTEEN WOMAN	35p plus 15, that's 50p please, darling.
SHEILA	50p.
CANTEEN WOMAN	Thank you, dear.
MARY	Hullo, Sheila.
SHEILA	Hullo, Mary. Phew! I'm tired!

1 *Listen.*
2 *Listen and repeat* Sheila.
3 *Listen and fill in* Sheila.

For men rewrite with Canteen woman using only 'dear'.
Afterwards students can make up similar dialogues in groups.
Note the use of forms of address such as 'dear', 'love', 'darling'.
These are not actively practised, but this is an opportunity to
explain that these are normal and friendly, but not over familiar
between equals in the factory.

c Money
If coins, expressions of money, and adding are not familiar to
students this is a good time to teach it.

Either take along a selection of coins or cards with amounts of
money written on them.

62 Game *spinning for food*

AIM **Further practice of material in Items 59, 60 and 61.**

Students sit in a circle. Each student is given a card with a
picture of food on it. A student spins the top and calls out:

Can I have some . . . . . ., please?

The person holding the card with the picture of the food called
out must reach the top before it stops spinning.

63 Reading a payslip

AIM **Reading and correct pronunciation of larger sums of money.**

Prepare a slide of a payslip or make multiple copies of payslips available.

First aim for all students to be able to read net amount on slip in response to:

How much have you got?

Further work can consist of opening dummy pay-packets containing dummy money. Check the amount on the slip and then count the money.

You may want to identify some of the other amounts on the slip as well as the name and the clock number. But more work is included on payslips in Item 108.

Part seven
Starting a conversation
Items 64 – 68

Language teaching points
a Questions with 'Are you'.
b Question form of present simple tense.
c Questions with present simple tense introduced by 'Where', 'What', 'Who', 'When'.
d Stress pattern in a reciprocal question.

Aims
To equip students with a simple formula for starting a conversation with a stranger.

To train students to give information about themselves clearly and accurately.

Teaching procedure
If the verb forms give the class difficulty, make up further material of the same type. Don't be limited by the material here or it will quickly become boring.

Equipment
Only standard items.

64 Dialogue *using questions in conversation*

AIM **To make students aware of how they can start a conversation with someone by asking questions. In this case about another person.**

Present the following dialogue with pictures of the characters.

⊗ Tape item 21

NARRATOR   Mary talked to the new girl Sheila at tea-break.
MARY   Hullo dear. Are you tired?
SHEILA   Yes, are you?
MARY   Not really.

SHEILA	Mary, who's that?
MARY	That's George.
SHEILA	What's his job?
MARY	He's on maintenance.
SHEILA	Where does he work?
MARY	The engineering department.
GEORGE	Who's talking about me?
MARY	Don't worry. George's always grumbling.

1 *Listen.*
2 *Listen and repeat* Sheila.
3 *Listen and fill in* Sheila.

Point out to students that Sheila asks questions all the time.
Ask them to try to ask an English-speaking person some questions that day.

65 Reciprocal questions

AIM **Practice in reciprocal questions as a way of carrying on a very simple conversation.**

Get over to the class the idea that 'I ask you a question, you ask me a question'. Demonstrate the following question sequences. Then go on to practise these and similar questions individually and in groups:

Are you married?
Yes, are you?

Are you hungry?
Yes, are you?

Are you thirsty?
No, are you?

Are you a machine operator?
No, are you?

Are you tired?
No, are you?

Do you work in the assembly department?
Yes, do you?

Do you have any children?
No, do you?

150

Do you like fish and chips?
Yes, do you?

Does your son go to school?
No, does yours?

Does your husband work in Southall?
Yes, does yours?

Does your mother live with you?
Yes, does yours?

Make sure students get the correct stress on 'you' in the reciprocal question.

⊗ Tape item 22

The same questions but with more extended answers can now be practised with better groups. It is suggested that the recorded questions should be a shock to raise interest and spur a student to give some comeback.

Examples

A   Are you married?

B   Yes, five times. Are you?

A   (pause for student response which can be yes/no or fuller).

At a later stage students can take B's part.

66 Reciprocal questions with *wh* – questions

AIM **Practice in reciprocal questions of another form as a way of carrying on a very simple conversation.**

Demonstrate the following type of questions, then go on to practise the following and other similar questions individually and in groups. Again make sure students stress the reciprocal question correctly. Items 65 and 66 are a good opportunity for doing some special work on stress.

Where do you live?
Hounslow. Where do you live?

What's your job?
Packing. What's your job?

What's your name?
Sue. What's your name?

Who do you work next to?
Mary. Who do you work next to?

Who is your supervisor?
Mrs James. Who is your supervisor?

When do you arrive at work?
8 o'clock. When do you arrive at work?

When do you have lunch?
12.30. When do you have lunch?

⊗ Tape item 23

The first questions above are recorded as a drill for students to answer.

67 Dialogue *using reciprocal questions in a conversation*

AIM **To demonstrate and practise the use of reciprocal questions in a conversation.**

Present this dialogue with pictures of the characters. Try to get over clearly to the class the way this dialogue is built up with questions and reciprocal questions.

⊗ Tape item 24

Version A

NARRATOR	Sheila and Gurmit were chatting in the canteen.
SHEILA	Are you married, Gurmit?
GURMIT	Yes, are you?
SHEILA	No, I've got a boy friend.
GURMIT	What's his name?
SHEILA	Peter. What's your husband's name?
GURMIT	Kulwant.
SHEILA	What?
GURMIT	*Kulwant.*
SHEILA	Oh yes. Where does he work?
GURMIT	At Lyons. Where does your boyfriend work?
SHEILA	At Hodkins.
GURMIT	What's his job?
SHEILA	He's an engineer. Where do you live?
GURMIT	In Hounslow. Where do you live?
SHEILA	In Hounslow too.

1 *Listen.*
2 *Listen and repeat* Gurmit.
3 *Listen and fill-in* Gurmit.

Equally students can practise and repeat Sheila's part.

By the end of this dialogue, some students should be capable of making up similar dialogues of their own. It might be possible to get some English-speakers to come along to this lesson, and then the students could have genuine conversations with them like this.

Version A is rather personal and, although it could be adapted for men, with some groups of men or women, the teacher may prefer a less personal situation for practising this language, such as Version B.

Version B

NARRATOR	Tony met the shop steward for the first time.
SHOP STEWARD	Hullo there, mate. I'm your shop steward. What's your name?
TONY	Goddard. Tony Goddard. What's your name?
SHOP STEWARD	I'm Danny Waters. What's your job Tony?
TONY	I'm a machine operator. What's your job?
SHOP STEWARD	I'm in the stores.
TONY	Oh yes.
SHOP STEWARD	Do you live near here?
TONY	In Hounslow. Where do you live?
SHOP STEWARD	Oh yes. I live in Hounslow too.

1, 2, 3. Tony.

68 Identifying yourself and making a request

AIM **Giving essential personal information clearly in a formal situation.**

Present this dialogue with pictures of the characters. This dialogue revises material on names, requests, and questions in a more formal setting.

⊗ Tape item 25

NARRATOR	Sheila went to the Personnel Office.
SECRETARY	Good morning. Can I help you?

SHEILA	Yes. Can I see the personnel officer, please?
SECRETARY	What's your name, please?
SHEILA	Richardson. Sheila Richardson.
SECRETARY	Miss or Mrs?
SHEILA	Miss.
SECRETARY	Thank you. And your clock number?
SHEILA	830624.
SECRETARY	And where do you work, Miss Richardson?
SHEILA	In the packing department.
SECRETARY	Right. Just wait a moment, please.

1 *Listen.*
2 *Listen and repeat* Sheila.
3 *Listen and fill-in* Sheila.

This dialogue could be adapted or similar ones made up for non-work situations such as hospitals or visiting a child's school to see a teacher.

Section three

Responding in more complicated situations
Measuring and accuracy

Introduction

There are two main aspects to the work of this section. Firstly the
student is involved in responding in quite complicated work and
language situations. The language and situations involved are far
more complicated and less set than in Sections One and Two. The
work includes such things as following unfamiliar instructions,
asking for help, using the telephone, and taking messages. These
represent genuine communication situations in which an immigrant often finds himself under pressure. It is worth spending a
good deal of time on making sure these items are really learned
because success with them will greatly increase the confidence and
motivation of students.

Secondly, the section contains important language for the job to
do with measurement, accuracy, and comparison. Also included is
a grammatical treatment of the past simple tense.

The different types of item in this section need mixing together
to give an interesting teaching order. It is unlikely this section can
be covered in less than twelve hours.

The job language present in the first three sections of the
materials has given no attention to how machines work. For
better groups, who are machine operators, there may be too much
emphasis in this section on the quality of the product and the
need for instructions, and not enough emphasis upon the relationship between these and the operator's machine. With such groups,
it is advised that Items 122 and 123 from Section Four are
brought forward and started during this section.

Contents *for section three*

156

Part one
Following instructions
Items 69 – 72

Language teaching points
a Further essential vocabulary for directions and instructions.
b Language used for controls.

Aims
a To understand and follow unfamiliar sequences of instructions.
And for better students to be able to give such instructions.
b Language for familiar controls.

Teaching procedure
As with all instruction work, this material is well suited for use
with groups. This part should be an opportunity for students to
develop and improvise from all the job instruction language so far
presented in the course.

Equipment
a Sets of job material if Item 69 is done.
b Large supply of squares of tissue paper.
c Slides may be required for Item 72.

69 Revision of factory instructions
If you feel some of the class are not entirely certain of the basic
sequence and essential language for job instructions go back and
revise Item 50 in Section Two. Alternatively revise the language
giving instructions for a different job but one which is very similar
to the jobs in Item 50.

For example: assembling a lampholder.

With a class which has fully grasped the work in Section Two
there is no need for revision.

70 Game *Where is it?*

AIM **To establish further essential vocabulary for directions and instructions.**

Present briefly the following vocabulary:

left, right
top, bottom, middle
a square
same again
top left corner
top right corner
bottom left corner
bottom right corner

Draw various items on the blackboard, or use prepared visuals. You can use this item to increase vocabulary – for example, the name of tools.

Each student has a number.

TEACHER   Number Six, where's the screwdriver?
STUDENT 6   It's in the top left corner.
            Number Two, where's the hammer?
STUDENT 2   It's in the middle.
            Number Seven, where's the knife? (etc.)

Or a visual can be made of a machine and some additional essential vocabulary introduced.

TEACHER   Number Two, where's the valve?
STUDENT 2   It's in the middle at the bottom.

71 Following unfamiliar instructions

AIM **To train students to be able to follow and carry out a set of instructions for a job they have not done before.**

Students are instructed how to make a paper object. The vocabulary involves common and useful words which often occur in factory operations. This item demonstrates how any job may be broken down into simple stages and language.

Each student needs a square of tissue paper (about eight inches square).
The following words should be taught or revised.

flap
fold
turn over
pull out
underneath

Making a paper flower

Put the square on the table
Fold the top left corner to the middle
Fold the top right corner to the middle
Fold the bottom right corner to the middle
Fold the bottom left corner to the middle
Do the same again
Turn it over
Do the same again
Look underneath
Pull out each flap from underneath

Suggested teaching procedure:
a Teacher demonstrates with the instructions.
b Teacher gives instructions while the class do the job.
c Teacher gives instructions while class repeat and do them.
d Teacher does the job; class repeats instructions only chorally.
e One student demonstrates while the class or group follow;
then better students instruct others in groups.

Having taught this sequence, go on to use other paper folding sequences. These can be done spontaneously and experimentally. Students as well as the teacher can come forward with ideas, but they must instruct someone *else* to do the actual folding. When done successfully this will represent real communication and will greatly boost the confidence of students. You may like to ask each student to prepare a sequence of instructions for the next lesson.

In a factory where making cartons, or wrapping form a part of the process, the language of these jobs should be taught and practised at this point because all the essential language has already been taught for paper folding.

72 Controls

AIM To teach vocabulary and simple instructions for controls that students use at their jobs.

Many jobs involve the use of foot controls or simple control panels. When you have considered the controls used by your students, demonstrate the essential language required in addition to the language in Item 71. This language can be demonstrated on a machine in the place you teach (for example, a vending machine) or with recognizable diagrams of controls:

Examples of vocabulary:

switch on/off, press, pedal, start button, stop button, power switch.

Add or substitute your own examples.

Slides

Then go on to teach the actual instructions for jobs either using slides (for complicated control panels) or going into the factory to look at simple controls.

Examples

Switch on the power.
Press the button in the top-left-hand corner.

Part two
Measurement
Items 73 – 75

Language teaching points
a Simple language for measurement of dimension and/or temperature.
b Comparative forms.
c Questions with 'how'.

Aims
To establish accuracy and use of language for simple measurement. Some of the language forms are used later in this section for work on weighing (Part Six). If no sort of measurement forms any part of the factory process, which is unlikely, this material should be dealt with very quickly.

Teaching procedure
This material is very straightforward and does not make any very active or interesting demands on students. For this reason these items will be best taught mixed in with work from other parts of this section. The one really essential point in this material is to insist upon real accuracy. After establishing the language and concepts of Item 73, the later items should be adapted for the type of measurement students require at work, excluding weighing dealt with later.

Equipment
Sets of rulers, pencils, rough paper.
A variety of numbered objects suitable for measuring.
Specially prepared diagrams of measures used on machines, for example, temperature dials and controls.

73 Simple measurement of length

AIM To establish accuracy and provide some basic vocabulary of measurement.

Students need rulers (with centimetres or inches as appropriate), pencils and pieces of paper.

Demonstrate centimetres on the ruler. Make sure the concept of measurement is familiar to the class, and some time may have to be spent on teaching people to read a measure.

Instruct the class:

Measure and draw a line two cms. long.
Measure and draw a line five cms. long.
Measure and draw a line six cms. long.

Class can then instruct one another in groups. Go round and check the measurements, saying:

This is right/wrong. Is this right?/wrong?

Later also establish:

Correct/incorrect

Now go on to give more complicated tasks.
Example: Demonstrate a rectangle on the blackboard.

Instruct the class:

Draw a rectangle two cms. wide (or broad) and six cms. long.
Draw a rectangle four cms. wide (or broad) and three cms. long.

Then students can set each other similar tasks in groups, and check one another.

Obviously many tasks like this can be given and students can also be asked to cut lengths if it is relevant to their work.

74 Comparing measurements

AIM To teach simple language for comparison.

Demonstrate the following comparative forms:
longer/shorter, higher/lower, taller/shorter, hotter/colder.
Concentrate upon comparisons relevant to the work situation.

Example. Measure two pieces of material of different length.
This (ribbon) is longer than that (ribbon).
This (ribbon) is shorter than that (ribbon).

Compare the heights of students:

Mr X is taller than Mr Y.
Mr Y is shorter than Mr X.

Prepare a variety of objects which can be measured for length. These objects should be numbered. Students measure them and write down these measurements on small prepared check sheets.

Then ask:

Is this shorter than that?
No, this is larger than that. (etc.)

Prepare piles of bricks of different heights:

These are higher than these.
These are lower than these.

All this material can be practised and reinforced with group work.

Note that the pronouns: 'this', 'that', 'these', 'those' are introduced for the first time in the course.

75 Measuring to a set figure

AIM Language for explaining whether something measures to a required figure.

Dimension

Assemble a variety of objects which can be measured for length and height.

This should be nine cms. long.
Please check.
This is too short.
These should be twelve cms. high.
Please check.
This is too low.

Go on with: too high, too long.

Temperature

Duplicate a diagram of the type of temperature gauge or control in use in the factory. Then mark different readings on each copy, and the control may or may not indicate the correct reading.

Practise sequences such as:

A This should be 420.
Please check.

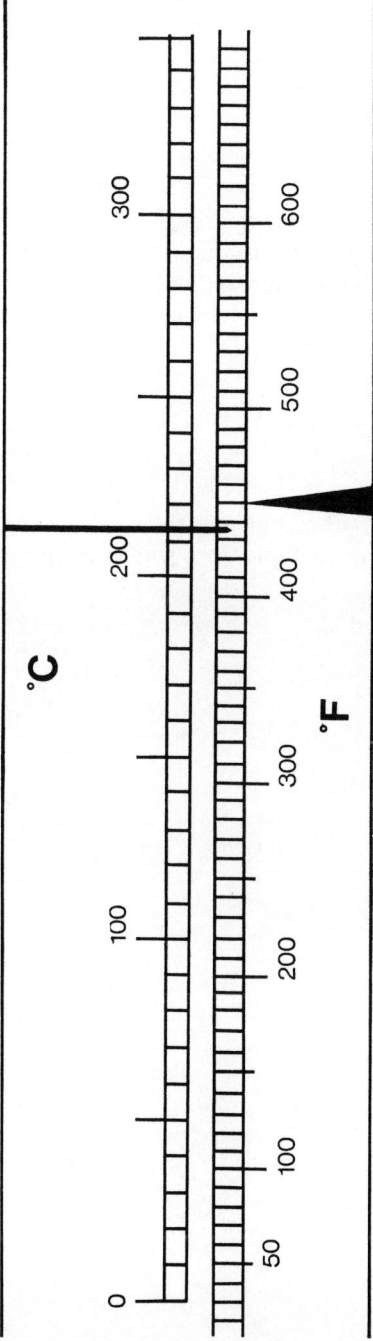

A thermo control

required temperature

°C

°F

actual reading

300

200

100

0

600

500

400

300

200

100

50

B It's 440.
It's too hot.

A This should be 450.
Please check.

B It's *nearly* 430.
It's too cold.

This work can be practised in groups.
Then present and practise the question form with 'How'?
Use the objects already prepared and measured for Item 74 on the same duplicated sheet but with only one temperature on it.

How long is this?
number six?
your pencil?
(etc.)

It's six cms long.

Repeat with 'wide' and 'high' or 'hot'.
This is the first time that questions with 'how' have been used in the course.

Part three
Understanding people
Items 76 and 77

76 How to behave if you're not understood

AIM **To provide a formula for responding when not understood.**

Teacher demonstrates with a glove puppet.

PUPPET   Good morning.

TEACHER   Morning.

PUPPET   (not clearly) Can I have twenty-five small boxes, please?

TEACHER   I beg your pardon? (and look blank)

PUPPET   (clearly and slowly) Can-I-have-twenty-five-small-boxes-please?

Go round the class, student taking the part of the puppet. Have variety of objects which the student can ask for, such as factory a objects, pens, books, keys, money.

The really essential point to get over to students is that they should repeat slowly and clearly what they said, and not change it or become silent. This may be an opportunity to get a class to understand that what they say may be correct, but the way they say it (the pronunciation) is the problem. Many immigrants assume that if they are not understood it is because the whole of what they said was incorrect English.

This could be a suitable occasion to do some minimal pair exercises on the recognition of phonemes and intonation patterns. But it may not be worthwhile troubling to get a class to understand the concept of such exercises.

77 How to behave if you don't understand

AIM **To provide a formula for responding when you cannot understand.**

It should not confuse students to present these items consecutively.

Students can then practise in pairs and groups.

Demonstrate with the puppet.

PUPPET   Good morning.

TEACHER   Good morning.

PUPPET   Where do you work?

TEACHER   (not clearly). I work in Southall.

PUPPET   I beg your pardon?

TEACHER   (slowly and clearly) I-work-in-Southall.

Teacher demonstrates by asking each student 'What's your job?' or 'Where do you live?' and students replying. The teacher uses one of the following:

> I beg your pardon?
> What did you say?
> Please say it again.

Having established a formula, then students can practise Items 76 and 77 in groups. Each group will need objects they can ask for, or prompt them to use questions practised in earlier sections.

Part four
Past simple tense
Items 78 – 82

Language teaching points
The past simple tense in statements, questions, and negative statements.
Certain adverbial phrases referring to past time.

Aims
a Establishing the basic forms of the past simple tense.
b Talking about past events.

There is little material in this part which a student can immediately use, but it is important to introduce the past simple tense by this point in the course if its linguistic forms are to be mastered. The past simple tense is used and exploited in Sections Five and Six although there are a number of incidental uses of it in earlier sections.

Teaching procedure
The pattern of this material is very similar to the work on the present simple tense in Section One so students should be able to cope with it fairly easily. The main points to get over are the notion of past time and the past simple verb forms.

This material is not linked to interesting work situations, and is entirely in the form of question and answer sequences. For this reason the material should be mixed in with other items in the section to give variety.

Equipment
Sets of visuals for Items 78 and 80.

78 Last weekend

AIM To present the English to talk about what you did at the week-end using the past simple tense.

First establish with a calendar the meaning of 'last weekend' and 'next weekend'. Make sure this is clearly understood, especially as Punjabi, Hindi, and Urdu use the same word for *yesterday* and *tomorrow*. Then go on to establish use of 'last' with days, months, years, etc.

> Last Monday, last Tuesday . . .
> Last week, last month, last year

General question

Ask the question:

> What did you do last weekend?

Then present and explain a series of answers. It will be helpful to prepare visuals for this. Base some of the answers on responses used in Item 43, and use other known verbs.

> I *went* shopping/to the cinema/to the temple/to the pub.
> I *visited* some friends/my family.
> I *cleaned* the house.
> I *cooked* the dinner.
> I *did* the washing/the ironing.
> I *bought* a scarf.
> I *read* the newspaper.
> I *drove* my family to . . . (etc.)

Make sure the generalized question 'What did you do?' is really understood. Then let the class ask and answer questions using the visuals as a stimulus.

'When' and *'Where' questions* to follow the general question:

> When did you go shopping?
> I went shopping in the morning.
>
> Where did you go shopping?
> I went shopping in Southall.
>
> When did you cook the dinner?
>
> Where did you cook the dinner?
>
> When did you clean the house? (etc.)

You may have to accept short answers, and guidance will be needed with the prepositional phrases of time and place. Practice in groups using visuals and clock faces is useful.

'What' question form

This is more difficult because it sometimes involves the introduction of a new verb.

What did you buy?
What did you clean?
What did you cook? (etc.)

Make sure you always present and drill a past form before expecting a student to reproduce it.

79 History of personal things

AIM **Further practice with past simple tense forms if required including new types of questions.**

This item is only for optional further structural practice. A quite amusing and interesting series of questions can be asked about personal objects of students, with the advantage that these questions clearly refer to the past.

X, where did you buy your coat/your watch/your handbag? (etc.)

When did you buy it?
How much did it cost?
Where did you get it?

A useful answer:
I can't remember.

The answers can be used for practice with other pronouns:

When did she buy it? (etc.)

With a better class it may be possible to start the questions sequence with a general question, using 'get':

Where did you get your watch, Mrs X?
I bought it.
Where did you buy it?
(and so on)

This question with 'get' could be confusing and requires a more difficult answer because the student has to supply his own verb.

80 Game

AIM **Further practice, if required, with past simple tense forms introduced in item 78.**

You will need the visuals prepared for Item 78 and preferably some new ones as well.

Divide the class into two teams.

Example

Teacher holds up a picture of shopping and a clock face:

TEAM A   What did you do last weekend/yesterday/(etc.)?

TEAM B   We went shopping.

TEAM A   When did you go shopping?

TEAM B   At three o'clock.

You can also use pictures of coming to work and leaving work and ask questions about 'yesterday', introducing the verbs 'begin', 'leave', 'speak to', etc.

81 Coming to England

AIM **To answer simple questions about coming to England. Use of questions with 'did' and negative forms of the past simple tense.**

Most students will be used to answering simple questions about coming to England, so it should be possible to insist upon real accuracy with verb forms.

Present the following type of sequence of questions and answers and then use them for individual and group practice.

When did you come to England?
Where did you live in India (etc.)?
Did you come by plane?
Where did you arrive in England?
Did you get a job immediately?
Where did you work?
Did your wife and children come with you?
When did they come to England?

In this sequence you will introduce the short answers 'Yes, I did', 'No, I didn't'. Explain the full form of the negative statement although it is not practised here.

Use the information obtained from the above questions to present and practise further questions with 'did' and short answers.

Examples

Did you come to England in 1963?
Yes, I did/No, I didn't.

Did you arrive at London Airport?
Yes, I did/No, I didn't.

82 Recorded drills

AIM **Practise with past simple tense forms.**

These drills are intended to introduce a number of new verbs which will require presentation.

Drill One

⊗ Tape item 26

Repeat the question and then answer it:

Did you begin work at 8 o'clock yesterday?
Did you eat in the canteen yesterday?
Did you come to work by bus yesterday?
Did you see your chargehand yesterday?
Did you leave work at quarter-to-five yesterday?
Did you go shopping last night?

Drill Two (mixed practice)

⊗ Tape item 27

Repeat the question and the answer.

Who did you come to work with yesterday?
I came to work with two friends.

When did you begin work yesterday?
I began work at 8 o'clock yesterday.

Did you begin work at 9 o'clock yesterday?
No, I didn't.

Where did you go last Saturday?
I went to Hounslow.

How did you go to Hounslow?
I went by car.

173

What did you buy in Hounslow?
I bought some furniture.

Did you buy a new house on Monday?
No, I didn't.

Did you watch television last night?
Yes, I did.

No attempt has been made to separate regular and irregular past tense forms in this work. However, at the end of this work a teacher may like to point out the existence of regular forms with some verbs, and to go back and check over with the class the past forms of the verbs used in this part and of other verbs in the course. It may also be worthwhile to contrast the forms of the present simple and the past simple, but without becoming involved in explanations.

Part five
Asking for help
Items 83 – 87

Language teaching points
Two formulae with which to ask for help when in difficulty or
needing instructions:

Excuse me.
Can you help me, please?

I can't . . .
How . . .?

The second formula involves the use of 'how' with the question
form of the present simple tense. This is the first time this type
of question has been overtly taught in this course.

Aims
To train students to ask for help, state their difficulty and follow
the instructions given.

Teaching procedure
First establish the essential opening line which identifies a student's
need: Excuse me. Can you help me, please?

Then go on to the formulae with 'can't' and 'how'. The 'how' question form will probably need quite a lot of additional work to
establish its meaning.

This section requires plenty of group practice. And try to get students
to use these formulae on the same day in the factory.

Equipment
Faulty or difficult objects for Item 85.

83 Asking for help

AIM **To provide two set formulae for asking for help.**

Present and practise the following formulae. Then practise in
groups. Generally use 'I can't . . . ' when physical help is needed.

175

Use 'How do you . . . ?' when a method or explanation is wanted and the need is less urgent. But at a later stage establish that the two forms are quite often interchangeable.

> Excuse me. Can you help me, please?
> (This line should preface all the following sentences).

Start with simple class demonstration:

> I can't lift this table.
> I can't find my pen.
> I can't move the blackboard.
> How do I stop the alarm, please?
> How do I open this box, please?

And make up other suitable examples.

Then move on to factory-related problems provided students have the vocabulary. If practical, use visuals or diagrams as prompts:

> I can't move the pressure valve.
> I can't adjust the temperature.
>
> How do I fill the hopper?
> How do I unblock the nozzle?
> How do I operate the bench machine?
> How do I clean the hopper?

See Item 122 for the type of diagram useful for this.
Practise further in groups.

This is the first time 'how' has been overtly taught as a question form. It is a particularly difficult question form for Asian learners and needs a lot of reinforcement and practice in the factory situation. It would be worthwhile for the teacher to get every student to ask someone a 'how' question on the shop-floor.

When starting on this question form, there is often immediate confusion with 'How are you?' and 'How many?'

84 Asking for help in the factory

AIM **How to ask for help with your work in the factory.**

Present the following dialogue with pictures of the characters.

⊗ Tape item 28

NARRATOR Sheila was on packing yesterday. She asked Mary to help her.
(Sounds of dropped cartons and annoyed exclamations)

SHEILA	Damn! I can't make this carton. Excuse me.
MARY	What's the matter?
SHEILA	Can you help me please? I can't make this carton.
MARY	Move over, I'll show you.
SHEILA	Thanks very much.

1 *Listen.*
2 *Listen and repeat* Sheila.
3 *Listen and fill in* Sheila.

Introduce a suitable expletive at the beginning of this dialogue. If practical, discuss briefly the use of swearing in English, or leave until Item 192.

85 Game

AIM **Further practice of material in Items 83 and 84.**

Use various items such as the following:

An envelope with illegible writing.
A locked or sealed box, or tightly done up jar.
Some child's puzzle or game.
Some piece of jewellery which doesn't undo.
A broken pencil.
A pen without ink.
A tin opener that it is not obvious how to operate.
Faulty parts from the factory.

Students can practise the following type of dialogues using these aids.

STUDENT A	Excuse me.
STUDENT B	Yes.
STUDENT A	Can you help me, please? I can't write with this pen.
STUDENT A	Excuse me.
STUDENT B	Yes.
STUDENT A	Can you help me, please? I can't read the writing (the envelope).
STUDENT A	Excuse me.
STUDENT B	Yes.
STUDENT A	Can you help me, please? How do I use this tin opener?

86 Recorded drills

AIM **Practice with the language formulae for asking for help.**

⊗ Tape item 29

Listen and repeat.

Excuse me. Can you help me, please?
I can't find my bag.

Excuse me. Can you help me, please?
I can't find my work sheet.

Excuse me. Can you help me, please?
How do I switch off my machine?

Excuse me. Can you help me, please?
How do I pack this box?

Excuse me. Can you help me, please?
How do I do this job?

Excuse me. Can you help me, please?
How do I get to the canteen?

Excuse me. Can you help me, please?
I can't find my overall.

87 Getting help with a job

AIM **To be able to ask for help with a job and follow the instructions given.**

Teach or revise the following vocabulary items:

flap, dab, packet, stick down, sticky tape.

These will be most easily taught by demonstrating how to assemble a packet with glue.

Present the following dialogue with pictures of the characters.

⊗ Tape item 30

Version A

NARRATOR   Sheila was on packing yesterday. She asked Mary to help her.

(Sounds of dropped cartons and annoyed exclamations)

SHEILA   Damn! I can't make this carton. Excuse me.

MARY   What's the matter?

SHEILA   Can you help me, please? I can't make this carton.

MARY   Move over, I'll show you.

SHEILA   Thanks very much.

1 *Listen* only.

Then continue the dialogue:

MARY   Fold the two small flaps.

SHEILA   Fold the two small flaps.

MARY   Then fold the two large flaps.

SHEILA   Then fold the two large flaps.

MARY   Turn it over.

SHEILA   Turn it over. Yes.

MARY   Put your packets in.

SHEILA   Put your packets in.

MARY   Put a dab of glue under the large flap.

SHEILA   Put a dab of glue where?

MARY   Under the large flap.

SHEILA   Yes.

MARY   Stick it down with sticky tape.

SHEILA   Stick it down with sticky tape.

MARY   See, it's easy.

SHEILA   Yes. Thanks, Mary.

1 *Listen.*
2 *Listen and repeat* Sheila.
3 *Listen and fill in* Sheila.

If the students are good enough, you might be able to use the pattern of this dialogue for students to instruct each other with jobs in their own factory. But this point is specifically dealt with in Section Four.

Version B

Example of an alternative dialogue using the same pattern:

NARRATOR Tony was on a new machine yesterday. He asked Fred to help him.

TONY   Excuse me.

FRED   What's the matter?

TONY   Can you help me please? How do I take this sprue out of the mould? It's stuck.

179

FRED	Move over. I'll show you. Put the switch to hand.
TONY	Put the switch to hand.
FRED	Open the mould with the switch.
TONY	Open the mould with the switch.
FRED	Take out the sprue with this brass.
TONY	Take out the sprue with this brass.
FRED	See, it's easy. Always use the brass.
TONY	Yes. Thanks, Fred.

1 *Listen.*
2 *Listen and repeat* Tony.
3 *Listen and fill in* Tony.

Part six
Weighing
Items 88 – 93

Language teaching points

a Ordinal numbers
b Vocabulary and expression used in weighing.
c Comparative adjectives.

Aims

a To teach students to weigh accurately and to carry out verbal instructions and weight checks.
b To train students to record weights accurately.

Accurate measurement and recording of measurement comes into many factory situations so that, even if students are not directly involved in weighing, a quick work through items 89, 90, 91 may be useful, and these should be followed by work on the types of measurement and recording that they are required to make, for example, worksheets.

In factories where weighing is part of the job, this material should be supplemented with additional specially written items covering those aspects of the process or the language not covered here.

Teaching procedure

There is not a lot of active language for students in this part, so these items will be best taught mixed in with other items from this section. In factories where weighing is important, active use of language in group work should be included.

Equipment

Sets of scales.
Sets of jars.
Sets of factory products for weighing.
Substances for making up weights (e.g. sugar, flour).
Sets of weight sheets and time charts for weights.

88 Revision of numbers

If any uncertainty amongst students, revise Items 1, 2, 6, and 7 in Section One.

89 Ordinals

AIM **To teach ordinal numbers which have many uses, and particularly are used in quality and weight control.**

Present and practise ordinal numbers:

1st, 2nd, 3rd, 4th, 5th, 6th, (etc.)

Demonstrate these with dates (revise Item 38). Go on to demonstrate and practise with sets of objects,

every second, every third, every fourth (etc.) every other.

Then demonstrate simple orders using any of the instructional language already presented in the course:

Pick up every second battenholder.
Take the cap off every third battenholder. (and so on)

This can be practised by the students in groups.
This may be an appropriate point to introduce such related formulae as:

One in fifteen.
Every two minutes.

90 Weighing of factory objects

AIM **Accurate reading of scales and recording of weight.**

Equipment

a Sets of factory products identified with code numbers (if used) or any numeral attached.
b At least two sets of scales – grammes or ounces depending on factory use.
c Prepared sets of weight sheets for each student.

Students will usually be able to write down numbers because Arabic numerals are in use throughout the Asian sub-continent. Anyway they will be able to read them out for others to write down.

Teach the vocabulary: 'scales'.

Then present and practise:

How much does it weigh?
It weighs . . . . . . grammes.

Students then weigh all their objects and enter them on their charts.

Weight sheet	
A110	20 g
A22	35 g
GR72B	400 g

91 Recording weights at intervals

AIM **To train students in accurate record keeping and to revise weighing procedures over a period of time.**

Prepare the following chart as appropriate for your classes.

Name	Mon 8.30	Tues 11.00	Wed 9.30	Thurs 8.45	Fri 9.40
Amarjit	25 g	30 g	15 g	20 g	19 g
Surinder	31 g	12 g	29 g	24 g	21 g

Present the chart to the class and revise the days of the week and telling the time.

This chart will be used for recording the weight of a jar containing beans. Each student weighs their own jar. Change the number of beans in the jar each day.

All the weighing items need to be well prepared and you should not allow students to linger too long over them. Encourage them to use language and ask the questions: How much does it weigh?

Weight control is normally carried out through regular checks by time or quantity and then recording the variations. If this is done in the departments where your students are working, make sure they fully understand and know the language used in the process. Teach it in the class and in the factory where the weighing is done.

92 Making set weights

AIM **Ability to follow instructions and to describe weight variations from a norm.**

Use sugar or any fine dry substance to teach the language of making weight.

Present and practise:

Weigh five grammes of sugar, a small amount at a time.
That's a little bit heavy/light.

Then go on to present and practise comparative forms which have already been presented with measurement in Item 74.

That's the right weight/correct weight.
This is heavier/lighter/than that.

93 Checking weights

AIM **Speedy and accurate weight checking with appropriate language.**

Give the class several jars filled with sugar (or other suitable objects). Some jars should be under or over a standard weight.

Revise the following instructions (as in Item 75)

These should weigh . . . . . . grammes.
Please check them.

Class then checks, rejecting those with the wrong weight.

What's the matter with this one?
What's wrong with this one?
This one is light/heavy.
Too light/too heavy.

Part seven
Taking a message
Items 94 – 100

Language teaching points

A series of language formula for use when taking messages. The language and behaviour essentials are as follows:

1 Listen to the message and repeat it.
2 Say you have a message and deliver it.
3 Repeat the reply if any.
4 Say you've delivered the message and deliver the reply.

Use of pronouns and simple reported speech is important.

Aims

To establish a method of language behaviour and make sure it is immediately reinforced and used.

Teaching procedure

This is the most ambitious piece of language teaching so far in the course. It is worth taking slowly and thoroughly because if students can then do this in a real situation their confidence and motivation will grow substantially.

Equipment

No special equipment needed.

94 Pronouns and reported speech

AIM **To revise pronouns if necessary and to establish the pronoun changes which occur in simple reported speech.**

If any difficulties are still occurring with pronouns revise some of the material in Items 20–23 and 26 in Section One.

Make sure in particular that students understand that 'him' and 'her' can be substituted for names. This point can be reinforced with simple classroom instructions such as the following carried out by a student:

Please, give Mr X a pen.
Please, give *him* a pen.
(say the two sentences together).

I want to give Mrs Y six packets.
Please give *her* six packets. (etc.)

The change of pronouns to the third person in reported speech causes particular difficulty for Asian learners. In Punjabi, Hindi, and Urdu, for example, no change of pronoun takes place when reporting what someone has said.

Present and later practise short sequences like the following. Initially demonstrate with a glove puppet.

PUPPET	I am 8 years old.
TEACHER (to class)	He says he is 8 years old.
PUPPET	I like fish and chips.
TEACHER (to class)	She says she likes fish and chips.
TEACHER (to a student)	Do you like chipatees?
STUDENT	Yes.
TEACHER (to class)	She says she likes chipatees.
TEACHER (to a student)	Where do you live?
STUDENT	. . . . . .
TEACHER (to class)	She says she lives in . . . . . .

95 Listening to and repeating a message

AIM **To train students to grasp and repeat the essentials of a message.**

Demonstrate and establish student response to a message:

TEACHER	(i) I've got a message for *Mrs Dhillon.* (name of a student)
	(ii) Go and tell her I want *500 lampholders.*
STUDENT	(Repeats essential parts only) Mrs Dhillon 500 lampholders.

Go on and practise this type of response with different students. Keep changing the wording in (ii) so that students can grasp that they only need to repeat the essential contents of the message.

Examples

I've got a message for *Mrs Y.*
Ask her for *20 labels.*

I've got a message for *Mr X.*
Can he give you *two red pens* for me?

Give this plenty of practice round the class until the idea of repetition is thoroughly grasped. You should not practise this in groups as the intention is only to teach language for *taking* a message.

96 Part One *receiving the message*

AIM **To demonstrate the formula for receiving a message.**

Present the following dialogue with pictures of the characters. This sequence of dialogues needs only minimal adaptation for a male situation.

⊗ Tape item 31

NARRATOR Yesterday Mrs James asked Sheila to take a message to the stores.

MRS JAMES Sheila.

SHEILA Yes, Mrs James.

MRS JAMES Can you help me, please?

SHEILA Yes certainly, Mrs James.

MRS JAMES Can you go and ask Mr Taylor for six thousand number tens?

SHEILA Mr Taylor – six thousand number tens.

MRS JAMES That's right. By three o'clock.

SHEILA Mr Taylor, six thousand number tens, by three o'clock

MRS JAMES That's right.

1 *Listen.*
2 *Listen and repeat* Sheila.
3 *Listen and fill in* Sheila.

Note that the formula: I've got a message for . . .' is not used in this dialogue so that students will not always expect such an obvious one.

97 Part Two *delivering the message*

AIM **To present and practise a formula for delivering a message.**

Present the following dialogue with pictures of the characters.
This dialogue is a continuation of Tape Item 31.

⊗ Tape item 32

MR TAYLOR	Hullo, Sheila.
SHEILA	Hullo.
MR TAYLOR	What can I do for you, darling?
SHEILA	I've got a message from Mrs James.
MR TAYLOR	Oh yes. What does she want?
SHEILA	She says she wants six thousand number tens by three o'clock please.
MR TAYLOR	Six thousand! What are you doing with them? Eating them?
SHEILA	That's what she said.
MR TAYLOR	O.K. I'll send them along.
SHEILA	Thanks. 'Bye.
MR TAYLOR	Cheerio.

1 *Listen.*
2 *Listen and repeat* Sheila.
3 *Listen and fill in* Sheila.

The really essential formula for students to learn from this
dialogue is:

I've got a message from . . . . . .
She says . . . . . .

The opening line establishes a clear context for the listener.
Contrast the use of 'from' here with 'for' in Item 95.

98 Part three *checking back with the sender*

AIM **To present and practise a formula for checking back with the
sender of a message.**

Present the following dialogue with pictures of the characters. This
dialogue is a continuation of Tape Items 31 and 32.

⊗ Tape item 33

MRS JAMES	You back, Sheila?
SHEILA	Yes. I gave your message to Mr Taylor.
MRS JAMES	What did he say?
SHEILA	He'll send the number tens.
MRS JAMES	Good, how many?
SHEILA	Six thousand.
MRS JAMES	Thanks, Sheila.

1 *Listen.*
2 *Listen and repeat* Sheila.
3 *Listen and fill in* Sheila.

The really essential formula for students to learn is:

I gave your message to . . . . . .
He'll . . . . . .

The past tense should not cause difficulty, and 'to' can be contrasted with 'for' and 'from' in the earlier items.

99 Recorded drills

AIM Practise with the various language formulae for taking a message.

⊗ Tape item 34

Listen and repeat the essential part of the message.

Can you help me, please?
Yes, certainly.
Go to Mr Mason and ask him for two boxes of pens.
Mr Mason – two boxes of pens.

Can you help me, please?
Yes, certainly.
Will you tell Gladys I want the time sheets?
Gladys – time sheets.

Can you help me, please?
Yes, certainly.
Can you go and ask Mr Taylor for forty boxes by this afternoon?
Mr Taylor – forty boxes – this afternoon.

Can you help me, please?
Yes, certainly.
I want you to tell Mrs Jones to see me at dinner time.
Mrs Jones – see you at dinner time.

Can you help me, please?
Yes, certainly.
Run upstairs and ask Mrs King for a new glue tray.
Mrs King – a new glue tray.

Can you help me, please?
Yes, certainly.
I want four blank time sheets from the stores.
Four blank time sheets from the stores.

100 Classroom practice

AIM **Accurate classroom practice of message taking language formulae.**

Teacher first demonstrates the complete message taking scheme with a puppet and a good student.

TEACHER   Can you go and ask Mrs X for a pen? (use the name of a student)

PUPPET   Mrs X – a pen.

PUPPET   (going over to Mrs X) I've got a message from . . . . . She says she wants a pen, please.

STUDENT   (gives the pen)

PUPPET   (going back to the teacher) I gave your message to Mrs X. Here's the pen.

Now demonstrate again with two students. Avoid group work until the idea is fully grasped by several demonstrations, with the teacher gradually dropping out, in front of the whole class.

These are the essential points in the formula:

a Receiving
Student repeats the essential part of the message he is to take.

i.e. *Who* he is to take it to?
What he has to get or say?

b Delivering
Student identifies what he is doing by saying:

I've got a message from . . . . . .
She says . . . . . .

c Checking-back
Student confirms he has given the message by saying:

I gave your message to . . . . . .

190

Only when students have accurately grasped this can they work in groups of three with better students giving messages.

Practical Communication exercise: message taking in the factory

AIM **To get students to use the message formula in a real situation.**

You will need to warn the supervisors that you will be doing this.

Each member of the class should be given a different message to carry to a supervisor or chargehand or English-speaker.

Examples of messages:
1 Supervisor has to tick off things (names, numbers) from a list.
2 Ask for a small part from the factory.
3 As for a spare time sheet.
4 Ask for the dates of holidays.
5 Teacher wants to borrow a red pen.

It is suggested that you might spread this item over several lessons.

This is a useful item for involving supervisory staff. Try to persuade supervisors themselves to use everyone on an errand or message in the coming few days.

Part eight
Incorrect and correct
Items 101 – 105

Language teaching points
Language formula for asking for an explanation when a student is doing some work in the wrong way. Obviously the formula is artificial, but in most situations it should be adequate. If in your factory it is not the type of language needed, rewrite this part substituting a more useful formula.

Aims
To get students to ask when in difficulty with a job and to be able to thank the person who has explained.

Teaching procedure
The main aim should be to establish a clear link in a student's mind between a situation of misunderstanding or difficulty over a job, and using the English presented here. Then as soon as possible yourself try students out with this language in the factory.

Equipment
a Prepare sheets for colouring, crayons, and coloured bricks.
b Sets of faulty parts from the factory.

101 Misunderstanding and needing an explanation

AIM **To illustrate situations where a student should ask for an explanation and to teach a language formula for this purpose.**

Equipment
a Prepare sheets of paper with triangles, squares and circles on them. Each sheet should be different (see top of page 193).
b Sets of crayons.
c Sets of coloured bricks.

First demonstrate with a good student. Give instructions to colour the paper in some way, speaking quickly. The student will do it

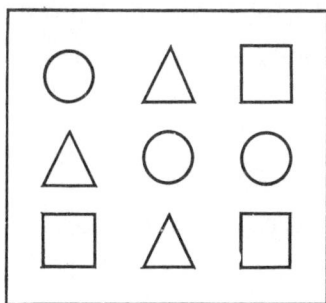

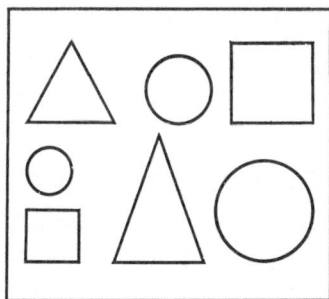

wrong or ask you to say it again. But just get him to try. Then give orders to arrange the coloured bricks in a particular order. Again, if you speak quickly enough and keep up a flow of irrelevant chatter the student will not be able to do it successfully.

Then the teacher says:

No! This is wrong.

Prompt student to ask:

I'm sorry. Can you explain what's wrong, please?

Then go around the class until everyone has practised and understood what they should say.

When the new formula is firmly established, revise from Item 93:

What's the matter with this one?
What's wrong with this one?

Or teach the first time if Item 93 was omitted. This should be fun to do in the class. You will not be able to get students to do this in groups because you have to give the initial instructions.

This item also gives an opportunity to revise the colours.

102 Saying 'sorry'

AIM **To establish fluency with set forms of saying 'sorry'.**

Use Item 101 to introduce:

I'm sorry.

This will be familiar to most students. Then go on to drill chorally on a prompt and response basis.

This is wrong!   I'm sorry.
                       I'm very sorry.
                       I really am very sorry.

This can just be treated as a choral game, which is frequently gone over in subsequent lessons. The point of this item is to establish clear and accurate habits of using these set phrases.

103 Asking for your work to be checked

AIM **To teach a language formula for asking someone to check one is working correctly.**

Repeat Item 84 and go on to prompt students with the responses for the lines in italics.

TEACHER No! This is wrong.

STUDENT I'm sorry. Can you explain what's wrong, please?

(Teacher explains and demonstrates)

STUDENT *Will you watch me, please?*

TEACHER Yes, that's right.

STUDENT *Thank you for explaining.*

You can go on now to practising in groups if the demonstrator just shows what to do, fairly fast, and does not speak.

104 Following an instruction incorrectly

AIM **To demonstrate and practise the language in Items 101, 103.**

a Present the following dialogue with pictures of the characters.

⊗ Tape item 35

NARRATOR Sheila was put on a new job in the assembly section.

MRS JAMES Now you're going to staple boxes.

SHEILA Yes, Mrs James, staple.

MRS JAMES You pick up the sheet.

SHEILA Pick up the sheet.

MRS JAMES You hold it under the machine. Press your foot down to start it.

SHEILA Press your foot down to start it.

MRS JAMES Then turn it over to each corner, see?

SHEILA Turn it over to each corner.

MRS JAMES That's right.

SHEILA Thanks Mrs James

1 *Listen only.*

(Students only need to grasp the situation, not all the details of what is said.)

b Present the following dialogue with pictures of the characters.

⊗ Tape item 36

NARRATOR   A few minutes later Mrs James came back. Sheila was doing the job wrong.

MRS JAMES   No! This one's wrong. And this one. And this one. Look!

SHEILA   Is this one right?

MRS JAMES   No it isn't.

SHEILA   *I'm sorry. Can you explain what's wrong, please?*

MRS JAMES   Yes. You're not stapling the right corners.

SHEILA   Oh I see.

MRS JAMES   Look, watch me. All right?

SHEILA   Yes, I see. *Will you watch me now please?*

MRS JAMES   Yes. That's right.

SHEILA   *Thank you for explaining.*

1 *Listen.*
2 *Listen and repeat* Sheila as italicized.
3 *Listen and fill-in* Sheila as italicized.

In this dialogue and some subsequent ones, the aim is to teach only the italicized language. On tape this has to be cued with a simple signal on the second version.

The dialogue in Tape Items 35 and 36 will be more useful if it is specially prepared and based on a job done in your students' factory. Otherwise difficulties of understanding what is being said in the instructions may detract from the essential learning points. In any case these dialogues will need to be altered for men.

105 Asking about faults in factory products

AIM **To practise the language taught in Items 101, 103, and 104 and to revise the names of faults.**

Revise the identification and name of faults taught in Item 49 and go on to teach the name of four or five more faults.

Sets of faulty materials and products will again be needed for this item.

Present and practise the following dialogue. You can use a glove puppet at first, but in any case all the language is now familiar.

A   This one's wrong.

B   Can you explain what's wrong, please?/What's the matter with this one.

A   Yes. Here is a short-moulding.

B   I see. Thank you for explaining.

Practise individually, chorally, and in groups.

Part nine
Some personal items
Items 106 – 108

Language teaching points

There are only minor new language teaching points in these items, limited to tone and vocabulary.

Aims

To consolidate and extend the work of Sections One and Two on numbers, names, and forms of address. Language is practised in the important new context of the telephone.

Teaching procedure

All the items call for some very simple discussion and information giving, particularly Items 107 and 108. But it is essential to keep this discussion very simple at this stage, or the material will be muddling and irrelevant to the students. If the teacher wants to to develop any of this information further, he should wait until Section Six.

Equipment

Prepare slides and dummy documents for Item 108.

106 Phoning

AIM **Revision of requests and other points within a telephone context.**

Present the following dialogue with pictures of the characters.

⊗ Tape item 37

NARRATOR	Tony wasn't feeling well. He phoned the doctor for an appointment.
TONY	(dialling) 846–7312 (Ringing sound)
SECRETARY	Hullo. Doctor Lister's Surgery.
TONY	Good morning. Can you help me, please?

SECRETARY	Certainly.
TONY	My name is Goddard. Tony Goddard.
SECRETARY	Yes, Mr Goddard.
TONY	I'm not feeling well. Can I see the doctor, please?
SECRETARY	Yes. Come at 7 o'clock this evening, Mr Goddard.
TONY	7 o'clock. This evening. Thank you.
SECRETARY	Thank you.
TONY	Goodbye.
SECRETARY	Goodbye.

1 *Listen.*
2 *Listen and repeat* Tony.
3 *Listen and fill in* Tony.

Use of the telephone tends to be a source of anxiety and difficulty for many immigrants.

The main points to bring out here are:

a General style of approach.
b Clear identification.
c Checking-back on essential information.

Clearly the telephone is very important to people, and a failure or reluctance to use it is inconvenient and time-wasting. List occasions to do with work when telephone is needed.

107 Nick-names and other forms of address

AIM To make students aware of the English custom of shortening names and using nick-names and other forms of address.

With a weaker class this item may be left to the end of Section Four. Present the following dialogue with pictures of the characters.

⊗ Tape item 38

NARRATOR	The lads were in the tearoom one dinnertime.
TONY	Come and play cards, Dave. DAVE!
DAVINDER	Look, Tony. Excuse me. But my name's Davinder, not Dave.
TONY	Oh yea. And my name's Anthony.
FRED	And I'm Frederick.
DAVINDER	What's the matter? What's wrong?

TONY   It's friendly to call someone by a nick-name or a short name. There's nothing wrong with Dave for you.

FRED   And we call Scotsmen 'Jock', or Irishmen 'Paddy'.

1 *Listening only*

Does anyone call any student by a short name or nick-name? Or do other people in the department have such names? The teacher should have established the facts. Then go on to deal more fully with other forms of address, such as 'dear', 'mate' (etc.), which were briefly presented in Item 61. Compare all these familiar forms of names and address with Asian practices; for example, the use of 'brother' (bhai), 'sister' (behn), 'uncle', and 'aunt' by your students; if it applies. Above all make sure that students understand that these English practices of address are friendly.

108 Payslips and other personal documents

AIM To understand and be able to supply the basic information from important personal documents.

The purpose of this item is to enable students to understand the meaning and purpose of essential personal documents rather than to teach new language.

At this stage, the teacher should concentrate on the essentials – understanding the broad purpose of the particular document and being able to identify it by name and number. If a teacher wishes to develop the work further (in terms of understanding taxation and social services), this should not be attempted until Section Six, which contains items of language and content which will tie in well.

Slides

Obtain specimens and preferably back up with a slide (for size) of the following:

    Payslip (from Item 63)
    Insurance Card
    Union Card
    Taxation form P.45.

Revise reading a payslip from Item 63. Establish briefly the different categories of deduction on the payslip and that this means people with the same gross pay will have different net pay.

Establish the vocabulary:

Insurance stamp, tax, net or 'take-home' pay, etc.

Give out simple dummy slips and practise in groups:

What's/How much is your tax/insurance/gross pay/overtime/ take-home money?

Is it right or wrong? (Item 101)

Go on to the other documents which are simpler and handle in the same way.

What's your insurance number?

Part ten
Dramatic listening dialogues
The message
Items 109 -- 112

These listening dialogues serve the same purpose and should be used in the same way as in Section One.

The main learning material revised is: language for messages, asking for help, measuring, and apologizing. The dialogues can also be used for teaching directions.

109 Dialogue One *The message*

Establish students understand:

go straight along
turn left/right

⊗ Tape item 39

(Door opens)

A Come in, B.

(Door closes)

Morning, B.

B Good morning, Mr A.

A Can you help me, please B?

B Certainly, Mr A.

A Can you take a message to Watkins?

B I'm sorry. I don't know where Watkins is.
Can you explain, please?

A Yes, it's a shop. Go straight along the road and turn left.

B Straight along and turn left.

A Yes – and then turn right.

B Turn right.

A And you'll come to Watkins.

B Straight along, turn left, then right.

A Yes. Go in and order fifty boxes.

B Fifty boxes, Mr A.

A That's right. I want boxes that measure fifteen centimetres square. They know what I want.

B Yes, Mr. A.

110 Dialogue Two *Delivering the message*

⊗ Tape item 40

(Noise of walking in the street)

B Go straight along.

(Bring up street noises)

   Turn right.

(Bring up noises)

   Turn left.

(Bring up noises)

   Now straight along.

(Bring up noises)

   Here's a big shop.

   There's no name, but it must be right.

(Going into shop)

D Good morning.

B Good morning.

D What can I do for you?

B I've got a message from Mr A.

D Mr A.

B Yes. He says he wants 500 boxes, please.

D 500 boxes!

B That's what he said, 500 boxes.

D Are you sure? 500?

B Of course.

D OK I'll send them to him at once.

B I'll tell him. Goodbye.

D Cheerio.

(Door closes)

202

111 Dialogue Three *The goods arrive*

⊗ Tape item 41

(Door opens)

A   You back, B?

B   Yes, I gave your message to Watkins.

A   Good. What did they say?

B   They'll send the boxes.

A   Thanks, B.

(B goes out)

A   Come in.

(Door opens)

MAN   We've brought the boxes, Mr A.

A   Good. That was quick.

MAN   Where do you want them?

A   In here.

MAN   Here! O.K.! Very good. Bring them in, lads.

(Great noises of lifting, straining, etc.)

A   Good heavens! What's this?!

MAN   The boxes.

A   But I wanted fifty. And these boxes are too big. I wanted
      boxes that measure fifteen centimetres square. These are very
      big.

MAN   You ordered 500 and we don't make small ones.

A   500!!

MAN   Yes.

A   Are you from Watkins?

MAN   From Watkins?

A   Yes, from Watkins?

MAN   No. I'm from Barnes and Barnes. I make big boxes.

A   Get out of here. I don't want them.

MAN   I'm sorry it's too late now.

A   Too late?!

MAN   Yes, and here's the bill, Mr A.

(Exasperated gasp)

112 Dialogue Four *Trouble*

⊗ Tape item 42

(Sound of telephoning)

A (into telephone) Send B in to me immediately!

(Distant footsteps. Knock at door)

Come in!

B Yes, Mr A. Oh, the boxes have come.

A B, how many boxes did you order?

B Five hundred.

A Five hundred!

B Yes, you said five hundred.

A B – you're a fool. I said fifty.

B Fifty?

A Yes – fifty. Five – o.

B I'm sorry, Mr A. I'm very sorry.

A And B.

B Yes, Mr A.

A Take this ruler.

B Yes, thank you.

A Measure this box.

B Mmh.

A How much does it measure?

B Oh? 20–30–40–42 Forty-two centimetres, Mr A.

A I said fifteen centimetres square, B.

B Oh dear. I really am very sorry.

A And B.

B Yes, Mr A.

A Where did you take the message?

B To Watkins.

A Are you sure?

B Well – I turned right, then left and then straight along.

A You're a bleeding idiotic fool. I said go straight along, then
   left and then *right*.

B Oh really, Mr A?

A GET OUT! – YOU'RE FIRED.

Section four
All about the factory

Introduction

This section is entirely concerned with teaching language needed
for the actual job. There is very little new structural work involved
in the section, but a great deal of new vocabulary, some of which
may already be known. It is important to insist upon accurate
mastery of all this vocabulary. There is less rigid insistence on
one particular structure in a situation. Often several alternatives
are given. It is hoped that in this section the student will see that
he often has a choice of things to say and that he can begin to
break out of the straight-jacket of the course.

Because this section deals altogether with the particular factory
and the particular jobs of students, it is only possible to provide
a teaching plan with examples rather than the actual teaching
material. This section provides a recipe and a teacher must provide
his own ingredients. The preparation of this section will require
quite a lot of time which is best spent at the very beginning of the
course because slides and photographs can take time to develop.
The factory may also want to see them and approve them before
they are used.

Students greatly enjoy this section because it is obviously
specially prepared to suit the situation in which they are using
English. The section, coming at this point in the course, will help
students to see the relevance and usefulness of a lot of what they
have learned in previous sections. The interest of the material is
greatly increased by the use of factory items, slides, photographs,
and specially prepared tape items. The mixture of activity and
presentation will be much enjoyed and, for this reason, it is well
worth putting in the time needed for preparation.

Unlike earlier sections, this one is best taught more or less in
the sequence suggested here because the subject matter is built
up in a logical order depending on information in earlier items.

The teacher may feel a lot of the material in this section is a
matter of induction and training rather than language teaching.
But with immigrants who have an elementary language problem,
it is unwise to assume that they understood much of their induction and training directly. Naturally they must already know their

205

job and the rules of the factory, but the purpose of this section is to make sure they understand them in English and learn enough English to be able to communicate about them in a simple way. It should be possible to work through this section at a good speed just because most of the content will be familiar.

Contents *for section four*

207

Part one
General information about the factory
Items 113 – 118

Language teaching points
There is no new structural material introduced in this part, but
there is some new vocabulary. Familiar structures are used in quite
new situations.

Aims
For students to start learning about the factory environment –
products, people, where things are – and talking about it in English.
The purpose of the material is to convey information about and
increase interest in the general work environment while at the
same time teaching and practising English.

Teaching procedure
All this material has to be specially prepared by the teacher to
suit the particular factory. We would strongly recommend the
preparation of colour slides of the factory and people in it,
and of general diagrams. These will prove very interesting and
enjoyable for students and result in the type of involvement which
makes for the best language learning and practice.

Equipment
a Specially prepared colour slides of the factory. The company is
most unlikely to have any but it is worth asking. Flash-light
equipment and a fairly good camera will be needed.
b Specially prepared diagrams of the factory and/or departments.

113 Talking to outsiders about your job

AIM **For students to be able to tell outsiders about the place where
they work.**

Students learn to make a number of statements about their
jobs which can be used in response to a variety of different questions with the same basic meaning. Naturally the answers given

here are only examples and will vary with each factory although the same structures should be appropriate in most cases. The work throughout this section will be much more interesting if slides can be prepared of the factory.

⊗ Tape item 43

Slides

First present and practise the correct forms in the class – if necessary on several occasions – and then use the tape for choral practice.

Where do you work? At a factory in Brentford.

What factory?
What's it called?
Which one? Ranton.

What do they make?
  It's a plastic moulding factory.
  They make plugs, light fittings, car ash trays.
  They make all kinds of plastic things.

Where's Ranton? In Commerce Road near the canal.

What do you do?
What's your job?

Slide I work in the machine shop. I make things. I'm a moulder.

Slide I work in the assembly section. I put the parts together.

Slide I work in the finishing section. I finish the parts.

Slide I work in the fluorescent section. I put the parts together for fluorescent lights.

Slide I'm a labourer. I move the materials and the finished products. I keep the shop clean and tidy.

(These slides should be general views of each section or department)

When this material is thoroughly known students can practise in groups.

114 Dialogue practice

AIM **To practise the material in Item 113 in the form of a dialogue.**

Prepare a taped dialogue of a new employee at the company and a friend talking about the new employee's work. Prepare pictures of the characters to use when presenting the dialogue.

⊗ Tape item 44

Example

NARRATOR	Sonia was chatting to her friend Anne at the weekend.
ANNE	Hullo, Sonia!
SONIA	Hullo!
ANNE	How's your new job?
SONIA	Fine. It's hard work.
ANNE	Where's the factory?
SONIA	In Brentford. In Commerce Road near the canal.
ANNE	What do they make?
SONIA	They make plugs, light fittings, car ash trays – all kinds of plastic things.
ANNE	What do you do?
SONIA	I work in the assembly section.
ANNE	Oh?
SONIA	I put the parts together.
ANNE	So you've made the plug on my Hoover!
SONIA	Maybe. I hope it works!

1 *Listen.*
2 *Listen and repeat* Sonia.
3 *Listen and fill-in* Sonia.

115 The immediate surroundings

AIM **To get students thinking and talking about what goes on around them,**

There is no special linguistic aim in this item. Present and practise the following type of sequence of questions and answers.

How many women work on your bench/line/etc.?
What are their names?

If the class do not know the names, they can find out for the next lesson. This will provide a chance to discuss English names and what people call one another.

Have you a friend in the factory?
What's her name?
What does she do? (Use material in Item 113 for the answer.)

Where do you work in the section/department/factory?
I work near the front/the back/the X machine/etc.

It will help to draw a diagram for this question.

In this section generally you will have to take a decision whether to talk about the whole factory or particular departments. Your decision will depend on the size of the site and where your students work.

116 People at work

AIM To be able to describe a person and to know the names and positions of key people in the factory

You can start off with a comic description recorded on tape to get over the idea of a description of a person. Play it straight off to the class and see if people can guess who it is.

Example – a description of the teacher.

⊗ Tape item 45

Who is this?
I'm short. I've got a long nose.
I've got two legs. I have brown hair and I wear glasses.
I'm very clever.

Then go on to descriptions of supervisors and chargehands. Building up descriptions of real people will be much easier and more interesting if slides can be taken and shown of them.

Slides

Examples

Who is your supervisor/chargehand/lineminder/etc.?
Gladys/Bill.

Make sure students know whether to use first names or surname when speaking to a supervisor and how to pronounce the name.

What does she look like?

Show *Slide* Gladys

Present and practise the following description:

Gladys: She's medium height.
She's got short brown hair
She wears a white overall.

The use of the verb 'have got' should not give difficulty because this has been used in various items in Section Two.

Show *Slide* Elsie – What does she look like?

She's short.
She's got short black hair.
She wears a white overall.

Go on to build up descriptions of other people well known to the class. Then people can give descriptions and other people can guess. The main phrases of height, and appearance of hair should be covered.

Then go on to slides of key people in the factory as a whole. Make sure the name and position is known.

Slide This is Grace. She's the shop steward.

Slide This is Mr Nicholls. He's the Personnel Manager.

Slide This is Mr Rose. He's the department manager.

Slide This is Mr Smiles. He's the works director.

If time permits and the class is good enough, practise questions and answers of the following type:

Who is the department manager?
What is he in charge of?

117 Where things are

AIM Language for showing someone around a place.

Present this dialogue with pictures of the characters. The purpose of the dialogue is to establish certain phrases for indicating position and direction. Some of these have already occurred. Make sure they are really understood with classroom demonstrations.

⊗ Tape item 46

NARRATOR	Mary has moved to a new house. On Sunday she showed Gurmit round her new house.
MARY	Oh, hullo. Come in, Gurmit.
GURMIT	Hullo, Mary. Thanks.
MARY	Well, this is our new house. This is the hall.
GURMIT	Mmm.
MARY	That's the sitting room next to the kitchen.
GURMIT	Where are the bedrooms?
MARY	I'll show you. Here's our bedroom. And there's another bedroom on the left.
GURMIT	Where's the bathroom?
MARY	Over there. Go past our bedroom and it's straight ahead.
GURMIT	It's a lovely house, Mary.

1 *Listen.*
2 *Listen and repeat* Mary.
3 *Listen and fill-in* Mary.

118 Where things are in the factory

AIM **Language for indicating where things are in the factory.**

Using the type of language practised in Item 117, get students to describe the factory or department they work in pretending they are showing a visitor around. It will be best to prepare a diagram of the factory, and duplicate it so that students have copies for group work (see page 214).

Example

Present and practise the following type of sentences using a plan and any of the slides prepared for this section.

That's the supervisor's office, between the assembly section and the fluorescent shop.
That's the finishing section over there.
That's the tea machine next to the supervisor's office.
That's the first aid room.
Some lockers are on the left. Some lockers are on the right in the assembly section.
The stores are on the right.

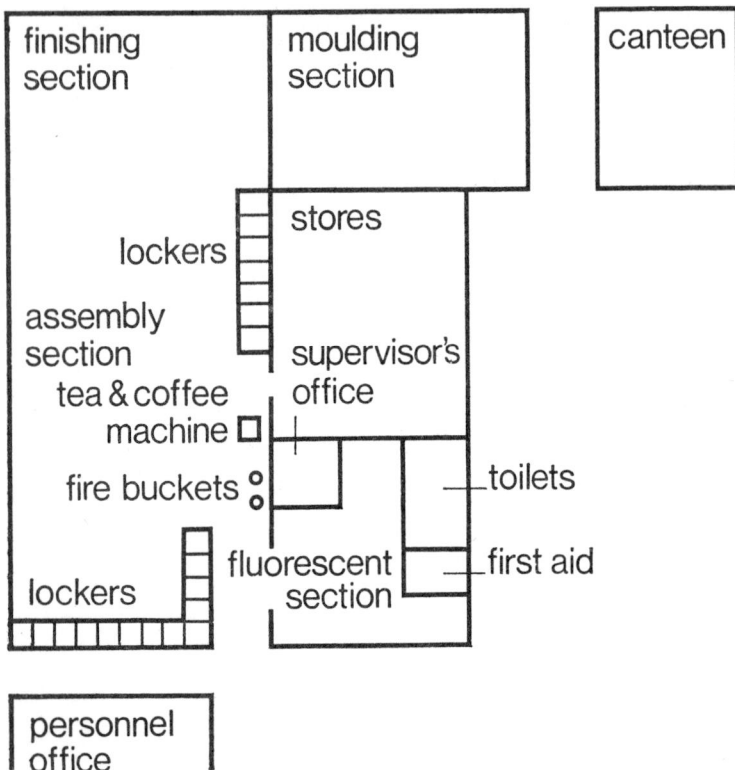

The moulding shop is straight ahead.

The canteen is outside. Go past the stores and turn right.

The amount of detail in this example is not necessary, and can be reduced for weaker groups.

Above is an example of the type of plan that can be prepared: The prepositions and adverbial phrases used in this sequence have all occurred previously in the course.

The sentences above assume the speaker is standing in a particular spot on the diagram. The speaker can touch the different things on the diagram and say 'This is . . .', 'Here's . . .' etc. Or at a later stage, students can pretend they are in different positions on the diagram and then make the necessary changes to their description. Once the language is known, students can practise in groups, taking it in turns to be the visitor and the person showing the visitor around.

A most valuable form of follow up would be for the teacher to go into the factory with small groups and pretend he or another student is a visitor. Of course, this would give an opportunity to practise freely quite a lot of other language as well.

If additional practice is needed with the prepositional phrases and adverbs, use a map of the local area for describing where things are. These are the prepositions and adverbs to practise.

between, over there, here, next to, on the right/left, straight ahead, go past, outside, inside.

With groups of students whose work involves moving things around the factory, this work offers an opportunity to revise and extend the work on 'fetching and carrying' in Item 51.

Part two
The overall manufacturing process
Items 119 – 123

Language teaching points
a The passive form in the present tense is introduced for the first time. Practice is only given in the third person forms and there are no drills.
b A great deal of probably unfamiliar vocabulary associated with the factory some of which is semi-technical.

Aim
Again the aim is to combine information about and interest in the work environment with language teaching. This part shows students how their own job fits into the overall processes in the factory and the department. By increasing understanding of and language for the factory, it is hoped the curiosity of students will also increase.

Teaching procedure
Again this material depends upon special preparation including colour slides and diagrams. At the end of this part it would be a good idea to take students on a tour of the parts of the factory that they have been talking about – probably in groups to give an opportunity to practise and reinforce the language.

Some of the material in Items 122 and 123 (when applicable) would be best introduced somewhat earlier in the course from about Item 83 onwards.

Equipment
Again specially prepared colour slides and duplicated diagrams.

119 Learning about the complete process

AIM **For students to understand where their job fits into the overall factory process and to learn a few sentences with which to describe this process.**

This item introduces the present form of the passive for the first time. No drill work is done on this verb form because it is felt better to confine the work on the passive to completely realistic contexts within the factory. Apart from the limited number of past participle forms used, the main difficulty for students will be agreement between subject (singular or plural) and verb.

Although students will have walked around their whole department and walked through other parts of the plant, they will very often have very little idea of what goes on anywhere other than their own job. This means they have little understanding of why their job exists or where it fits into the overall process. To get this over, slides are really essential and diagrams will also be needed (possibly the same one as in Item 118).

To prepare this item, a teacher will need to tour the plant and record brief descriptions of each stage of the process, and he must make sure of the key vocabulary. Then he can go around again and take a few colour slides. The company may want to see the slides before they are used and retain them afterwards. For further advice see the Introduction to the course.

Example of complete process

The following example is based upon a fairly small plastic moulding company. But even in a very large company it should be possible to show a slide of each department and to explain very simply what is done there.

Note the use of the passive verb forms.

Slides

Slide Goods inwards area.
   What's this?
   The materials are brought to the factory by lorry.
Slide Warehouse.
   What's this?
   The materials are stored in the warehouse.
Slide The powder shop showing feeder and rumbler.
   Where's this?
   What's this?

The powder is mixed in the powder shop (by the feeder and rumbler).

Slide Moulding shop.
    What's this? It's the moulding shop.

The teacher then explains and demonstrates what a mould is, and what pellets are.

    The pellets are put in the mould.
    Later the moulding is taken out of the press.

Slide Finishing section.
    What's this. The finishing section.
    The moulding is sent to the finishing section.
    The mouldings have rough edges.

Teach 'parts' as interchangeable for 'mouldings'.

    The parts are finished.
    Some parts are flashed.
    Some parts are filed.
    Some parts are drilled.

Slide Assembly section.
    What's this? The assembly section.
    Then some parts are sent to the assembly section.
    They are put together.
    Lampholders, battenholders (etc.) are assembled here.

Slide Fluorescent section.
    What's this? The fluorescent section.
    Some parts are sent from the finishing section to the fluorescent section.
    The parts are put together.
    Bi-pins (etc.) are assembled here.

Slide Packing.
    Then the products are packed.

Slide Despatch department or company lorry.
    Then the products are despatched.

In this particular example more is said about the finishing, assembly, and fluorescent section because this is where the students work. Do not attempt anything elaborate with an elementary class. In a factory where each department has a moving line with many different types of jobs, very great generalization will be necessary.

The amount of detail given will be varied according to the

218

language and jobs of the students. Far more can be given than in this example, and in many factories 20–25 slides are needed. But particular emphasis should always be given to the students' own jobs.

120 Describing the complete process

AIM **To practise the language presented in Item 119.**

Having presented, explained, and given some practice with the language of the overall process, now go on to practise without using the slides as a stimulus. The sequence, at this stage, is best re-presented on tape for purposes of choral practice.

⊗ Tape item 47

A   Tell a visitor what happens at Ranton.

B   The materials are brought to the factory by lorry.
The materials are stored in the warehouse.
This powder is mixed in the powder shop.
First the pellets are made in the moulding shop.
Next the pellets are put in the mould.
Later the moulding is taken out of the press.
Then the moulding is sent to the finishing section.
It is flashed, or filed, or drilled.
Then the parts are sent to the assembly section.
The parts are assembled.
Then the products are packed and despatched.
You can buy a lampholder from Ranton in a shop.

Then students can practise in groups; one student being a visitor and another showing her around. The duplicated diagram will be a useful prompt. Encourage 'the visitor' to ask questions, preferably not to a set pattern because it is important at this stage that students start trying language out themselves and not always using the set formula they have been given.

121 The departmental process (if applicable)

AIM **For students to understand each stage on the line in their department and be able to describe what is done at each stage.**

In a department where each employee is doing a complete job – for example, assembling plastic parts into a product– the next stage is for students to learn to describe their own jobs – descriptions of some of which have already been built up in Sections One and Two.

However, in a department where a series of processes are carried out on a machine-timed moving belt, a simple process description for the department will be needed. This will be different from the individual jobs described in Sections One and Two because a process description will consist of one general statement for each stage. Again we suggest the description should be in the passive.

Example of department process
The following example is based on a packing room in an instant coffee company. A slide is needed for each stage in the process together with an overall diagram of the line of the following type:

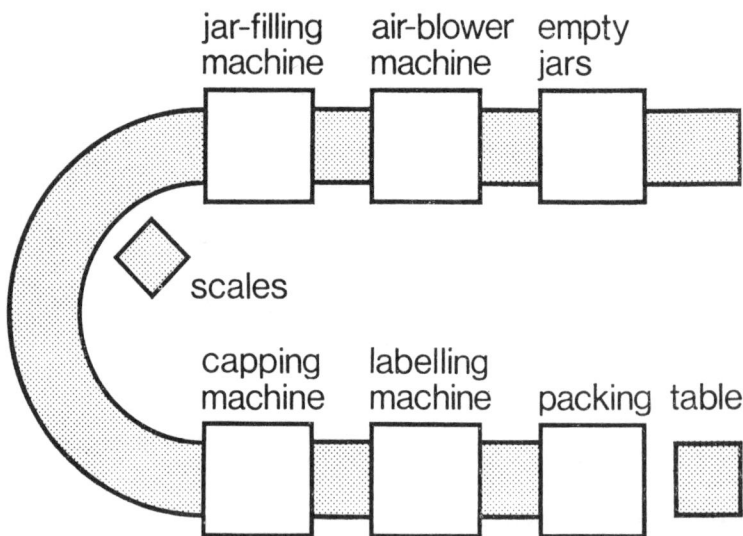

Slides

Slide Jar-feeding.
 The empty jars are put on the line here.

Slide Air-blower machine.
 The jars are cleaned here.

Slide Jar-filling machine.
 The jars are filled with coffee here.

Slide Table and scales.
 The weight of some jars is checked on the scales.

Slide Capping machine.
   The caps are put on the jars here.
Slide Labelling machine.
   The jars are labelled here.
Slide Packing area.
   The jars are packed here.

Then go on to group practice using the diagram as a stimulus in the way suggested for the overall process in Item 120.

122 A Machine Process (if applicable)

AIM **For students to understand and be able to describe how their machine works.**

Operating a large machine is a more complex and responsible job than being on a line or doing simple assembly work. When an operator's English is poor, it will be difficult for him to grasp or talk about the sequence and working of the machine inside the sections which are not visible. However, it is these sequences and processes which determine the quality of the product, and they need to be discussed when things go wrong.

To explain in English the operation of a large machine, each student will need a good cross-section diagram. The presentation should be supplemented with slides and a visit to the factory. It is also necessary to help the students read a diagram which may involve unfamiliar concepts and conventions (see diagram on page 222).

First establish the basic vocabulary (probably known), using the diagram on page 222, and then build up a description of the process using the present passive or present simple tense.

When the process is understood, present the description on tape and practise it chorally.

⊗ Tape item 48
Example
How an injection moulding machine works
   Listen:
   The hopper is filled with powder.
   The powder is fed into the machine.
   It is heated in the heating chamber.

221

An injection moulding machine

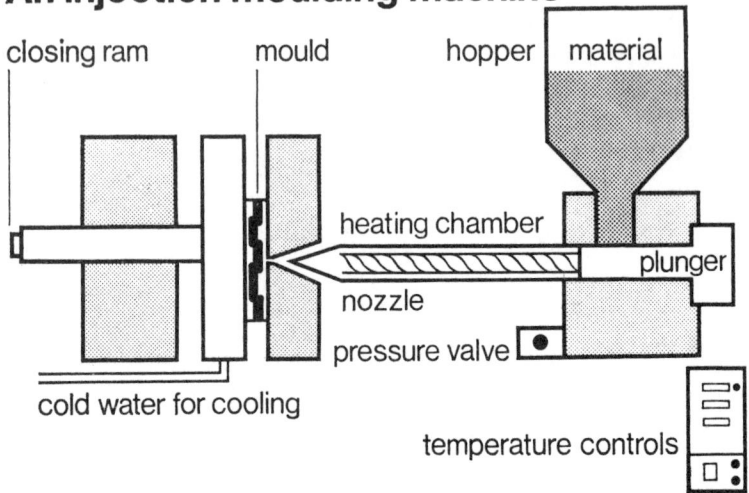

closing ram   mould   hopper material

heating chamber

plunger

nozzle

pressure valve

cold water for cooling

temperature controls

The liquid plastic is pushed through the nozzle by the plunger.
The mould is filled with the plastic.
The mould is cooled with cold water.
The shot is taken out of the mould.
The process is controlled by the time-clocks and temperature controls.

Go on to group work with students describing the process to each other using their diagrams as a prompt.

123 Key points on machine operating (if applicable)

AIM **To understand and be able to describe the key points in the operation of a machine.**

This item moves from the passive understanding of the machine process of Item 122, to stressing the key points in the operator's responsibility.

⊗ Tape item 49

Example
Working a moulding machine

I must make sure the temperature is correct.
I must make sure the pressure is correct.
I must make sure I have the correct material.

I must make sure the mould is clean.
I must make sure there is nothing stuck in the mould.
I must *not* interrupt the cycle.
I must open the gate at the correct time.

The language of this item is a development of the work on faults in Items 49 and 50, and of the work on controls in Items 72 and 75. But a new piece of language is the use of 'I must . . .' to stress responsibility. This can be initially presented and practised using some of the earlier material in Sections One and Two.

You *must* clock-on when you arrive at work. (etc.)

Example

Here is a much more complicated discussion about a machine operator's job. This could only be handled with very successful and receptive students.

The dialogue would have to be built up in stages, but nearly all the language has been presented earlier in Items 113, 122, 28 and 123.

NARRATOR X has been working in the factory.
Y asked him about his job.

Y   Hullo – where do you work?

X   I work in the machine shop. I'm a moulder.

Y   What?

X   A moulder.

Y   What's that?

X   I'm a machine operator. I operate an injection moulding machine.

Y   What do you do?

X   Well, the process of the machine is controlled by the time clocks. I have to open the gate when the cycle is finished. And I take out the shot.

Y   Is that all?

X   Then I break the shot up. And I put it in a plastic bag. And I seal the bag.

Y   Does the machine ever go wrong?

X   Sometimes.

Y   What happens?

223

x   There are five things.
    The temperature; the pressure; the material; the
    mould and the time.

y   It sounds difficult.

x   I must make sure the temperature is correct. I look
    at the thermo-control.

y   Mm.

x   I must make sure the pressure is correct.
    I must make sure there is no rubbish in the material.
    I must make sure it is the correct material.
    I must make sure the mould is clean, and there is
    nothing stuck in the mould.
    I must open the gate at the correct time.

y   Why?

x   Because the plastic becomes too hot in the heating
    chamber.

1 *Listen.*
2 *Listen and repeat* X.

In this second example of a dialogue, 'why?' and 'because' are
introduced (in passing) for the first time. 'Why' and 'because' are
dealt with in Section Six (Item 171), but teachers may find with
some groups explaining reasons can be introduced earlier – say at
this point.

Part three
Jobs
Items 124 – 125

On the language side there is little new structural material presented in this part; but there is quite a lot of new vocabulary. Aims, teaching procedures, and equipment are fully described under each item.

124 Talking about a job

AIM **To introduce the idea of talking about your own job.**

In previous sections job descriptions have been built up in the form of instructions. Only two or three typical jobs have been dealt with. In this item the idea of being able to describe your own job is established. Then in the next item every student will build up a description of his own job.

The structure and vocabulary required should be known by this stage.

Prepare a taped dialogue of someone in the factory describing their job to an outsider.

⊗ Tape item 50

Examples

a Here is a simple job discussion drawing on material present in Items 113 and 28.

NARRATOR   A has been working in the factory.
B asked her about her job.

B   Morning – where do you work?

A   I work in the assembly section on heat-sealing.

B   What?

A   Heat sealing.

B   What's that?

A   I put the pieces of brass into a bridge.

B   Mmm.

A   Then I put the bridge on the base.

B Yes.

A And put the base in the machine.

B Yes.

A And pull down the guard and seal it.

B How many do you do every day?

A About 500,000!

B You're not very quick, are you?

1 *Listen.*
2 *Listen and repeat* A.

Make sure that essential vocabulary for most people's jobs, which can be demonstrated in the classroom, is known or taught. There will be some vocabulary items which will be better established with the individual in the factory. Make a list of vocabulary for checking in the classroom, and another list for dealing with in the factory.

Example for plastic moulding assembling department.

LIST A Put, like this, first, then, pull down, switch on/off, pedal, press, brass, terminal, nut (plus the vocabulary in earlier job descriptions).

LIST B Contacts, soldering, soldering iron, clear, drill, jig, fibre, (etc.).

125 Describing your own job

AIM **For each student to be able to describe his own job accurately and in detail.**

It is usually better to teach the language of each individual's job actually in the factory. Otherwise there is no real check-back on mistakes.

Divide the class into group with four students in each. Finish the class fifteen or twenty minutes early, and then spend fifteen or twenty minutes with each group in the factory.

Get each student, with your help, to explain exactly what he does while demonstrating it to you. Other students listen, observe, and join in. In addition to describing their own jobs accurately, students should pick up the main language of a number of jobs, which will increase their flexibility.

At the next lesson get students to mime their jobs in the classroom and to describe them. The best stimulus is good colour slides showing each person doing his job – these always cause interest and enjoyment. After a student has given a description of his job, ask another student to describe it while the other one mimes again – (using 'she' or 'he' and the present simple tense).

The students can divide up and do this in groups. Black and white photographs are a very good stimulus to group work.

When students are miming their jobs, get the class to count the number of movements involved. Also get students to be aware of whether they use the right or left hand for a particular movement where it is relevant.

At some stage, record each student describing his or her own job. As well as causing great satisfaction and amusement these recordings can be used in the class for correction and generally to make students more self-critical and aware of the need for accuracy. This awareness is something which it is most important to develop at this stage in the course.

Obviously the work on this item will be spread over several lessons, and will take some time. However, because it is so closely related to what students do, it is very well worth the time.

Example

Here is an example of a simple personal job description a student might build up in the end.

Job: a woman who flashes ceiling roses.

First I switch on the power.

Then I press the green button.

I sit down.

I put the tray on my lap.

I put a glove on my left hand.

I press the pedal with my right foot.

I pick up a ceiling rose with my left hand.

I pick up a file in my right hand.

I put the ceiling rose on the jig.

I flash it with the file.

I put it in the tray.

227

Part four
Safety and accidents
Items 126 – 132

Language teaching points
a A lot of new vocabulary.
b Some parts of the body.
c One use of the present perfect tense.

Aims
a Make students aware of safety and their responsibility.
b Establish a minimum language for identifying safety hazards, and warning others.

This part contains little real language teaching; the aim is to use the opportunity of the classes to make sure safety is really understood.

Teaching procedure
Again a mixture of factory and classroom presentation is called for. It will prove well worthwhile to prepare the special photographs because these will greatly increase interest and provide much more varied practice in class and in groups.

Equipment
Multiple copies of black and white photographs specially prepared or any other suitable visuals.

126 Awareness of safety

AIM **An introductory item to develop awareness of safety.**

Safety is as much a matter of alertness and general attitude as it is of having every single dangerous situation in factory explained.

The first point to get over is 'dangerous' and 'safe'. This can be done with simple simulated situations in the classroom and with photographs or slides of familiar dangers in the home. Black and white photographs or drawings are most suitable for this because they can be handed around and examined by the class.

Photographs

Examples

1 Leaning over a hot iron while ironing.
2 Standing too near an electric fire.
3 Kneeling down to an oven, with danger of knocking saucepan on top of stove when getting up.
4 Walking on a wet floor carrying a tray of things.
5 An unguarded paraffin heater.

Is this dangerous?
Is this safe?

Students can perhaps mark area of danger on picture with a wax marker that can be rubbed off later. Go on to get an explanation of the danger from students, accepting anything in intelligible English.

An iron and an electric fire in the classroom will give possibilities for acting all sorts of dangerous situations for this and later items.

127 Warning someone

AIM To teach a rapid response and use of English to warn someone in a dangerous situation.

Again using the photographs of dangers at home and acted situations in the classroom, teach students useful phrases to shout out in order to warn someone of the danger.

Examples

Look out! The frying pan.
Look out! The iron.
Be careful! The electric fire.
Watch out! The floor.
Mind out of the way!

It is important that some situations are acted and that students are forced to *shout* these things out. Group practice can be given with multiple copies of the photographs.

128 Dangers at work

AIM **To apply Items 126 and 127 to the factory situation.**

Initially it may be best to go into the factory with groups to demonstrate and discuss dangers. But for the classroom work a series of black and white photographs are needed of all the principal hazards. In teaching these a good deal of new vocabulary will also have to be established.

Photographs

First of all present the situations in the factory or with the photographs:

Is it safe?
Is it dangerous?
Is it all right?

Get or offer some very simple explanation of the hazard – this is not for language learning. Then establish the appropriate warning to be shouted out:

Look out! Your finger.
Be careful! Your eyes.
Look out! Your scarf.

Examples for photographs in assembly department of plastics factory.

Long hair that can catch in a machine.
Not wearing goggles.
Using a machine without a guard.
Leaving a box sticking out dangerously into a gangway.
Holding a part wrongly and so getting your fingers too near the machine.
Putting your hand or finger in a dangerous place.
Not looking at your work.

British Safety Council posters may provide good illustrations for some of the situations which can occur in your factory. You should be able to obtain these through the firm.

129 Being responsible about safety

AIM **For students to observe safety rules themselves and take action when they see rules being broken.**

Present and practise the English for the most essential rules of safety in your factory. Once these rules are understood, they can simply be run through chorally on a number of occasions more or less as a game.

Examples

DRESS

Make sure you tie back your hair.
Make sure you wear the right clothes/goggles/the right shoes/
gloves.

MACHINES

Make sure you understand the machine.
Make sure you can turn off the machine.
Don't work with the guard up.

Then present and practise language to use to another person
when they are breaking safety rules, but there is not an immediate
danger requiring a shouted warning. The photographs prepared
for Item 128 can be used again here. For speaking to a friend:

Excuse me. Your scarf/hair (etc.) is dangerous.

Where there is something wrong with a machine, the operator
will need to speak to the charge-hand.

Excuse me. The machine has no guard.

Group practice can be given with the photographs showing
safety hazards and people breaking safety rules. The following
dialogue can be used:

What shall I do?
Move the box.
Speak to X.

Obviously the language needed for this item will vary a great deal
depending on the type of factory.

130 Accidents

AIM **To know and be able to tell someone what to do when
there's been an accident.**

This item teaches the names of some parts of the body and a
restricted use of the present perfect tense. These language points
are dealt with much more fully at the beginning of Section Five
so there is no need for systematic work to be done upon them at
this point.

Present and practise the following type of statement and response.
For later choral practice it will be a good idea to record the items.
To present these sentences act some of the situations in the class,
take photographs for others, and use the photographs from Item
128 as a stimulus for others.

231

⊗ Tape item 51
Student holds appropriate photographs:
  I've hurt my hand.
  I've cut my finger.
  I've strained my back.
  I've bruised my knee.
  I've burned my arm.
Response:
  You need some sticky plaster/(etc.).
  You'd better go to First Aid.
  You'd better go to the supervisor.

131 Printed safety notices

AIM **To explain the meaning of any very prominent and frequent safety notices in the factory.**

In an elementary class, a good number of students may not be able to read at all. In any case long and involved safety notices are probably not important in ensuring safety. However if there are a limited number (three or four) simple notices in frequent use throughout the factory, recognition and understanding of these can be taught even to students who can't read.

132 Fire precautions

AIM **Comprehension of fire regulations and procedures.**

There is no active language-teaching in this item. This is a small information item which can be dealt with very quickly. Use the plan of the factory that you have prepared for Item 118.

Then get over in any suitable way the following information:
  What do you hear if there is a fire?
  A bell/siren/hooter/etc.
  Can you do anything?
  Mark where the fire buckets are on the plan.
  Where do you go?
  Indicate exits.
  How do you go?
  Walk calmly.
  Don't go to your locker.
  Don't shout.
  Don't run.

Part five
Quality and faults
Items 133 – 138

Language teaching points
a Language for 'same' and 'different'.
b Names of principal faults for everyone's job.

Aims
For students to understand the importance of quality and to be able to name all faults that occur in the work.

For food factories, work on hygiene is also included.

Teaching procedure
The recorded dialogues in this part are only intended to get over general awareness and concepts. But close and repeated language work will probably be needed to build up an adequate vocabulary of all the faults which can occur.

Equipment
a Sets of faulty parts from the factory. In cases where the product is too bulky to bring into the class, groups will obviously have to go to the factory.
b Prepared sets of cards for Item 133.

133 Bad quality

AIM **General awareness of faults and the importance of quality to anyone buying something in a shop.**

Present the notion of 'same' and 'different' with various subjects of your choice.

Then prepare a number of cards which are the same colour, but different shades. Present and practise the following short dialogue.

A Look at these cards.
   Are they the same colour?

B   Yes, they're the same.
No, they're different.

Practise individually and in chorus. Then give out cards for group practice. Colour has been chosen here, because shade variations are the type of differences within a category which have to be watched out for in any manufacturing process.

Present and practise the following dialogue:

⊗ Tape item 52

NARRATOR	Mary went shopping on Saturday. She wanted to make her daughter a new dress.
MARY	Good morning. Have you got any green cotton, please?
SALESMAN	Good morning. Yes, madam. This is £1.50 a metre.
MARY	Good. Can I have three metres, please?
SALESMAN	Yes, madam.
MARY	Excuse me. Look at this. It's not the same colour here and here.
SALESMAN	Oh, no. I'm very sorry.
MARY	I can't use this piece.
SALESMAN	No, madam. I'm very sorry. There is a fault in this material.

1 *Listen.*
2 *Listen and repeat* Mary.

Make sure everyone understands the point that no one will buy something with a fault in it.

134 Bad quality in the factory product

AIM **Awareness that a student's own work cannot be sold if it contains faults.**

Use the language at the beginning of Item 133 with factory parts.

A   Look at these two rings. Are they the same?

B   No, they're different.

A   What's the difference?

B   There's a crack on this one.

You can use any of the faults established in Items 49 or 105.

Note the use of the pronoun 'one' here.

Present and practise the following type of dialogue. This will have to be prepared for a particular product in your factory.

⊗ Tape item 53

CUSTOMER	Good morning. Have you got any plastic lampholders, please?
SALESMAN	Good morning. Yes, madam. How many?
CUSTOMER	Can I have three, please?
SALESMAN	Yes. There you are. That's £1.80, please.
CUSTOMER	Excuse me. Look at this. There's a crack on this one.
SALESMAN	Oh. I'm very sorry. Here's another one. I'll send this one back to the factory.

1 *Listen.*
2 *Listen and repeat* customer.

135 Identifying faults

AIM **Ability to identify and name all the more common faults which occur in the factory.**

Already a number of important faults have been presented in earlier sections in Items 49 and 105. Quickly revise all these faults with the class.

Now that everyone's job description has been taught in detail, the faults likely to occur on all jobs can be established. Prepare sets of parts in which one has something wrong. Present and practise the following type of dialogue:

A Are these all the same?

B No. This one is different.

A What's the difference?

B The holes are blocked. (singular or plural answer)

A What shall I do?

B Put it in the scrap box. (as appropriate)
   Speak to X.

Note that the answer to the question 'What's the difference?' may require a question in a different grammatical form from 'Can you explain what's wrong, please?' in Item 105.

At a later stage identification and explanation of faults should also be practised in the dialogue form of Item 105.

Students might like to act out dialogues similar to the one in Item 134 in groups.

136 Memory game

AIM **To learn the names of as many different faults as possible.**

The game is played by placing a number of objects on a table. Each object is named and then the objects are covered over. The game is to see how many of the different things each person can remember.

Gradually build up a complete range of faults for Item 135 which can be practised and revised in this game.

Examples

This is a chipped moulding/a bad moulding/a short moulding.
The inserts fall out.
There is too much flash.
This is cracked.
The holes are blocked/rough.
There is baked-in flash.
There are file marks.
There are blisters.
There are sharp edges.
It hasn't been flashed properly.

137 Awareness of hygiene

AIM **General awareness of the importance of hygiene to someone buying the product.**

In the food industry, hygiene is an important aspect of quality, and the rules that have to be enforced need to be approached in a way similar to the problem of safety.

Present and practise the following dialogue which should be made up about the product manufactured in your factory.

⊗ Tape item 54

CUSTOMER   Good morning.

SALESMAN   Good morning, madam.

236

CUSTOMER   Yesterday I bought a jar of coffee here.

SALESMAN   Yes, madam.

CUSTOMER   I've brought it back.

SALESMAN   Oh. Can you explain what's wrong, please?

CUSTOMER   Yes. I found a hair inside the jar.

SALESMAN   I'm very sorry.

CUSTOMER   It's disgusting.

SALESMAN   I really am very sorry. Here's another jar.

CUSTOMER   Thank you.

SALESMAN   I shall telephone the factory immediately.

1 *Listen.*
2 *Listen and repeat* customer.

138 Rules of hygiene in the factory

AIM To establish a minimum language for hygiene regulations.

Again this item is only for use in food companies. One can assume that students already observe hygiene rules even if they do not always understand the reasons for these rules.

Black and white photographs or other visuals can be prepared showing hygiene hazards and non-observance of rules. The work can be approached along the same lines as safety in Items 128 and 129 of this section.

Section five

Explanations and apologies
Cultural differences of behaviour
Solving problems

Introduction

This section is primarily concerned with three areas of language
behaviour: the language to use to explain mistakes and to
apologize; the language to use in order to solve problems before
they cause real difficulty; and certain differences of behaviour
between Asians and non-Asians which may cause difficulty. Asian
immigrants are often criticized by British workers for their failure
to communicate successfully in these three areas so it is particularly
important to include them in a course like this.

There is not a lot of new language material in this section. The
main structural items of language dealt with are the present
perfect tense and quantitive determiners and pronouns.

It may not be appropriate to teach some of the items in this
section. In any case not more than about eight hours should be
spent on this material on an intensive in-company language course.

At this point in the course it becomes imperative that students
should start to feel able to cope with free conversational situations.
For this purpose it may be useful to hold back a couple of students
after each lesson and chat to them for a few minutes. Visitors
to the class can also be most useful in this way.

238

Contents *for section five*

Part one
Present perfect tense
Items 139 – 142

Language teaching points

The present perfect tense: a thorough treatment of the positive form and a brief introduction of negatives and questions.

Aims

To use the present perfect tense to state that something has happened. After the present simple tense, the present perfect is probably the most useful tense in a work situation. It is needed to explain changes in circumstances at work, personal conduct, accidents and illness, and for many other important uses.

Examples

The electricity has failed.
I've finished my job.
I've cleaned up.
I've hurt my back.

Teaching procedure

Once the positive form has been established, the rest of the work in this part can be mixed in with later items. Items 141 and 142 are not of much functional value, but are included to establish form and meaning. At the end of this part, it may be useful to revise the present simple and past simple tenses.

Equipment

Set of visuals for Item 141.

139 Stating what has happened

AIM Use of the present perfect tense to state that something has happened.

Various uses of this tense have occurred earlier in the course, especially in Section Four, Item 130. At the very beginning of teaching this tense we suggest that the teacher uses the uncontracted forms because they are easier to hear. Then he can introduce the contracted forms, I've, she's, etc.

First revise the formula for asking for help (Items 83 and 84):

A   Excuse me. Can you help me please?

B   What's the matter?

A   I have lost my purse.

Go on to present a whole series of troubles:

I have lost my purse/handbag/coat/overall/(etc.)

Teacher can then ask:

What have I done?
What have you done?
What have they done?
What has she done?

Students need not practise these question forms. They should reply

I've/You've/She's/He's lost my/your/her/his . . . . . .

Make sure students understand the full forms and the contracted ones. Use this opportunity to revise possessives. Give plenty of practice round the class.

140 Accidents or illness

AIM To teach useful vocabulary items and to give further practice with the present perfect tense.

Revise Item 130 in Section Four and then go on to demonstrate a wider variety of afflictions.

A   What's the matter?

B   I've (have) *hurt* my *hand.*

A   You'd better go . . . . . .
    You need some . . . . . .

verbs: cut, strained, bruised, burned

nouns: wrist, arm, shoulder, foot, ankle, leg, thigh, knee, eye(s), ear(s), nose, mouth, neck, head, finger, thumb, stomach, back

With a better class you may also teach the expression which allows for more types of illness:

I've got something the matter with my . . . . . .

242

Teacher can ask third person questions:

What's the matter with her?
She's hurt her hand.

Give plenty of practice round the class and in groups.
Encourage students to act out their various afflictions.

The names of all the different parts of the body can be dealt with in this item.

141 Classroom demonstration and practice of present perfect tense

AIM Practice of the present perfect tense of familiar verbs and vocabulary.

Teacher demonstrates with various obvious classroom activities where the results are visible. Use both uncontracted and contracted forms.

I've opened the door/window/box (etc.)
I have closed the door/window/box (etc.)
She has put the chair on the desk/the box on the floor (etc.)
She's picked up the folder/the bricks (etc.)
She has dropped the bricks/the pen/the purse.
She's turned on/off the lights/the tape recorder (etc.)

Teach comprehension of the general question form introduced in Item 139:

What have I done?
What has she done?

Introduce new words and situations. Visuals are useful for this:

Examples

I've spilt the tea.
She's knocked over the cup/glass (etc.)
He's crashed his car.
I've written my name.

You must make sure students complete their actions before describing them.

The form of the main verb used may give difficulty although in all the cases here (except one) it is the same as for the past simple. It may be useful to draw attention to the forms by contrasting the present, past, and present perfect.

142 Questions, short answers, and negatives in the present perfect

AIM To familiarize students quickly with question and negative forms of the present perfect so that they can see it follows the same pattern as other verb tenses.

This item is optional and can be omitted if time is short. But as students have already mastered the positive, negative, and question forms of the present and past simple tenses, this material has been included to show that the present perfect tense follows the same pattern.

Students can begin to ask questions in the present perfect:

One student demonstrates by dropping a pen. Teacher asks:
    Has she dropped the pen?
Students reply:
    Yes, she has.

Demonstrate a negative answer too.
Give plenty of demonstration using different verbs.

Students go on to work in groups:

Example

    STUDENT A   (touches something)

    STUDENT B   Has she touched the book?

    STUDENT C   Yes, she has.

When students have thoroughly practised the forms, you can introduce some more realistic uses:

    Have you seen my purse?
    Have you got my pen?

And a game can be played along the following lines:

While a student is outside, someone takes something of his.
    Who has taken my folder?
Everyone must answer truthfully:
    I haven't/I have.

Part two
Mistakes – apologies and explanations
Items 143 – 150

Language teaching points

a Revision of set phrases for apologizing.
b Explanations in the past simple tense.
c Negative orders and forms of acknowledgment.

'Why' and 'because' could also be usefully introduced at this point with better groups (see Item 171).

Aims

To equip students with language for politely apologizing and explaining behaviour when they make a mistake or there is a misunderstanding.

The behaviour and language essentials covered are as follows:

Statement of mistake (passive understanding: often present perfect).
Set apology formula.
Covering excuse or explanation (often past simple).

Immigrants often find themselves under pressure for the right language when they are rightly or wrongly accused of doing something wrong. So although this material is rather negative, it is most important that Asians should be able to explain and justify themselves when something has gone wrong. It is also most important that when at fault they should apologize clearly and politely because lack of this type of language understandably often irritates English-speaking colleagues.

Teaching procedure

Just because it is rather negative this material needs to be handled briskly. These items do not usefully lend themselves to group work so most of the work must be done as individual and choral practice.

Equipment

Visuals if required for Items 145 and 146.

143 Dialogue *Upsetting someone's tea*

AIM **Illustration of a situation where a mistake has been made. Language for apology.**

Present the following dialogue with pictures of the characters.

⊗ Tape item 55

NARRATOR	Yesterday Sheila spilt her tea in the canteen. It went all over Betty.
TEA LADY	There's your tea, dear. Sugar?
SHEILA	Yes, please. Thanks.
GURMIT	Come over here, Sheila.
SHEILA	O.K. (Sheila trips on Betty's foot)
BETTY	Look out! (Sound of tea cup crashing to floor)
SHEILA	*Look out! The tea. Betty!*
BETTY	God! Your tea's gone all over me!
SHEILA	*Oh dear. I'm very sorry.*
BETTY	Look your tea's spilt all over me!
SHEILA	*I'm very sorry, Betty.*
BETTY	Huh! You'd better be careful.
SHEILA	*I'll be very careful next time.*

1 *Listen.*
2 *Listen and repeat* Sheila for the lines in italics.
3 *Listen and fill-in* Sheila for the lines in italics.

144 When to apologize

AIM **To get students first to identify situations where apology is appropriate and to provide a simple language formula to use.**

First revise the expressions of apology in Item 102.

Get each student to do things in the classroom which should be followed by a simple apology. This will be difficult because often Asian immigrants do not seem to be sensitive to things which cause offence to English people. Throughout this part you should therefore try and draw their attention to behaviour which gives offence. If possible get over the idea that these are matters of manners, not of something right or wrong. But beware of going on too long, or students will switch off.

Appropriate classroom situations,
Slamming a door (contrast with closing it quietly).
Scraping a chair (contrast with lifting it).
Knocking over someone's things.
Dropping something.
Leaning across someone (contrast with walking round or saying 'excuse me').

145 Explanations of mistakes using the negative

AIM To give a quick explanation of something that has gone wrong using the past simple negative verb forms.

Having established situations requiring a simple apology, this item deals with situations which require an apology and an explanation. Lateness should be included in this item.

This Item and Item 146 require an explanation using the past simple tense. If you haven't revised this, you may want to now (see Items 78–82).

Present situations in the classroom and use visuals whenever possible:
You're late.
Your machine is broken.
Your file is blunt.
This work is bad.
You've packed the wrong parts.

Students respond with a negative explanation:
Sorry, I didn't think.
Sorry, I didn't look.
Sorry, I didn't understand.
Sorry, I didn't know.

It is not very realistic to practise this work in groups so aim for speed of response instead. For fun you could time how long it takes to go round the class, each student giving an explanation of the type above.

146 More explanations of mistakes

AIM **To give quick explanations using the past simple positive form.**

This Item practises explanations using positive forms of the past simple. Absence should be included in this Item.

On the whole the situations suggested here are ones where the mistake carries more personal responsibility, and therefore a more specific apology and explanation is needed.

Present situations such as these in the classroom:

You've packed the wrong box.
You're late.
You've broken the box.
You've spilt the tea.
Your machine is dirty.
You were away yesterday (etc.).

Present and practise the following replies:

Sorry, I forgot.
Sorry, I sat on it.
Sorry, I broke it.
Sorry, I dropped it.
Sorry, I was in a hurry.
Sorry, I was sick. (etc.)

Use visuals whenever needed and practise round the class.

147 Recorded drills

AIM **To practise a variety of apologies and explanations.**

These drills practise a mixture of the forms of explanation and apology presented so far in this section.

Drill one

⊗ Tape item 56

Listen and repeat the answer:

Have you got my pen?
Sorry, no, I haven't.

Have you got any change?
Yes, I have.

You haven't got an overall.
Sorry, I left it at home.

You've filled up your card wrongly.
Sorry, I didn't understand.

You're late.
Sorry, I missed the bus.

Have you checked the number?
Sorry, I forgot.

You aren't wearing gloves.
Sorry, I didn't understand.

Did you break this box?
Sorry, I dropped it.

Drill two

⊗ Tape item 57

Now you give the answer:

Have you got my pen?
Have you got any change?
You haven't got an overall.
You've filled up your card wrongly.
You're late.
Have you checked the number?
You aren't wearing gloves.
Did you break this box?

148 Dialogue *incorrect weighing*

AIM Practise with apologizing and explaining within a recorded dialogue situation.

Don't spend long on this Item. Write an appropriate dialogue for your students as an illustration of a situation where an apology is needed.

Present the dialogue with pictures of the characters:

⊗ Tape item 58

NARRATOR   Betty did a stupid thing yesterday. She filled up a jar of coffee with her hands.

(Factory machine noises)

IRIS   These jars look a little light.

BETTY   I'll put a bit more powder in.

IRIS	You shouldn't do it with your hand, Betty. Use the measure.
BETTY	It's all right. No one will see me.
IRIS	You fool. Mrs James saw you.
MRS JAMES	What's going on here?
BETTY	*I'm sorry, Mrs James. I was in a hurry.*
MRS JAMES	It's dangerous.
BETTY	*I'm very sorry. I didn't think.*
MRS JAMES	Well, don't do it again.
BETTY	*No, I won't.*

1 *Listen.*
2 *Listen and repeat Betty* for the lines in italics.
3 *Listen and fill in Betty* for the lines in italics.

149 Prevention of mistakes

AIM A language formula for acknowledging a negative instruction.

Set up a precarious arrangement of objects, probably easiest to use bricks, then issue instructions. Make sure the meaning of the main verb is really understood in each case.

Don't knock it over!
Don't touch it!
Don't pick it up!
Don't move the table!
Don't move!
Don't put your hand there!

Students respond and acknowledge all these with:

No, I won't!
Don't worry, I won't.

You could do this item in the form of a game, alternatively issuing positive and negative instructions with students responding as above.

150 Recorded drill

AIM To practise the response forms of Item 149.

⊗ Tape item 59

Listen and repeat the answer.

250

Don't be late tomorrow.	No, I won't.
I don't want you to begin this job yet.	Don't worry, I won't.
Don't forget to wear gloves.	No, I won't.
You must not work with the guard up.	Don't worry, I won't.
Don't touch this switch.	No, I won't.
You won't pack these in the wrong box, will you?	No, I won't.

Part three
Indicating and contrasting quantity
Items 151 – 155

Language teaching points
a A formal but simple presentation and practice of the following quantitive determiners and pronouns:

some, any, none, no, all
a lot of, a little, a few
others as appropriate

These determiners have all occurred in earlier items, particularly in Section Three, but they have not been specifically taught and it is unlikely that they can be understood or used accurately by the majority of students.

b Questions with 'How much/many?'

c The structure: 'There is/are . . .'

Aims
Accurate handling of these determiners and distinguishing in usage between countable and uncountable nouns is a most important aspect of English nominalization. However, in the factory situation, these are only really important for immigrants handling materials and ingredients particularly if weighing or measuring is involved.

All the items in this part should be omitted from the course if the class is not of a high enough standard.

Teaching procedure
The distinction between countable and uncountable nouns can be strongly established by always initially presenting the determiners with standard substances for each. Here it is suggested you use beans and sugar (both previously used), but you may prefer something used in the factory. Or you may use something instead of sugar, such as rice, sawdust or sand. Then go on to practise with a variety of different substances.

This material is particularly suitable for group work. These items will be most tedious if taught all together so they should be mixed with material from later in the section.

Equipment

Jars, sugar, beans.
Sets of factory parts or products.
Materials or ingredients from the factory.
Two sets of scales.

151 Some, any, none, no, all

AIM Classroom presentation and practice with familiar objects.

Always demonstrate first with your basic countable and uncountable substances. Then go on to practise and extend with everyday factory objects – preferably ingredients, parts, or products.

First put beans on most people's desks. Present and practise the following type of sequence with the class:

Look, there are some beans on A's table.
There are some on B's table.
Are there any on C's table?
No, there aren't any.

Then fill some of the jars on your desk with sugar. Present and practise the following type of sequence:

There's some sugar in this jar.
There's some in this.
There's some in this.
Is there any in this jar?
No, there's none/no sugar.
No, there isn't any.

Then repeat either or both of these sequences with familiar objects
Practise the sequences in groups.

Then present the determiners again with a new sequence and bring in 'all'. Practise individually, chorally, and in groups.

Examples

A pile of mixed battenholders.

Some of the battenholders have H.O. skirts.
Some of the battenholders have short skirts.
All the battenholders have bases.
None of the battenholders have caps.

Alternatively, this could be presented with 'some', 'all', and 'no'.

A pile of packets of cake mix.

Some of the packets weigh 200 grammes.
Some of the packets weigh 400 grammes.
All the packets contain sugar.
None of the packets contain sugar.

This type of short sequence can be learned off by heart with the appropriate objects there.

152 Many, much, a lot of, a little, a few

AIM As for Item 151.

These items have been partially taught in Section Three, Items 90–93.

Present and practise with basic structures:

Are there any beans on A's table?
Yes, there are a lot of beans.
Yes, there are a few beans.
No, there aren't any beans.
No, there are none/no beans.

Is there any sugar in this jar?
Yes, there's a lot of sugar.
Yes, there's a little sugar.
No, there isn't any sugar.
No, there's none/no sugar.

Then extend the practice as appropriate with factory objects.

Then go on to question with 'many' and 'much'.

How much sugar have you got in your jar, Mrs Grewal?
How many beans have you got on your desk?

Replies should be with 'a lot', 'a little', 'a few'.

You can go on to count the countable substance and to weigh or measure the uncountable substance if you want to revise weighing or measuring.

'How many' and 'how much' have often been used in earlier items in the course, so make sure they are now really accurately understood and grasped.

153 Game *Instructions*

AIM To reinforce Items 151 and 152.

This can be played as a game with the class in two teams and a

254

point for each successfully carried out set of instructions. Or the
instructions can be given in groups.

Use basic substances or factory products, parts, or ingredients:

Pass me a few beans.
Pass me a lot of beans.
Pass me all the beans.
Weigh a little sugar.
Weigh a lot of sugar.
Weigh all the sugar.

154 Dialogue practice

AIM **More realistic practice with determiners from Items 151, 152.**

Present to the class some dialogues of the following type. For
example, how to ask for sugar in your tea.

A   Can I have some sugar, please?
B   How much?
A   A little, please/A lot, please.

A   Can I have some biscuits, please?
B   How many?
A   A few, please/A lot, please.

These dialogues will help to establish that these determiners do not
indicate absolute quantities, but relative quantities.

155 Other quantitive determiners

AIM **To teach any other essential quantitive determiners.**

The quantitive determiners so far presented are probably the most
important. But any of the following may also be important:

many, much, each, every, both, half.

If any of these are important in your factory, teach them in a
similar way to the earlier items.

The following type of phrase of quantity should also be dealt with
if any of them are relevant in the factory and have not been
taught already:

a piece of, a pound of, a cup of, a spoon of, a tray of, (etc.)

Part four
Talking an Asian language
Items 156 and 157

Language teaching points
A simple formula to use to English-speaking people when speaking
to a fellow Asian in a foreign language:

Excuse me speaking my language.
Say at the end what has been talked about.

Aims
In England, which is a monolingual society, many people tend to
be paranoic about immigrants speaking their own languages in
front of them. Often when language classes are started, indigenous
supervisors and employees quite unrealistically expect that the
trainees will immediately stop using their own language. The
teacher must try to educate them on this point.

However, most Asians appear quite oblivious of the fact that
English people may be offended, or that it is considered rather
rude in Britain to talk away in a foreign language without any
explanation. This problem would be eased if immigrants used a
simple polite formula and the aim of these items is to provide one.

Teaching procedure
These two items contain very little language teaching, so do not
spend much time on this part. It will be counter productive if
students think their language is being attacked.

Equipment
Slides may be needed for Item 157.

156 Dialogue *Talking an Asian language*

**AIM A language formula to use when using another language in
front of English-speaking people.**

This dialogue should be recorded in a relevant language as well as
English.

Present and practise the following dialogue:

⊗ Tape item 60

NARRATOR	When she sees English people near her, Gurmit is careful to say something in English when she is talking to her Indian friends.
GURMIT	'Bye, Mrs James. Have a nice weekend.
MRS JAMES	Yes, 'bye, Gurmit. And you.
SHEILA	Come on, Gurmit.
MRS GREWAL	(in Punjabi) *Gurmit, can you help me over the weekend?*
GURMIT	Excuse me speaking my language, Sheila.
SHEILA	That's all right.
GURMIT	(in Punjabi) *Yes, what's the matter?*
MRS GREWAL	(in Punjabi) *Can I leave my son with your mother on Sunday morning?*
GURMIT	(in Punjabi) *Yes, I'm sure you can.* (in English) Mrs Grewal wants my mother to look after her baby on Sunday.
SHEILA	Oh, yes. Well, 'bye, 'bye. Have a nice weekend.
GURMIT	And you! 'Bye.
MRS GREWAL	Goodbye.

1 *Listen.*
2 *Listen and repeat* Gurmit in English.
3 *Listen and fill in* Gurmit in English.

If you cannot easily record the dialogue, just practise the essential part of the dialogue:

Excuse me speaking my language.

157 Discussion

AIM **To bring out some essential points of behaviour about speaking English or an Asian language.**

Be careful not to let this discussion drift on to wide-ranging cultural differences. Try and be precise and make points of behaviour which students will be able to remember and follow. Don't go on too long with a discussion like this.

These suggestions might help in the discussion:

1 Use slides or visuals to show places where you should speak English or your own language.
(in the factory/on the bus/at home etc.)

2 Use slides or visuals to show which people you should speak English to.
(supervisors, groups of English people, when English people near you, etc.)

3 Tell students that English people may feel angry if someone speaks another language in front of them because they think they are being talked about.

4 Ask students to remember when they first came to England. What did they feel? Found themselves somewhere where everyone was speaking English.

From now on you should rigidly insist on the formula:

Excuse me speaking my language.

whenever a student speaks his own language. Try and make this as constant as 'please' and 'thank you'.

Part five
Faults analysis and correction
Items 158 – 160

Language teaching points

A behaviour and language formula for taking action on faults,
particularly for machine operators:

Stage 1 Report fault. Ask questions about remedial action.
Stage 2 Report continuing fault. Say what you have done.
Stage 3 Find fitter. Report action already taken.

The present perfect tense is used and a limited number of new
phrases.

Aims

Language needed for discussing and reporting upon major faults –
the examples given here are from injection moulding. These items
involve students in an appreciation of the responsibilities of
their job as well as in using language.

This material is particularly appropriate for machine operators.
In many other situations an employee only has to report faults and
is not required to take action in which case most of this material
can be omitted.

Teaching procedure

The main emphasis is on dialogue presentation backed up with
classroom group-work.

Equipment
Sets of faulty products.

158 Dialogue *Reporting and discussing a fault*

AIM **To present and practise the overall language needed for
reporting and discussing the action needed to overcome key faults.**

Revise key points on machine operating using diagram from Item
122. The expression of possibility, 'perhaps', needs initial
presentation.

⊗ Tape item 61

Example

NARRATOR   Yesterday Tony's machine went wrong. He got a lot of short mouldings. So he spoke to Mr Carr, the foreman.

TONY   Can you help me, Mr Carr?

MR CARR   What's the matter?

TONY   My machine is wrong.
Look at these shorts.

MR CARR   Yes I see.
Well, perhaps the pressure is too low.
Perhaps the temperature is too cool.
Perhaps the nozzle is blocked.

TONY   Where do I adjust the pressure?

MR CARR   Use the pressure valve. It's in the middle near the floor.

TONY   OK. Adjust the temperature and the pressure.
And check the nozzle.

1 *Listen.*
2 *Listen and repeat* Tony.
3 *Listen and fill in* Tony.

⊗ Tape item 62

Example

TONY   My machine is still wrong, Mr Carr.

MR CARR   Have you adjusted the temperature and the pressure?

TONY   Yes, I've turned up the temperature.
And I've turned up the pressure.

MR CARR   What about the nozzle?

TONY   I've checked the nozzle.

MR CARR   Have you interrupted the cycle?

TONY   No, I haven't.

MR CARR   Well, you'd better find a fitter.

1 *Listen.*
2 *Listen and repeat* Tony.
3 *Listen and fill in* Tony.

Main language points: present perfect; 'still'; turn up and down, 'interrupt the cycle'.

⊗ Tape item 63

Example

NARRATOR	Tony found a fitter.
TONY	Excuse me. Can you help me, please?
FITTER	What's the matter?
TONY	My machine is wrong. Look at these shorts.
FITTER	Oh yes.
TONY	I've turned up the temperature and the pressure. And I've checked the nozzle. It's still wrong.
FITTER	Hang on. I'll come over in a minute.

1 *Listen.*
2 *Listen and repeat* Tony.
3 *Listen and fill in* Tony.

159 Classroom practice of faults analysis

AIM **To practise the language contained in Item 158 in groups and to apply it to other faults and difficulties.**

A set of products with the relevant faults is needed. The teacher must obtain a faults analysis chart from the factory and will probably need to record fault descriptions and instructions on how to overcome them.

Group practice dialogue

Build this up around the second dialogue of Item 158 (Tape Item 62) Allow and encourage variations as needed.

Start: My machine is still wrong.
      Look at this ...... (name fault)

160 Recorded drill on major faults

AIM **To drill the language and the sequence of action on faults practised in Item 159**

Prepare a question and answer sequence on five or six major faults. Record these as drills and get students to listen and repeat and then answer the questions.

⊗ Tape item 64

Example

FLASHING

Have you adjusted the injection pressure?

Yes. I've turned down the pressure.

Have you adjusted the temperature?

Yes. I've turned down the temperature.

Have you adjusted the locking pressure?

Yes. I've turned up the locking pressure.

Have you interrupted the cycle?

No, I haven't.

or

Yes, I've left my machine for five minutes.

Part six
Solving problems
Items 161 – 164

Language teaching points

No new structural material is presented in this part, but students are shown how they can use English they've already learned to take the initiative in their work situation and solve problems which may present themselves.

A basic behaviour and language formula for getting something needed on the following lines is established:

Stage 1 State what has happened (usually present perfect tense). Ask where to go and who can help you.

Stage 2 Report what has happened to the right person. Say exactly what you want.

Aim

The aim in this part, and increasingly in the remainder of the course is to show students how they can use the language they have now learned not only to respond, but to take the initiative in situations and relationships. Naturally they will not be able to do much at this point, but if their English is to go on increasing after the course they must become experimental and enterprising.

Teaching procedure

The main emphasis is upon recorded dialogues, but there is some opportunity for games and group work. This material can well be mixed in with some earlier material in the section.

161 Dialogue *Running out of parts*

AIM **To present and practise the language needed to avoid running out of something.**

This dialogue demonstrates the need to take action when about to run out of something. Although the student is responding to the

263

situation, verbally he has to take the initiative by going and asking.
The language of the dialogue is all familiar except for the
question 'What do I do then?' Note the need to repeat
instructions which should be familiar from the work on messages
(Items 95–100).

Present and practise the following dialogue:

⊗ Tape item 65

NARRATOR Sheila nearly finished all the parts she had yesterday.

SHEILA Can you help me please, Mary?

MARY What's the matter?

SHEILA I've nearly run out of parts.

MARY You'd better go and get some more.

SHEILA Where do I go, please?

MARY Go to the stores.

SHEILA What do I do then?

MARY Ask for some more parts.

SHEILA Go to the stores and ask for some more parts.
OK. Thanks.

1 *Listen.*
2 *Listen and repeat* Sheila.
3 *Listen and fill in* Sheila.

162 Classroom practice

AIM **Classroom practice of the language contained in Item 161.**

Give a demonstration in front of the class first.

TEACHER Can you help me, please?
I've nearly run out of *labels* (etc.).

(Try and get across the idea of 'nearly' here, by still having something left in your hand.)

STUDENT Where do I go for more, please?
Go to the cupboard/etc.

Now get the class working in groups. Give vocabulary stimulus by
having prepared visuals of new items which students can run out of.

Some ideas: ink, wool, tea, anything appropriate to the factory.

163 Dialogue *Getting the new parts*

AIM **The language of requests. This has already occurred earlier in the course.**

This dialogue is a continuation of Tape Item 65.

⊗ Tape item 66

MAN   Hullo, there!

SHEILA   Excuse me, can I have some more parts?

MAN   Take your pick, love. There's 2,500 different parts in here.

SHEILA   Can I have 500 G31's, please?

MAN   That's it. Here you are.

SHEILA   Thank you very much.

1 *Listen.*
2 *Listen and repeat* Sheila.
3 *Listen and fill in* Sheila.

164 Dialogue *Torn gloves*

AIM **Further illustration of getting something needed for the job.**

Again, this dialogue should not involve language difficulties. The main thing to establish by this stage is a very clear behaviour formula.

Stage 1   State what has happened.
            Ask where to go and who can help you.
Stage 2   State what has happened.
            Say what you want.

Present and practise the following dialogue:

⊗ Tape item 67

NARRATOR   Gurmit tore her gloves yesterday.
            She asked for another pair

(Factory noises)

GURMIT   Oh dear. I've torn my glove.

MARY   You'd better get another pair.

GURMIT   Where do I go for another pair?

MARY   Go to the canteen.

GURMIT   What do I do then?

265

MARY   Ask Mrs Quickly for another pair.

GURMIT   The canteen – Mrs Quickly.

(Door being closed)

MRS QUICKLY   Hullo, dear.

GURMIT   Mrs Quickly?

MRS QUICKLY   That's right. What can I do for you?

GURMIT   I've torn my gloves.

MRS QUICKLY   Yes, you have, haven't you?

GURMIT   Can I have another pair, please?

MRS QUICKLY   What size, dear?

GURMIT   I don't know.

MRS QUICKLY   Well, what size are you wearing?

GURMIT   Um . . . size M7.

MRS QUICKLY   Right, here you are.

GURMIT   Thanks very much.

MRS QUICKLY   Don't tear them again.

GURMIT   No, I won't.

1 *Listen.*
2 *Listen and repeat* Gurmit.
3 *Listen and fill in* Gurmit.

Classroom Practice

Prepare a series of visuals on cards of objects which students could run out of, tear (etc.). These students can practise asking for things in groups.

Use the language formula established in earlier items.

A   I've nearly run out of . . . . . .
    I've torn my . . . . . .
    Can I have some . . . . . . ?

B   How many/what size/ (etc.).

A   (precise statement).
Change over the teams.

Part seven
Behaviour which can cause offence
Items 165 and 166

This material does not contain any new language learning points but illustrates a couple of points of Asian behaviour which quite often irritate British people, and provides an opportunity for a very simple discussion of such misunderstandings if the class is good enough. In some factories it may be unnecessary to deal with these points, but the teacher should make sure.

165 Laughing inappropriately

AIM **To draw attention to a point of behaviour which causes offence and to provide the language for an explanation.**

Many Asian women laugh when being spoken to or ticked off as an expression of embarrassment. This is often misunderstood by British people. If this appears to be a regular problem in your factory, it is worth trying this item. Otherwise ignore this item.

First establish the idea of '*polite*'. Explain that British people do not think it is polite if you laugh when they are talking to you. And they may think you are laughing *at* them. British people don't usually show embarrassment in this way.

Present the following dialogue:

⊗ Tape item 68

NARRATOR	Yesterday Mrs James was angry. Gurmit wasn't checking the weights of packets properly.
MRS JAMES	Who is sealing these packets?
GURMIT	I am, Mrs James.
MRS JAMES	They're all light – underweight.
GURMIT	Oh (starting to giggle) I'm sorry.
MRS JAMES	You must check the weight.
GURMIT	Yes, Mrs James (still giggling).
MRS JAMES	Don't you laugh at me!

GURMIT	I'm not. I'm sorry, Mrs James.
MRS JAMES	You stop laughing. You're very rude, Gurmit.
GURMIT	I'm sorry, Mrs James. I felt embarrassed.
MRS JAMES	Well, you check the weights.
GURMIT	I will.

1 *Listen* only.

This is a behaviour problem only for women.
Asian men under pressure or embarrassed do not giggle, but, in so far as one can generalize, tend to become very formal and even aggressive. This again may make problems for an English person, but it is not so easily demonstrated or discussed with a group of Asian men.

166 Speaking a foreign language

AIM **To explain and discuss how British people often misunderstand Asian behaviour.**

If the speaking of Asian languages appears to be a real source of tension amongst British people, it is worth dealing with this item in addition to Items 156 and 157. This item has been deliberately separated from the earlier ones as it is not a good idea to overdo a point like this on one occasion. After students have listened to this dialogue and the previous one, have a general discussion about misunderstanding and difficulties which arise for students in dealing with indigenous people.

Present the following dialogue:

⊗ Tape item 69

NARRATOR	Gurmit and some of her friends were talking and laughing together in Punjabi. Mary was with them.
GURMIT	See you tomorrow, Sheila.
SHEILA	Yes, 'bye 'bye, Gurmit.
MRS GREWAL	(in Punjabi) *How's your brother?* *Does he still not like working?*
GURMIT	(in Punjabi) *Oh yes. He complains every day!* (laughing)

268

MRS GREWAL	(in Punjabi) *What does your father say?* (laughing)
MARY	Stop talking about me!
GURMIT	We're not talking about you.
MARY	Yes. Mrs Grewal was looking at me and laughing.
GURMIT	We were talking about my brother, Mary.
MARY	Well, why don't you *tell* me what you're talking about?
GURMIT	Sorry, Mary.

1 *Listen* only.

Section six

Taking the initiative
Responding in difficult situations
Cultural matters
Revision

Introduction

The emphasis in this situation is less upon routine job or social situations, and much more upon situations which are likely to be important or stressful to an individual. The full aim of the section, which would require a group with considerable fluency in elementary English, is to equip students with the language they need to express themselves and stand up for themselves in terms of social and work situations and in terms of general behaviour and culture.

There is not a lot of new language in this section; but the situations and behaviour posed are much more difficult and the intention is to stretch the students' language as much as possible. Again many of the items are rather open-ended and it is left to the teacher to develop the idea further in the light of the time available and the ability of the group (e.g. Items 173, 174, and 181).

On the other hand, there are some straightforward items which are quite elementary (e.g. Items 188 and 190), but there will be little time for this section with a group who started at a very elementary level in any case. With a group who have been able to move very quickly through the early sections of the course, there is much in this section for them and there are many items which can be taken further by the teacher. Indeed, this section contains some of the essential materials for a fairly advanced industrial course – for example, contrasting effective and ineffective language (Item 174) and the ideas for real recording at the very end.

270

Quite a lot of revision is built into this section and a teacher should add other necessary items. The final part of the section contains suggestions for putting together revision materials authentic to the particular situation of a group of students.

Contents *for section six*

272

PART FIVE Talking about Asian and English customs

PART SIX Revision

Part one
Solving personal problems
Items 167 – 174

Language teaching points
These items aim to train students in working through a number
of language transactions which together give a pattern of
communication for getting effective help with some personal
requirement.

a greeting and gaining attention
b overcoming reluctance
c stating the subject
d asking for a solution
e reasons and justification

In this and later parts of this section, we have tried first to present
the language in situations which are straightforward, and next with
difficult or unco-operative people.

Aims
To provide the necessary language and confidence for students to
feel able to present and press their point of view to people in
authority over them on matters of personal importance.

Teaching procedure
Throughout this section there is a lot of use of dialogues for
presenting language in complex situations. But it is essential to
back this fully in the classroom with group work. Try to discover
some personal need or problem for each student, and arrange for
that student to raise the matter with the appropriate person.

Item 174 introduces an important new method to the course;
contrasting two uses of language which are linguistically both
correct, but one of which is the more appropriate and effective
for the situation. Teachers should use this technique throughout
the rest of the section.

Equipment
Set of prompt visuals for Item 170 and onwards.
Appropriate forms for Item 173.

274

167 A pay problem

AIM **How to approach someone for help with a personal problem.**

Revise basic points about payslips from Item 108 using a visual or slide.

Demonstrate main point of dialogue.

TEACHER   This is my payslip. But I think my money is not right.
(To a student acting as a supervisor)
Excuse me, X. I think my money is wrong.
What do I do?

STUDENT   (I don't know.)

Discuss with class what they would do. Who they would speak to (etc.).

⊗ Tape item 70

NARRATOR   Tony had a pay problem. He spoke to the supervisor.

TONY   Hullo, Mr Carr. Can you spare a moment?

MR CARR   Oh yes. What's the problem?

TONY   I think my money is wrong. I'd like to talk to you about it.

MR CARR   Yes, all right. See me at four o'clock in my office.

TONY   Thanks.

1 *Listen.*
2 *Listen and repeat* Tony.
3 *Listen and fill in* Tony.

Practical work: Does everyone understand their payslips? Ask someone from the company to come in and explain simply.

Bring out the difference between:

My money is wrong.
I think my money is wrong.

168 Making sure someone is co-operative

AIM **Practice of some phrases for making an effective initial approach when seeking someone's co-operation.**

First establish fluency in one attention-phrase:

Can you spare a moment?

This is an alternative and more useful phrase than:

Excuse me. Can you help me, please? (Item 83)

Then go on to establish:

I'd like to talk to you about ....

Point out this is slightly more polite than, 'I want to talk to you about ......'

Practise these phrases in class and groups with students bringing up their own ideas of possible problems:

...... about my payslip/my holidays/my shift time/sick pay/ etc.

Make sure a student always greets the other speaker or at least uses his name at the beginning:

Hullo, Amrik. Can you spare a moment?
Amrik, can you spare a moment?

Drill

⊗ Tape item 71

Listen to the example

A Money.

B Can you spare a moment?
   I'd like to talk to you about my money.

Now begin:

holidays/shift time/sick pay/a day-off/my back

When this work is reasonably fluent, introduce some alternative opening phrases:

Can I have a word with you?
Can I see you for a moment?

169 Changing shift

AIM **How to persist in asking for help with a personal problem when the other person is uninterested.**

Polite persistence is a very subtle skill. Foreign-language speakers usually lack such skill and become ineffective communicators as soon as they meet resistance or indifference.

⊗ Tape item 72

NARRATOR	Fred had a problem over the time of his shift. He spoke to the supervisor.
FRED	Hullo, Mr Carr. Can you spare a moment?
MR CARR	Not now, mate!
FRED	Well, can I see you later?
MR CARR	Not today. Look out over there!
FRED	Mr Carr, I'd like to talk to you about my shift time.
MR CARR	I've told you I'm busy.
FRED	Can I see you at five o'clock?
MR CARR	OK. OK.
FRED	At five o'clock in your office.
MR CARR	All right. Gor! What a day!

1, 2, 3 Fred.

Establish the technique of asking suggestion questions:

Can I see you later/at five o'clock?

And the suggestion and establishing of a solution:

At five o'clock in your office.

170 Getting your point of view over

AIM **Practice and development of language techniques of Item 169.**

Classroom practice in groups should be organized around a series of personal problems. These problems can be cued with visuals on cards that are given out to groups.

Example

Time-off for a hospital visit.
Visual can show red-cross or a hospital.

Do not at this stage spend time on students explaining the problem. Simply deal with the difficulty of getting an appointment to speak to someone.

171 Reasons and justifications

AIM **To establish question and answer sequences with 'why?' and 'because'.**

For discussion and questioning, 'because' clauses are very useful.

277

The teacher should present and practise question and answer sequences on the basis of some earlier items such as: personal documents (Item 108), job language (Items 124 and 125), the material on safety (Items 126–132), and explanations of mistakes (Items 143–150). This will also give a good opportunity for revision.

Examples

> Why must you make sure the pressure is correct?
> Because the wrong pressure produces shorts.
>
> Why must you make sure the guard is down?
> Because the machine is dangerous.
>
> Why are you late?
> Because my husband is sick.

Then move on to reasons and justifications for raising problems in Items 167–170. Use the visuals for Item 170.

Examples

> I think my money is wrong.
> Why do you think your money is wrong?
> Because I have no overtime money.

172 Explaining about a problem

AIM Using language (including Item 171) to put forward reasons convincingly and clearly in a difficult situation.

This dialogue introduces a further form of request:

> Is it possible to . . . . . . ?

⊗ Tape item 73

NARRATOR	Fred went to the supervisor's office at five o'clock.
FRED	Hullo, Mr Carr. Can you spare a moment now?
MR CARR	Yes. Come in, Fred, and sit down.
FRED	Thanks.
MR CARR	Now, what's the problem?
FRED	I'd like to talk to you about my shift time.
MR CARR	What about it?
FRED	Is it possible to go on the morning shift?
MR CARR	Why?

FRED	Because my wife has a new job. She's working in the afternoon.
MR CARR	What am I going to do when everyone wants to change their shift?
FRED	My children come home at four o'clock.
MR CARR	Leave it with me, Fred. I'll tell you tomorrow.
FRED	Thanks a lot.

1 *Listen.*
2 *Listen and repeat* Fred.
3 *Listen and fill in* Fred.

Classroom practice

Stress the need to sometimes push the case for something. Develop further group practice bringing in the new form of request:

'Is it possible to . . . . . .?'

173 Help with filling in a form

AIM **Reinforcement of the language of earlier items and practice in giving personal information for forms.**

Find out what forms students may need to fill in from time to time. Bring along specimens and work out the common basic information. This is also an opportunity for revising numbers – such as National Insurance number. There is no new language in this item.

The following dialogue involves a shop steward for only the second time. In companies with a strong union organization, shop stewards should appear in any appropriate earlier dialogues. But generally an employee will need to communicate with his shop steward on rather complex matters which is why we have introduced a steward at this point. This item also emphasizes that help should not only be asked for from supervision.

⊗ Tape item 74

NARRATOR	Tony had been away sick for five days. He asked his shop steward, Danny Waters, about sick pay.
TONY	Hullo, Danny. Can you spare a moment?

279

SHOP STEWARD	Yes sure, Tony. What's it about?
TONY	I've been sick. I'd like to talk to you about my sick pay.
SHOP STEWARD	Have you got the form?
TONY	Yes. Can you help me fill it in?
SHOP STEWARD	Yes, sure. Meet me in the canteen at one o'clock.
TONY	Thanks. Canteen at one o'clock.

1 *Listen.*
2 *Listen and repeat* Tony.
3 *Listen and fill in* Tony.

Form-filling

Develop language work for this.

> Can you help me fill this form in?
> I can't write English very well.

Then establish that everyone can orally supply basic information. Some people will also be able to write it down given a bit of practice.

174 Effective and ineffective use of language

AIM **To increase students' awareness of the importance of using the right language rather than just crudely getting over meaning.**

There is a constant danger that students will not appreciate the importance of using the correct phrase in terms of its politeness, appropriateness, and tone. It is very difficult to appreciate the nuances of politeness and attitude in a foreign language, when wrestling with more basic elements of the language. On the other hand these apparently finer factors often determine whether someone can use the language effectively.

In this later part of these materials, we suggest that the teacher constantly contrasts polite, effective, friendly use of language with their opposites. Students should identify the more effective of the two and the teacher should try and explain the reasons in very simple terms.

⊗ Tape item 75

NARRATOR	Listen. Say who talks in the best way.
1 MRS JAMES	Here's your pay packet, Mary.

| MARY | I must talk to you. |
| | My money is wrong. |

Contrast this with Tape Item 70.

2 MARY	Mrs James. Can I see you for a moment?
MRS JAMES	Not now, Mary. I'm busy.
MARY	I must see you.
MRS JAMES	Look, I said I'm busy.
MARY	It's your job to see me.

Contrast this with Tape Item 72.

The teacher should make up as many similar contrasts as seem useful.

Part two
Solving work problems
Items 175 – 182

Language teaching points
a Further development of language in Part One with application to work and grievances.
b Language formulae for politely questioning instructions and treatment and stating own view.

Aims
To bring together the many different aspects of students' jobs presented in the course and to help them to recognize the full scope and responsibilities of their work and where English is most needed in it. To develop the language work of Items 167–174 so that students can insist upon fair and reasonable instructions and treatment.

Teaching procedure
Again a lot of dialogue presentation. Many of these dialogues contain much familiar language for the students so should be handled quickly. In any case, at this stage in the course, students should be encouraged to experiment with a number of ways of saying things when they are practising in groups and not to follow slavishly the phrasing of the dialogues. Suggestions for classroom development are left vague in many items and must be developed by the teacher according to the importance of the item for his group.

Equipment
A collection of faulty products for Item 175.

175 Queries about faulty work
AIM **Extending the use of language in Items 167 and 168 and revising faults.**

Use the faulty products and diagrams from Items 49 and Items

158–160. Students first to approach the teacher and then other students in their group and point out what is wrong.

Examples

X, Can you spare a moment?
About this packet. I think it's underweight.

176 Game *Find the fault*

AIM **Further informal practice of language in Item 176.**

At the beginning of a lesson, make sure something is obviously wrong – for example, not enough chairs in the room. Then get a student to raise the matter with you and point out what is wrong.

Develop a game by sending a student out of the room and then making something wrong – for example, someone takes off one of his shoes.

This sort of game can be played for a few minutes in several lessons to provide relaxation as well as revision.

177 Nearly running out and getting some more

AIM **Language for clear explanation of work behaviour.**

This item is mainly included to put over the behaviour, but one important new piece of language is introduced, 'need'.

Present and practise 'need' first with the class. Give out things that are incomplete and get students to say:

'I need . . . . . .'

Also concentrate on accurate identification of *precisely* what they need.

⊗ Tape item 76

NARRATOR   Mrs James thought Sheila had left her job. But Sheila came back.

MRS JAMES   Who is working here?

VOICE   Sheila.

MRS JAMES   Where is she?

(Noise of packets being put down)

SHEILA   Phew! There!

MRS JAMES	Where have you been, Sheila?
SHEILA	I've got some more packets.
MRS JAMES	Who told you to go and get more packets?
SHEILA	No one, but I nearly ran out. I needed some more 500 gramme packets.
MRS JAMES	Are these the right packets?
SHEILA	Yes. I made sure I got the right packets.

1 *Listen.*
2 *Listen and repeat* Sheila.
3 *Listen and fill in* Sheila.

178 Querying an instruction

AIM **Language to query a direct instruction without provoking a difficult confrontation.**

The key new phrase is:

It's very difficult to . . . . . .

Structurally this develops from 'Is it possible to . . . . . .?' in Item 172.

First demonstrate this phrase to the class by getting a supervisor to come into the class and say something like this to the teacher:

'MRS H I want you to start the class at 7 a.m. tomorrow.'

As she goes out the teacher says:

'MRS G. Can I see you for a moment?
It's very difficult to start at 7 a.m.
I live a long way from the factory.'

Go round the class, ask the students to do difficult things such as staying in the class, coming ridiculously early to class. Students should respond as above.

Then ask for some real examples of difficult instructions in the work situation.

The essential formula to get over to students is:

1 Make a polite approach.
2 Say they can't do what is asked. (It's very difficult to . . . . . .)
3 Explain why.

179 Asking for an explanation

AIM **To equip students to ask for explanations and to demand reasonable treatment.**

When an employee feels unreasonably treated, he should have the language to take the matter up immediately and ask for an explanation. Otherwise grievances fester. An added difficulty for Asian immigrants is that they may be given no explanation of an instruction because their English is thought to be inadequate to understand one.

The language in this item is built up from earlier in this section and from Items 76 and 101. The use of 'I beg your pardon' is weak, but it has occurred earlier, and we cannot find a better alternative.

⊗ Tape item 77

NARRATOR   The supervisor moved Davinder yesterday. Davinder was unhappy.

MR CARR   You (clicks fingers). Over to number two line.

DAVINDER   I beg your pardon?

MR CARR   You heard. Number two line.

DAVINDER   Excuse me, Mr Carr. Can you explain why? You moved me yesterday.

MR CARR   Sorry, Davinder. Yes I'll explain.
A man has gone to the personnel office from number two line. I only need you for half an hour, please?

DAVINDER   Thanks for explaining.

1 *Listen.*
2 *Listen and repeat* Davinder.
3 *Listen and fill in* Davinder.

In this dialogue, the supervisor changes his behaviour and is reasonable. Consider what an employee can do if this is not the case. But a teacher should not encourage students to take action which is in breach of conditions of employment even if someone is rude or unreasonable.

Develop classroom and group practice for this situation. Contrast this dialogue with examples of language which Davinder might have used and which would have been ineffective. Use the contrast technique of Item 174.

180 Raising a grievance

AIM To give students the confidence to raise a grievance through the correct channels.

For grievances 'unfair/fair' are very important words and concepts. Establish them with the class.

This item aims to get over these essentials:

1 Enough English for someone to put forward a grievance on his own.

2 How to argue his case in a reasonable and polite way to give more credibility to it even with his own shop steward.

3 The importance of producing good reasons or evidence.

⊗ Tape item 78

NARRATOR	Tony was very unhappy about overtime. He went to Danny Waters, the shop steward.
TONY	Hullo, Danny. Can you spare a moment?
SHOP STEWARD	Yes. What's the problem, mate?
TONY	I'd like to talk to you about my overtime.
SHOP STEWARD	Overtime? Go on.
TONY	Danny, I think the supervisor is unfair. He doesn't give me enough overtime.
SHOP STEWARD	Why?
TONY	Because other operators get more overtime.
SHOP STEWARD	Can you prove it, mate?
TONY	Here are my payslips. Three hours' overtime last week. And the same on this one.
SHOP STEWARD	Can I keep your payslips?
TONY	Yes.
SHOP STEWARD	I'll see the supervisor and I'll talk to you tomorrow, mate.
TONY	Thanks, Danny.

1 *Listen* only.

This dialogue is inevitably simpler than reality. Tony would be asked how much overtime other people get and how it is allocated. But the language needs of such situations are quite unpredictable.

With a better group who could spend some time on Section Six, a longer listening comprehension dialogue should be developed. Note the characteristic use of the 'will'—future by the shop steward when giving an undertaking of action. The future tense has not been included in these materials for elementary learners, but, with a more intermediate group, contents could be developed from these later sections and the future tense should be brought in early in this section.

181 The full scope of a job

AIM **To bring together the wide range of items covered in the course so that students form a clearer picture of the full scope of their job.**

Using earlier job-language items from the course, the teacher can build up a complete picture for a student of what his job involves.

Immediate job routines
Quality
Faults
Responsibilities
Knowledge of department and factory
Social contact
Personal needs
Trade union (etc., etc.)

This will offer a good opportunity for some useful revision. The overall picture of a job will be best presented with the aid of a visual. The teacher can also identify all the points at which English is needed by an immigrant (as in Item 157).

182 Other suggestions

There are endless possibilities as to the problems that can face a person in their work, or the situations in which they may need to take the initiative. Here are some further suggestions as to situations which might be more appropriate for teaching items than some of the items included in this part.

Jobs are allocated each morning. You keep on getting the same one and you would like a change.
Someone is doing something the wrong way. You put them right. 'It's quicker/easier/better/etc . . . . . .'
Someone is in difficulty and needs advice – 'You'd better . . . . . .'

Part three
Formal situations at work
Items 183 – 186

Language teaching points
a Phrases for overcoming difficulties of understanding by either speaker.
b Style of language in a formal interview and over the telephone.

Aims
Again the main aim is to change attitudes towards a situation so that linguistic skill can be fully used. The two situations presented are the telephone and formal interviews with management.

Teaching procedure
Rather long dialogues which should be cut for weaker groups. But these dialogues offer useful listening comprehension if the teacher cannot or does not wish to exploit them fully.

Realistic follow-up should be offered by creating opportunities for students to the telephone and have a real interview. This will prove invaluable in realizing the aims of this part.

Equipment
Two telephones if possible for Item 183.

183 Using the telephone

AIM Extension of Item 106 and application in the work situation.

Telephoning: Find out whether ordinary employees ever have to use the internal telephone. Even if none of your students do at present, use of the telephone may be essential for any upgrading.

Holidays: The next three items are built around a request for extended leave because this is very important for Asians. Every few years Asians want to go home; at other times they are not very interested in holidays. Find out what the company procedure is on annual holidays (close down, staggered, possibility of money instead). Establish meaning of 'extended holiday/leave', 'unpaid leave of absence', and 'terminate'.

⊗ Tape item 79

NARRATOR	Davinder was planning a trip to India. He needed an extended holiday. So he spoke to the supervisor.
DAVINDER	Hullo, Mr Carr. Can you spare a moment?
MR CARR	Yes, certainly Davinder. What is it?
DAVINDER	I'd like to talk to you about my holidays.
MR CARR	Yes?
DAVINDER	Is it possible to have extended leave? I'm going to India.
MR CARR	Nothing to do with me. Speak to Personnel.

Listen only.

Before moving on to the telephone, revise Item 106.
Point out differences between internal and external styles if appropriate.

⊗ Tape item 80

NARRATOR	So Davinder phoned the Personnel department. (Dialling sound)
SECRETARY	Personnel
DAVINDER	Hullo. My name is Bhullar. Machine-shop.
SECRETARY	Yes, Mr Bhullar.
DAVINDER	This is about my holidays.
SECRETARY	Yes, your holidays.
DAVINDER	I'd like to talk to a personnel officer about extended holidays.
SECRETARY	I see. What's your clock number?
DAVINDER	8 1 1 2 8 1
SECRETARY	You should see Mr Prentice. Can you come to the personnel office at four-fifteen today?
DAVINDER	I'm sorry. Can you repeat that, please?
SECRETARY	Yes. Mr Prentice, in the personnel office at four-fifteen.
DAVINDER	Mr Prentice at four-fifty.

289

SECRETARY No. four-fif*teen*.

DAVINDER Oh yes. Thank you, four-fifteen. 'Bye.

SECRETARY 'Bye.

1 *Listen.*
2 *Listen and repeat* Davinder.
3 *Listen and fill in* Davinder.

Classroom work

One of the most important points for classroom development is what to do when a person does not understand.

I'm sorry. Can you repeat that, please?

Also revise Items 76 and 77.

Set up a series of real or simulated telephone conversations (including phoning up when you cannot come to work). If this work is important, teach language for students to use when they are not understood or misunderstood.

e.g. 'I'm sorry. You didn't understand me.'

Practical

Try to arrange for everyone to use the internal telephone.

184 An interview

AIM Behaviour and language in a formal interview situation.

The following dialogue is rather long and with weaker groups inessentials could be cut. But there is no new language in the target role (Davinder).

⊗ Tape item 81

NARRATOR	So Davinder told the supervisor and went to see Mr Prentice the Personnel Officer at four-fifteen.
PERSONNEL OFFICER	Come in, Mr Bhullar. Good afternoon.
DAVINDER	Good afternoon, Mr Prentice.
PERSONNEL OFFICER	Now sit down. What can I do for you?
DAVINDER	I'd like to talk to you about my holidays.
PERSONNEL OFFICER	Yes. Your holiday is due in September. (Secretary comes in)

SECRETARY	Tea, Mr Prentice?
PERSONNEL OFFICER	Yes please. And one for Mr Bhullar. With or without, Mr Bhullar?
DAVINDER	Milk and sugar, please.
PERSONNEL OFFICER	Yes, your holidays?
DAVINDER	Is it possible to have an extended holiday?
PERSONNEL OFFICER	Well, why?
DAVINDER	I'm visiting India.
PERSONNEL OFFICER	Are your family in India?
DAVINDER	Yes, my father and mother.
PERSONNEL OFFICER	Now let's see. How long have you been with the company?
DAVINDER	Three years.
PERSONNEL OFFICER	Three years. That's all right then. You can have up to three weeks unpaid leave.
DAVINDER	So I can have six weeks' holiday.
PERSONNEL OFFICER	No, Mr Bhullar. I said *three* weeks.
DAVINDER	I'm sorry. You didn't understand me. I said six weeks because I can have three weeks' holiday and three weeks' unpaid leave.
PERSONNEL OFFICER	Yes. That's correct. If you want more, you must terminate and you can re-apply when you return.

1 *Listen.*
2 *Listen and repeat* Davinder.
3 *Listen and fill in* Davinder.

Bring out the essential points:

Greeting
Statement of subject
Tea idiom
Request and reason
Correction of misunderstanding.

Develop classroom practice as appropriate. The teacher would best take the formal interviewer role, and it may be possible to get some visitors to help.

185 Holidays

AIM **Where there is choice over holidays, to equip students to discuss their wishes fully.**

If the holiday situation is complicated, develop some work for discussing needs. First revise dates from Items 38 and 89.

186 A difficult interview

AIM **To practise language for a stressful formal situation.**

With a good group in some companies, it is worth developing an item for a more difficult situation than the one in Item 184.

Example

Davinder and another Indian worker are called to the Department Manager's Office to be questioned about an incident in which another worker refused to carry out an instruction. Also present at the interview are the supervisor and shop steward. At some point Davinder and the other Indian need to discuss something in their own language (revise Item 156).

Part four
Social behaviour
Items 187 – 193

Language teaching points
a Phrases of congratulation and condolence.
b The verbs 'borrow' and 'lend'.
c Set phase: 'Don't talk to me like that.'
d Examination of tone and stress.
e Revision of politeness tags.

Aims

To equip students to respond appropriately in situations of personal emotion, towards more trivial things and events, and towards rudeness and coarse language.

Teaching procedure

The relevance and importance of this material will depend on the atmosphere and attitudes in the work situation towards Asian employees and whether there is any opportunity for people of different ethnic groups to mix. In some places it would be a waste of time to teach these items except Items 191, 192, and 193.

Equipment
Visual prompts for Item 187.

187 Saying the right thing on a personal occasion

AIM **A language formula for an important personal event.**

The English mark important personal occasions with little comment, even so, it is necessary to say something to a colleague on an occasion such as, an engagment, wedding, birth, family sickness, death.

Asians have far more expressive and formalized behaviour for such occasions and may find English ways strange and apparently callous. Discuss with students what the English would say, representing each occasion with a visual.

I'm very sorry about your. . . . . .

Congratulations about your . . . . . .

And between people who know each other reasonably well, for a sad event:

Can I do anything?

Then move on to a dialogue presentation.

⊗ Tape item 82

NARRATOR	Fred's son, David, was very sick in hospital.
MAN	Did you hear about Fred?
TONY	No.
MAN	His son's sick.
TONY	Is it bad?
MAN	Yes, I think so.
NARRATOR	Later Tony saw Fred.
TONY	*Hullo, Fred.*
FRED	Hullo, mate.
TONY	*I'm sorry about your son.*
FRED	He's in hospital. I'm seeing him tonight.
TONY	*Can I do anything?*
FRED	Thanks. I'll let you know.

1 *Listen.*

2 *Listen and repeat* Tony for the lines in italics.

3 *Listen and fill-in* Tony for the lines in italics.

Develop group work for a number of such situations using the visual prompts. Other things can be added to these phrases, such as:

When's the wedding?

How's the baby? (etc.)

188 Responding to something personal

AIM **A few useful phrase responses for less serious occasions than in Item 187.**

That's nice!

That's a pity!

Such phrases are trivial but useful when a person has nothing to say, or in order to start off a conversation. But we hope at this stage in the course students can go on to say more or ask questions.

Practise these phrases with prompts, such as bits of news or a visual of something.

Examples

I've bought a new dress.	That's nice.
Sheila's lost her purse.	That's a pity.

189 Recorded drill

AIM **To practise fluency with material in Items 187 and 188.**

⊗ Tape item 83

Listen to the example.

A   Mary's child is sick.
B   I'm sorry about your child, Mary. Can I help?

Now begin:

A   Sheila's getting married.
B   Congratulations about your engagement, Sheila. When's the wedding?

A   Gurmit's sister has had a baby.
B   Congratulations about your sister's baby, Gurmit. Boy or girl?

A   This is my new coat.
B   That's nice.

A   My car's broken.
B   That's a pity.

190 Simple borrowing and lending

AIM **Language to request the loan of something.**

Establish the meaning and use of 'borrow' and 'lend'. Discuss the type of things which can freely be borrowed in a work situation.

⊗ Tape item 84

NARRATOR   One of the women at work had a baby daughter. Mrs James asked everyone to sign their name on a present to send her.

MRS JAMES	Just sign your name here, Sheila.
SHEILA	Right. There you are.
MRS JAMES	Now you, Gurmit.
GURMIT	Oh. I haven't got a pen. Sheila, can I borrow your pen, please?
SHEILA	Sorry?
GURMIT	Can you lend me your pen, please?
SHEILA	Yes, of course I can.

1 *Listen.*
2 *Listen and repeat* Gurmit.
3 *Listen and fill in* Gurmit.

Using familiar objects, go around the class and each student asks another to lend her something. Within the work situation, there are some things you can borrow, and other things which you cannot – for example, items necessary to work which can be obtained from the stores should not be borrowed. Make this distinction.

191 Rudeness

AIM **Some language to cope with rudeness.**

It is very difficult for a foreigner to judge the degree of rudeness and to react in the right way. Establish with the class what 'rude' means. Discuss examples, preferably from their experience. Then play this dialogue.

⊗ Tape item 85

NARRATOR	There was an argument in the factory yesterday. Another woman was very rude to Gurmit.
WOMAN	Whose overall is this?
GURMIT	It's mine.
WOMAN	Well, get your ruddy overall off my bench. You keep out of here.
GURMIT	Please don't shout. I didn't know.
WOMAN	Well, keep out.
GURMIT	Don't talk to me like that.

1 *Listen.*
2 *Listen and repeat* Gurmit.
3 *Listen and fill in* Gurmit.

Practise the last line of dialogue in classroom and group situations.

192 Swearing

AIM **An opportunity to understand something of the use of coarse language in a workplace.**

This is more of a problem for Asian men than Asian women. But even so, there is a tenedncy to overreact to fairly mild language because

a The meaning is taken literally.
b The use of such language is thought to represent a very personal insult.

In reality, there are some English people who cannot use more than four or five words without one of them being an expletive, and such use is often neither literal nor personal.

Rural peasants in the sub-continent use good-humoured obscenity as well, but practice and manner are different. Then again, many Asian immigrants consider such language socially or educationally below them and are therefore as unhappy at having to tolerate British working-class practice as Indian peasant practice.

A teacher may feel this is a difficult subject, but he can start at an innocent enough level. Ask the class whether the following words are rude:

silly, stupid, foolish, fool, bastard.

The answer is that it depends how they are said and to whom and by whom. Demonstrate with some taped examples:

⊗ Tape item 86

Listen. Is this rude or quite friendly?

A   Don't be silly. You don't need to move over. (friendly)
B   Don't be silly. I decide. (aggressive)

A   Hullo, you old bastard. What are you drinking? (friendly)
B   You rotten old bastard. (insulting)

A   That's a stupid thing to do. (rude)
B   George – you're really stupid, aren't you. (irony)

193 Drill *Politeness phrases*

AIM **Revision of politeness tags.**

With most groups of learners automatic use of the standard politeness tags takes a long time to establish.

⊗ Tape item 87

There is a word missing. You say the word when you hear the buzzer.

A Can you help me . . . . . .?

B Can I have some tea . . . . . .?

A Careful, you've broken the handle.

B Oh. I'm . . . . . .

A Here's your money.

B Oh . . . . . .

A Do you understand now?

B Yes . . . . . . for explaining.

A I told you not to wear high heels.

B . . . . . . I forgot.

Part five
Talking about Asian and English customs
Items 194 – 199

Language teaching points

A few phrases and some vocabulary items are the only new language points. It is intended that these items are mainly used for free conversation and discussion in which students stretch their existing language.

The subjects and situations presented here could be used for far more extensive language work if time and situation called for it.

Aims

To introduce cultural topics and the idea of differences and comparisons. To enable students to say something simple about their own customs and beliefs.

To make students aware of some of their customs which cause tensions with English people.

Teaching procedure

These items are rather tentative and open-ended because they should be approached in an exploratory manner with any group, and the teacher should respond to students' interests and needs rather than have precise language objectives.

With some groups neither time available, level of language, or the atmosphere of the work situation will make much of this material appropriate. But again there are some very simple points which could be covered with any group (for example, Item 196).

Equipment

Loan or preparation of contrasting Asian and English slides for Item 195. Visual chart of relationships for Item 199.

194 The idea of background differences

AIM To establish some vocabulary for, and the idea of talking about differences of background, custom, and culture.

Revise 'same' and 'different' from Item 74 or present for the first time. The teacher will know where students are from:

Is the village of Bhuttar in Jullundur district the same as Southall?
No, it's different.
What's different?

The introduction of this subject will cause a lot of interest amongst students and they will want to talk. The object of this item is to establish the subject, so let the conversation run on a bit and establish the basic topic vocabulary and the main areas of interest. Establish the meaning of 'customs'.

Are English and Indian customs the same or different?

If necessary use a few contrasting slides to establish some of the obvious differences. With women students, a woman teacher can contrast her own dress. Some of the major differences are:

houses, kitchens, bathrooms, hygiene customs, food, dress, make-up and jewellery, hair, family life, marriage, religion.

195 Comparing and criticizing

AIM **For students to think about cultural differences and to establish some limited language for discussing them.**

Slides
Prepare a series of contrasting slides of English and Asian things.

Examples
Food.
Weddings.
Nuclear and extended families.
Dress (or demonstrate).
Bathrooms.
Religious buildings.

Discuss the differences (using comparative forms from Item 74) and make the distinction between demonstrable differences:

Indian food is hotter than English food.
English baths are larger than Indian showers.
English houses are smaller than Punjabi houses.

And differences which are value judgements:

Indian food is nicer than English food.
Indian marriages are better than English marriages.

Ask the question, 'Who for?' Help students to see these statements represent a particular point of view.

Then move on to asking for explanations (from Item 171):

'Why do Indian women wear trousers?'
'Why do Indians not use handkerchiefs?'

In many cases a student cannot give an explanation in English and anyway may not know it. In such cases the following phrase is useful:

This is my custom.
or It is an Indian custom.

In other cases a simple explanation may be possible:

We think a shower is cleaner.
We like the taste of garlic.

Establish the importance of the phrase 'we think' (compare Item 167).

196 Religion

AIM **For students to be able to identify themselves by religious beliefs and present a few important points.**

Present and practise:

What is your religion?
I am a Sikh/Moslem/Hindu/etc.

There is some difficulty in establishing this concept of a religion, which is sometimes (understandably) confused with nationality and culture. Establish (with a good group) whether they wish to be able to describe any essential features of their religious beliefs or practices.

197 Questions about culture and customs

AIM **To practise simple discussion of cultural differences.**

Tell the class that Gurmit's sister or Davinder's brother has just come to England and is going to start work in the students' factory. Ask them what they would tell her/him about:

Food.
Dress.
Hygiene.

Slides

Present slides of the canteen, locker room, break room, washrooms, and lavatories. This will make the discussion much easier. Then the teacher tells the class he is just going to India or Pakistan.

What will you tell me?

Having opened up the subject, now present the following dialogue which is intended to suggest to students that these things could be discussed at work.

⊗ Tape item 88

NARRATOR	Sheila asked Gurmit some questions about her customs yesterday.
GURMIT	What's the time, Sheila?
SHEILA	Quarter-to-one. We've got another fifteen minutes before we start again.
GURMIT	I need the rest.
SHEILA	Gurmit, why do you always wear that silver bangle?
GURMIT	It's part of my religion. I'm a Sikh.
SHEILA	Oh yes. But why do you wear the bangle?
GURMIT	Because all Sikhs wear this bangle. It's our custom.
SHEILA	Oh, I see.
GURMIT	Can I ask you a question about customs, Sheila?
SHEILA	Yes, of course.
GURMIT	Why do lots of English girls cut their hair?
SHEILA	I don't know. We think it looks nice, that's all.

Listening only.

Some of the language of the dialogue could be exploited in question and answer practice if a teacher wishes.

198 Disgust at cultural habits

AIM An opportunity to discuss any aspects of English behaviour the students find upsetting and to inform students of any of their behaviour or customs which upset English employees.

This is a sensitive subject. There is usually some tension surrounding Asian habits in the washrooms (blowing out of the nose and mouth) and the smell of Asian food. Asian immigrants may be quite unaware of this. The best way to approach this subject is to make students aware of the fact that there are some British customs which they find unpleasant although they are probably more tolerant than most English people.

What English customs do you dislike?

Typical points might be flirting, swearing, and eating beef.

Then move on to the idea:

Do English people dislike Indian customs?

Ask students on what points English people have been rude to them or asked them to change. Discuss in simple terms how far this is understandable and how far it just represents hostility.

199 Present giving and families

AIM **To establish British customs about present giving in the work place.**

⊗ Tape item 89

NARRATOR George was leaving, so the other men decided to give him a present.

FRED Tony, are you going to make a contribution?

TONY What for?

FRED George's leaving present.

TONY Yes. Of course. How much?

FRED Well, most people are chipping in 50p.

TONY Yes, I'll give you 50p. George is all right.

FRED Thanks, Tony. Ah! there's Davinder. I must catch him.

1 *Listening only.*

Ask students for their opinions about when and how you give presents in Britain. Is it different from India?

Prepare a visual showing the main relationships within which presents are given in Britain. Contrast Asian habits of hospitality and present giving, which tend to be more generous and also to involve formal relationships in which presents are considered very inappropriate in Britain.

If a teacher wishes to, this is also a good opportunity to compare and contrast family structure and obligations.

Part six
Revision
Items 200 and 201

Constant revision of earlier language material and its extension in new situations has been a systematic feature of these materials. However, the two last items contain suggestions for other sorts of revision work.

200 Revision of recorded material

The tape items provide a record of most of the language and situations presented in the whole course. The playing through of these items therefore represents a revision of most material. It is suggested that towards the end of the course, a tape item is played and quickly revised at the beginning and end of each lesson. Ideally, students would be lent tapes to revise at home on their own.

201 Real recordings in familiar situations

A very interesting and worthwhile form of revision is to record real dialogue in some of the key factory situations for which language has been taught on the course.

About ten situations should be recorded, and the language used should be as near genuine as possible. There may be difficulties which will require things to be specially set up and the English used to be kept under control.

The following are some suggestions for situations:

Arriving at work.   A work problem.
Starting up work on the floor.   An interview with supervisor
Being instructed on a new job.   or personnel officer.
Lunchtime.   Leaving work.

Play the recorded item through two or three times (the quality will not be perfect). Then ask the students comprehension questions: When is this? Who are the speakers? What are they talking about? Then compare the genuine recording with some of taped dialogues in earlier items.

Appendix one
Language functions and language forms contained in teaching items in part two

This appendix provides a complete guide to the content of the teaching materials in Part Two of this book. Each teaching item is described in two ways. The functional purpose of the language is described in the first column, headed 'Language Functions'. The second column, headed 'Language Forms' indicates the main grammatical features of the language in the same items.

By consulting this appendix, a reader can see clearly what features of language code or form are being practised in conjunction with what language functions. A teacher can then make decisions as to whether he needs to supplement or reduce the amount of work associated with particular language forms or functions according to the needs of his particular students. More importantly, the teacher has an overall view of the materials from two standpoints which will enable him to organize and use them in any way he chooses.

A few vocabulary areas are listed under the column of 'Language Forms'; but no attempt has been made to indicate overall vocabulary, which will vary considerably between courses. Regretably this appendix does not indicate the range of stress and intonation used in items. These aspects of phonology have significant relationship to language functions.

While we have tried to describe the contents of each item fairly thoroughly, as later items become longer and more complex, it has been impractical to list every re-occurrence of language functions and forms, either because they are so frequent or because they are not features given prominence in the teaching suggestions.

We have faced difficulties in providing simple descriptions of language functions because of the lack of any agreed classification. The labels used simply aim to be relatively self-explanatory. In the case of the grammatical labels, we have used whatever seems clearest without regard to consistency of descriptive system.

Item number	Language functions	Language forms
Section one		
1–8	numbers: counting	numerals: 1–100, hundreds, thousands
	accurate listening comprehension switching between speech and writing	strings of numerals
9 10	letters of the alphabet: switching between speech and writing	alphabet: upper and lower case
11	spelling your own name	pronunciation and spelling of names
12	identifying objects by codes accurate listening comprehension switching between speech and writing	numerals and alphabet
13	identifying yourself at work	names, alphabet, numerals
14 15 16	simple physical instructions listening comprehension	imperative verb forms phrasal verbs (with particles) politeness phrases: *please, thank you* prepositional phrases of place determiners: *a, the, your*
17	correcting someone politely pronouncing and spelling your name clearly	determiners object pronouns names and alphabet politeness phrase: *excuse me*
18 19	greetings and farewells	greeting sequences farewell sequences
20 21 22 23	—	subject pronouns verb *be*: present tense prepositional phrases of place questions: *what? where?* determiners: *a, the,* zero vocabulary: factory objects
24 25	—	possessive determiners and *'s* prepositional phrases of place questions: *where? whose? who* determiner: *the*
26	simple physical instructions	object pronouns vocabulary: factory objects determiner: *a*

Item number	Language functions	Language forms
Section one—*continued*		
27	identifying a personal object	possessive pronouns vocabulary: personal work objects
28	instructions for a simple manual job	vocabulary: immediate job present simple tense in affirmative with *you* determiners: *the, your*
29	—	short answers with *do*
30	—	present simple tense: third person questions: *where? when? what?* vocabulary: travel, work and time
31	talking about your family	present simple tense (third person): including negatives questions: *what time? when? where?*
32	talking about your own daily routine	present simple tense forms
33	—	present simple tense forms (third person) questions: *when?* and *where?*
34 35 36 37	listening comprehension: revision	revision
Section two		
38	greeting: after a weekend	vocabulary: days and months *did you have . . . ?* *is/was/will be* contrasted
39 40	telling the time asking and answering questions about timing	time telling phrases present simple tense *what time . . . ?* sequence words: *first, then*
41	reading printed times	time telling phrases
42	listening comprehension	present simple tense noun + *be* + . . .
43	greetings: at the start of the day	greetings sequence *early/late/on time* comprehension of *did* questions

Item number	Language functions	Language forms

Item number	Language functions	Language forms
44 45	greeting and responding according to someone's mood	greetings sequence *I'm* + adjectival
46 47	instructions linked to colours	vocabulary: colours imperative verb forms phrasal verbs (with particles)
48	revision of item 28	—
49 50	instructions for a job sequence alerting someone to look out for something in a job sequence	vocabulary: product faults *make sure . . .* *there are . . .* determiner: *no* *have got . . .* present simple tense phrasal verbs (with particles)
51	instructions for collecting, moving and delivering objects	imperative verb forms prepositions of place noun + *of* + noun: *a bag of boxes* vocabulary: more instruction verbs
52	listening comprehension	mixed tenses noun + *be . . .*
53 55 56	introducing yourself introducing other people farewell at the end of the day indicating location of an object responding to a question about location	pronouns: *that, one* questions: *who? where?* *I'm . . .* prepositional phrases of place farewell sequence
54	—	vocabulary building
57	listening comprehension use of English names	farewell sequence
58	use of English names and titles use of Asian names in England	pronunciation of English name
59 61 62	polite requests understanding familiar forms of address	*can I have . . . ?* politeness phrases: *please, thank you* vocabulary: money, food question: *how much?*
60	instructions	imperative verb forms + *pleas*

Item number	Language functions	Language forms

63 payslips: switching between written and spoken
counting money
payslip vocabulary
how much have you got?

64 making personal contact with a colleague
short questions: *are you . . . ?*
questions: *what? where? who?*

65 —
are you + noun phrase?
do/does questions
reciprocal short questions
pronouns

66 —
questions: *where? what? who?*
+ present simple tense
+ verb *be*
short answers

67 exchanging personal information with a colleague
as for items 65 and 66

68 identifying yourself in the factory
making a request
use of English names and titles
names and numerals
can I see . . . ?

Section three

69 revision of item 50
—

70 indicating location
vocabulary: indicating position
prepositional phrases of place

71 72 instructions
imperative verb forms
prepositional phrases of place
vocabulary for folding and packing
phrasal verbs
vocabulary: machine controls

73 instructions
vocabulary: accurate measurement of length

74 —
-er comparatives
is + comparative + *than*
vocabulary: physical qualities
demonstrative pronouns

75 talking about measurements
too comparatives
questions: *how?*
comprehension: *should, nearly*

Item number	Language functions	Language forms
Section three—*continued*		
76	repeating and responding when not understood	pronunciation
77	indicating failure to hear or understand	clarification formulae
78 79 80	—	past simple tense: mixed regular and irregular forms question forms with *what, when, where, how much* adverbs: *last, next, yesterday*
81	talking about settling in England	past question form: *did* short responses: *yes, I did; no, I didn't* negative forms
82	—	past simple tense – various forms
83 84 85	requesting help	politeness phrases: *excuse me, please, thanks* *can you . . . ?* *can't* questions: *how?*
86	—	drill as for items 83 84 85
87	requesting help repeating instructions back	as for items 83 84 85 imperative verb forms
88	revision: counting and numbers	—
89	instructions	ordinal numbers expressions: e.g. *one in, every two, every third*
90 91	writing down measured quantities	vocabulary: weights questions: *how much*
92 93	talking about weight	expressions of weight – *er* comparatives
94	repeating what someone has said to a third person	pronouns reported speech: present simple tense
95 96 99	listening and repeating the basic essentials of a message responding to a request for help	response phrase: *yes, certainly*

Item number	Language functions	Language forms

Section three—*continued*

97 — passing on information to a third person — message delivery formula: *I've got a message from . . .* reported speech: present simple tense

98 — reporting back on a message — message check-back formula: *I gave your message . . .* reported speech: *he'll . . .*

100 — listening to, repeating, and passing on information and messages — message formulae reported speech

102 — apologizing — phrases with *sorry*

101 103 104 105 — asking for an explanation about something wrong / asking for attention and acknowledging it — various question forms politeness phrase: *thank you for explaining* vocabulary: job faults

106 — simple use of the telephone for business: approaches, identification, essential information — revision including names *can* questions

107 — understanding the use of nicknames and other familiar forms of address — —

108 — understanding certain documents and talking about them — vocabulary of payslips and other documents

109 110 111 112 — listening comprehension: revision — revision

Section four

113 114 115 — giving information about your workplace and job — present simple tense vocabulary: the place of work prepositional phrases of place

116 — describing a person's appearance — *be* +adjective/noun vocabulary for describing people present simple tense

117 118 — indicating physical position and directions — prepositional phrases and adverbs of place vocabulary: rooms and areas at home and at work

Item number	Language functions	Language forms

	showing someone around home and workplace understanding and talking about a diagram	
119 120 121 122	describing mechanical processes indicating sequence and logical relationships in a process understanding and talking about a diagram	passive third person forms of the present tense vocabulary: factory departments and processes sequence words: *first, then, next, later* prepositional phrases of place prepositional phrases indicating cause (*by, with*, etc.)
123	indicating important personal responsibilities explaining how you carry out a process	*I must make sure . . .* present simple tense *when* and *because* clauses vocabulary: factory jobs
124 125	describing the actions in sequence of your own job	present simple tense vocabulary: factory jobs sequence words
126 127 128	giving warning of danger enquiring about possible dangers	warning phrases: exclamations vocabulary: hazards
129	instructions on safety for jobs pointing out a hazard	*make sure . . .* attention phrase: *excuse me*
130	reporting a minor personal injury advising action on an injury	present perfect tense: *I've* *you'd better . . .* vocabulary: parts of the body
131	understanding safety notices	recognition of certain posters
132	understanding fire precautions	—
133	listening comprehension	*same, different*
134	listening comprehension	vocabulary: product faults pronoun: *one*
135	asking for and giving an explanation of a fault	vocabulary: product faults present passive and imperative forms *same/different/difference*
136		vocabulary: product faults *there is/are* present passive

Item number	Language functions	Language forms
Section four—*continued*		
137 138	giving warning of hygiene hazards	vocabulary: factory hygiene structures: unspecified
	instructions about hygiene	
Section five		
139	reporting a personal difficulty requesting help	present perfect tense forms
140	reporting a personal injury or illness	present perfect tense forms question: *what's the matter?*
	advising action on injury or illness	vocabulary: parts of the body, illness
141 142	—	present perfect tense forms
143 144	apologizing	apology phrases with *sorry*
145 146 147 148	apology and explanation	present simple tense forms present perfect tense forms apology phrases
149 150	understanding and acknowledging warnings	negative imperative: *don't* . . . phrases with *I won't*
151	—	determiners and pronouns: *some, any, none, no, all* *there is/are* countable and uncountable nouns
152	—	determiners and pronouns: *many, much, a lot of, a little, a few* *there is/are* questions: *how much, how many* countable and uncountable nouns
153 154	asking for quantities	as for 151, 152
155	—	other quantitive determiners
156 157	polite acknowledgment when talking in a foreign language	formula: *Excuse me speaking in my own language*
	farewells	farewell sequences
	passing on information to a third person	reported speech (present simple tense)

313

Item number	Language functions	Language forms
Section five—*continued*		
158 159 160	requesting help over a job reporting and answering questions about action taken on a machine repeating instructions	present perfect tense: various forms *Can you . . . ?* attention phrase: *excuse me* adverb: *still* imperative verb forms
161 162	requesting information to solve a work problem reporting the problem repeating instructions	present simple tense (questions) *Can you . . . ?* present perfect tense imperative verb forms
163	polite requests	*Can you . . . ?* politeness phrase: *excuse me,* formula for thanks
164	as for items 161, 162, 163 and further revision	
165 166	understanding and dealing with embarrassing situations listening comprehension	—
Section six		
167 168	gaining someone's attention stating an opinion tentatively understanding a pay slip	requests: *can you . . . ? I'd like to . . .* introducing statements with: *I think* language for payslips names preposition: *about*
169 170	insisting on someone's attention politely making sure someone has noted a fact	requests: *can you . . . ? I'd like to . . . ?* emphatic repetition names
171	giving reasons	questions: *why?* *because* clauses
172	gaining someone's attention making a personal request giving reasons	requests: *can you . . . ? I'd like to . . . Is it possible to . . . ?* *because* clauses present simple tense

314

Item number	Language functions	Language forms
Section six—*continued*		
173	supplying personal information required for official forms making a personal request repeating instructions	requests: *can you . . . ? I'd like to . . .* vocabulary: personal circumstances emphatic repetition
174	listening comprehension: distinguishing between polite and impolite language	—
175 176	gaining someone's attention stating an opinion tentatively	requests: *can you . . . ?* prepositional phrases with *about* introducing statements with: *I think*
177	explaining and justifying behaviour	modal: *need* past simple tense
178	explaining a difficulty in doing something	*it is* + adjective + *to* polite request: *Can I . . . ?*
179	asking for an explanation of an instruction	*I beg your pardon?* request: *Can you . . . ?* past simple tense
180	raising an anxiety or grievance listening comprehension	revision
181 182	synthesis and revision	open-ended
183	use of the telephone: identifying yourself and your purpose asking for something to be repeated repeating essential information	request: *I'd like to . . .* emphatic stress names and numbers *This is about . . .* formulae for repetition vocabulary: holidays
184 185 186	requests to, and discussion with, a superior in an interview being offered tea or coffee correction of misunderstanding	requests: revision *because* clauses misunderstanding formula vocabulary: holidays
187	commenting upon an important personal occasion	phrases of congratulation and condolence preposition: *about*
188	friendly comment on news or objects	phrases: *that's nice*, etc.

Item number	Language functions	Language forms
Section six—*continued*		
189	—	drill as for 187 and 188
190	requesting the loan of something	*can* questions with *borrow* and *lend*
191	responding to rudeness	imperatives: *don't* . . .
192	understanding English use of swear words	vocabulary: insults and swear words intonation: contrasting the friendly and the rude
193	—	revision of politeness phrases and tags
194 195 197	discussing and explaining some differences between English and Asian customs	vocabulary: custom and culture *same/different* comparative forms questions: *why*, *can*, *what* present simple tense phrases for identifying customs
196	identifying your religion	vocabulary: religions structure: open-ended and revision
198	understanding English dislike of some Asian habits	vocabulary structure: open-ended and revision
199	understanding English customs on present-giving	open-ended and revision
200 201	suggestions for revision	

Appendix two
Language tests for assessment, selection and evaluation

Four specimen tests are given here; two for pre-course assessment and two for evaluation. These are not standardized or fully validated tests and are better described as suggestions for assessment techniques for use by experienced language teachers.

The scoring schemes simply give one mark to each point for scoring. In actual use, the scoring of each item needs to be weighted according to priorities and difficulties. Certain items require tape recording in order to score them accurately. These are marked with the word 'record'.

The following are the aims of each test:

1 *Elementary assessment interview*
This is intended to diagnose elementary problems. Above a fairly elementary level, the assessment does not grade people clearly. This interview also supplies a number of items for post-course comparative evaluation.

2 *All levels assessment interview*
This includes most of the items contained in the elementary interview but goes on to items suitable for testing and grading people with a higher level of English. This test is suitable for grading a much wider range of interviewees, say from a random sample.

3 *Final evaluation test*
This is a specimen of a final language assessment given at the end of a 12-week elementary in-company course. The test starts off with various items from the pre-course interview and then expands and adds new items more specifically related to course teaching.

4 *Supervisor language performance evaluation.*
This is for administration by a chareghand or supervisor during work after the end of a course. The tasks are to be set and performance recorded without the trainees being told.

This type of evaluation has several important advantages: it measures successful communication in the real work situation and it does so secretly so that the trainee suffers no anxiety or tension.

1 Elementary assessment interview

There are more suggested items than it would usually be necessary to use.

Item A

Social Conversation (record)

Purpose and instructions

To be asked rapidly, but repeated if necessary.

To put interviewee at ease and judge simple conversation, allow conversation to develop if possible. Give all encouragement possible. Never correct an interviewee in any item.

Interviewer's questions	*Student's replies*	
	Acceptable	Unacceptable
1 Good morning. How are you?	1	0
2 What's your name?	1	0
3 Could you spell it for me?	1	0
4 What's your clock number?	1	0
5 Where do you live?	1	0
6 How do you come to work?	1	0
7 What time do you start work in the morning?	1	0
8 Where (in what shop/section/dept.) do you work?	1	0

Time about 1½ minutes   *Score*

Personal information (not for scoring)

As part of Item A or whenever seems appropriate in the interview.

A   When did you come to England?

B   Where did you come from? Which district or town?

C   Did you go to school or college?
    What class did you finish/What certificate did you get?

D   When did you start work at this Company?

Item B

Following simple instructions (score at the time)

Purpose and instructions

Accurately comprehending and following simple instructions.

A box of coloured crayons is needed and make sure interviewee understands 'crayon'. Avoid visual clues. People with a high score on Item A but a low score on Item B may give the impression of being much better at English than they are.

Interviewer's instructions	*Student's response*		
Here is a box of crayons.	None/Wrong	Hesitant	Good
1 Open the box.	0	1	2
2 Pick up a green crayon.	0	1	2
3 Give me the crayon	0	1	2
4 Now, take a red crayon.	0	1	2
5 Put it down near the box.	0	1	2
6 Touch two yellow crayons.	0	1	2
7 Don't pick them up.	0	1	2
8 Put back the red and the green crayons in the box.	0	1	2
9 Close the box.	0	1	2

Time $1\frac{1}{2}$ minutes.   *Score*

Item C

Describing immediate job (record)

Purpose and instructions

Assess ability to describe and explain immediate job. Measure pronunciation, accuracy, and speed in speaking.

Some patience and care may be needed to get over to interviewee what is wanted in his reply – keep prompting and encouraging.

Interviewer's questions

What's your job here at this factory?

Can you tell me what you have to do?

(If there are several jobs, select one to be described. Prompt where necessary.)

	Bad	Fair	Good
Accuracy with structure and vocabulary	1	3	5
Pronunciation and intelligibility	1	3	5

Score for student's reply

Number of complete acceptable sentences (open-ended).

Unable to reply	0

Score

Note on scoring: In scoring give one point for each complete acceptable sentence or clause. Example: After I switch on my machine, I pick up the file.   *Score* 2 points.

Time 1½ minutes

Item D

Giving an explanation of a familiar process (record)

Purpose and instructions

An alternative to Item C but a more general item for accurate explanation and description. This is an unexpected thing to ask and will therefore need prompting. A visual cue will be useful.

Interviewer's question

Can you tell me what I must do (choose only one)

– to make a cup of tea?
– to make a chippatee?
– to make a chicken curry?

Start from the beginning.

Score for student's reply

	Bad	Fair	Good
Accuracy with structure and vocabulary	1	2	3
Pronunciation and intelligibility	1	2	3

Number of complete acceptable sentences (open-ended)

Unable to reply	0

Score

Time 1½ minutes   (maximum 9+)

Item E

Repetition of sentences (record)

Purpose and instructions

Accuracy in spoken skills. Don't break up the sentences, but say them at a reasonable speed. Don't say the sentences a second time or try to correct a mistake.

Interviewer says	*Student's response*		
Repeat these sentences after me:	Poor	Fair	Good
1 Give me 14 sheets.	1	2	3
2 Bring her the cups.	1	2	3
3 I can't wait five minutes.	1	2	3
4 Switch it on and turn it up.	1	3	5
5 Turn right. Take the 2nd door on the left.	1	3	5

Score

Time ½ minute   (maximum 19)

Item F

Reading (record or score at the time)

Purpose and instructions

Test levels of reading. A reading card is required. With a non-reader note whether he can recognize letters.

Reading card	*Student's reading*		
	Poor	Fair	Good
1 Five, Four, Three, Two, One.	0	1	2
2 Take off! A great noise and the rocket lifts off the pad.	0	2	4
3 It rises, slowly at first, then turning slightly shoots into the sky.	0	3	5

Score

Time 1½ minutes   (maximum 11)

Item G

Writing (score at the time)

Instructions

Hand the interviewee a prepared sheet.

Interviewer says	Score for student's writing		
		(1.)	(2.)
(1) Write your name here (indicate on sheet).	Unable	0	0
	Block letters	1	1
	Long-hand	2	2
(2) Copy this sentence.	Reasonable speed	1	1

Time 1 minute

2 All levels assessment interview

This interview progressively gets more difficult. With an interviewee with fairly elementary English, the interviewer should cut off when he reaches the more difficult items. When using the interview with someone who is more advanced at English, full marks can be credited for items which prove embarrassingly simple without working right through them.

Items A and B (as for Elementary Assessment items A and B)

Item C

Describing immediate job (record)

Start with *Item C* of Elementary Assessment. After student has identified a few main facts, hand him a diagram or picture of the main machine or piece of equipment with which he works. Ask what each part is and its function. Also ask what can go wrong.

Score: Similar scheme to earlier Item C.

Item E (as for Elementary Assessment item E)

Item F

Guided conversation (record)

Purpose and instructions

To test a variety of levels of spoken English up to difficult levels of hypothetical discussion. A clock card is needed. Omit questions 1 and 2 with very good speakers and allow maximum marks.

Interviewer says	Student's replies
1 What's this? (point to time stamp and place for clock no)	(1) 0 1 2
2 You've got a card Where is it now? Where is the time-clock?	(2) 0 1 2
3 When do you need your clock-card? (beginning and end of work)	(3) 0 1 2
4 I don't work in a factory. So can you tell me exactly what you do with it in the morning? (mark all acceptable sentences)	(4) 0 1 2 3 4 5
5 How do you know where to put your card when you leave work? (by the number on the rack)	(5) 0 1
6 What happens if you lose your card?	(6) 0 1
7 What would you think if your card was not in its place? (e.g. it might have been taken by mistake)	(7) 0 1

Score _____

Item G

Situational response (record)

Purpose and instructions

To test social adequacy of response in a potentially difficult or tense situation. Explain each situation (a picture prompt often helps) and ask interviewee to say what he would say to his foreman/shop steward/fellow worker.

Interviewer says	Student's response		
	None/Wrong	Poor	Adequate
1 You're late!	0	1	2
2 Where were you yesterday?	0	1	2
3 Ask for permission for a day off.	0	1	2
4 Say you are willing to work overtime this week.	0	1	2
5 Ask the shop steward about your pay slip.	0	1	2

6 Are you coming to the Union meeting this evening?	0	1	2
7 A fellow worker has been away for three days. What would you say the first time you saw him?	0	1	2

Score

Scoring: 'Wrong': would be a social and communicative failure, however grammatically correct. 'Poor': would be communicatively acceptable, but is difficult to understand. 'Adequate': is a response which would be acceptable.

Item H (as for Elementary Assessment item F)

Item I

Silent reading test (score at the time)

Purpose and instructions

To test reading comprehension and logical thinking. A set of six cards are needed.

Hand the Cards to the interviewee. Say:

'Here are some cards giving the programme of the first morning for a new operator in the factory. Arrange them in the best order.'

These should be adapted in content for the particular situation.

Note approximate time taken, and in any event stop after $1\frac{3}{4}$ minutes – even if the interviewee hasn't finished.

Score

Cards in correct order   0 1 2 3 4 5 6

Time taken under 1 minute   3
between 1 and $1\frac{1}{2}$ minutes 2
over $1\frac{1}{2}$ minutes   1 (score only if a start on the cards has been made)

Sentences on cards in correct order:

◇ Programme for first day
☐ Operators are picked up by the Instructor in Personnel Department at 8.30 a.m.
○ First the Instructor shows the new operators the clocking in and out procedure.
☐ The Instructor then takes the new operators to the linen room where they are supplied with protective clothing.

△ The operator is then shown how to wear the protective clothing.

⊂⊃ At tea break the Instructor takes the new operators to the canteen and explains the ordering of lunch.

Item J

Writing (score at the time)

Purpose and instructions

Test levels of writing. Hand out prepared form.

Interviewer says

Fill in this form please.
Read out if necessary and give help.

(1) Name
(2) Work hours
(3) Job
(4) Department
(5) How did you find your job here?

Score

		(1)	(2)	(3)	(4)
(1–4)	Unable	0	0	0	0
	Reasonably accurate (either u/c or l/c)	1	1	1	1
	Reasonable speed	1	1	1	1
		(5)			
5	Unable	0			
	Long-hand	1			
	Reasonably accurate	1			
	Reasonable speed	1			

3 Final language assessment

This is just an example. Any final assessment has to be based upon the actual course taught and the work situation. This was prepared at the end of an elementary course in a rubber-packings company.

Item A

As for Elementary Pre-Course Assessment item A
With the following additional items.

Interviewer's questions	Student's reply
	Score
9 Where is this factory?	1 0
10 Where is (name answer to 9)?	1 0
11 What do X make?	1 0
12 What's your job?	1 0
13 Where is the first aid room?	1 0

Item B

As for Elementary Pre-Course Assessment item B

Item C

As for Elementary Pre-Course Assessment item C

Item D

Job language (score at the time)

a *Purpose and instructions*
To test language for accuracy and measurement.

Props: three strips of rubber packings each marked '9 ins.' but one is accurate, one is too short, one is too long.

Interviewer says	Student's replies
Here are 3 strips of cloth.	
They should be 9 ins. long.	
Please check them.	
Is that the right length?	Yes, it is. It's the right length.
If 'no' What's the matter	No, it isn't.
with this one?	It's short/ long. Wrong size.

Repeat for other two strips.

Score

Accept reasonable accuracy.
One point for each acceptable answer.

Total score   0   1   2   3

b *Purpose and instructions*
To test language for message taking.

Prepare a card for interviewer's reference with a variety of possible messages.

Interviewer says	Student's replies
I want you to take a message to . . . Ask her for . . . What is the message?	He should repeat essentials of the message as in Items 94–100

Example
Miss Brown/twenty-five serpent strips/by three o'clock.

Score
One point for each part of the message which is accurate.

Total score 0 1 2 3

c *Purpose and instructions*
To test language for asking for advice and help.

Interviewer says	Student's replies
Imagine that you cut your finger/hurt your leg/etc.	
What do you say to your supervisor?	*Example* I've cut my finger.
Ask two questions.	

Score
Accept only complete accuracy.
One point for each part of the sentence.

0 1 2 3
0 1 2 3

Total score

d *Purpose and instructions*
To test correct language for warnings and safety.

Props: hazard photographs from Item 127.

Interviewer says	Student's replies
Look at this picture. This is dangerous.	
	Example Watch out!/the iron.
What do you say? Ask twice with two different photographs.	

Score
Reasonable accuracy. One point for each part.

$$0 \quad 1 \quad 2$$
$$0 \quad 1 \quad 2$$

Total score _____

e *Purpose and instructions*
To test that students have the language to identify common faults in their work with reasonable accuracy. This can be based on a number of different items in the course.

Props: a collection of faulty objects from the factory or photographs.

Interviewer says	*Student's replies*
He shows student an object. Look, is this all right? What's wrong?	Name of the fault is minimum acceptable answer.
Do this three times.	

Score
One point for each answer.

Total score 0 1 2 3

Item E

Social language (score at the time)

a *Purpose and instructions*
To test language for making a police request.

props: a box of assorted factory objects.

Interviewer says	*Student's replies*
Points to an object. Ask me for this politely.	*Example* Can I have a screwdriver, please?

Score
One point for each part of the answer if completely correct.

Total score 0 1 2

b *Purpose and instructions*
To test language for asking for help.

Prop: illegible address or other aids as suggested elsewhere.

Interviewer says	*Student's replies*
Ask me to help you read the address.	*Example* Excuse me. Can you help me? I can't read this address.

Score
One point for each acceptable sentence.

Total score   0   1   2   3

c *Purpose and instructions*
To test the language needed for apologies and explanations.

Interviewer says	*Student's replies*
Examples You're late today. What do you say to your supervisor? Your machine is dirty. Ask twice.	*Examples* I'm sorry. I missed the bus. I'm sorry. I forgot.

Score
One point for each acceptable answer.

0   1   2   3
0   1   2   3
―――――――――
Total score

4 Post course assessment to be administered by supervisors

This is an example from the same company as the final language assessment.
Please test the following items during the week.
Don't tell the person that he/she is being tested.
Do the items over a period of time preferably when an opportunity for using the language comes naturally.
You can use the weekly summaries as a guide to simple English.

Social Language

Tick where
appropriate

A Can the person reply to greetings at the beginning or at the end of the working day?

Yes ......
With difficulty ......
No ......

B Can the person chat about his/her family and your family?

Yes ......
With difficulty ......
No ......

Example
You can ask: Where does your son go
to school;
or: Is your brother better?

C Does the person usually say 'Thank you' if you give him/her something?

Yes ......
With difficulty ......
No ......

Note next time you give the person anything.

Work Language

D Ask the person to fetch something connected with the work he/she is doing.

Carried out correctly ......

Example
You could say: 'Fetch some S/A cores.' Speak in your usual way as to an English person.

Carried out incorrectly ......

E Ask the person to measure or weigh a strip of cloth accurately.

Carried out correctly ......

F Tell the person to ask another English-speaking employee in your department how many rings/packings etc. he/she has made during the day.
Expect the person to report back to you.

Carried out correctly ......
Carried out incorrectly ......